Democratization in the Middle East

Changing Nature of Democracy

Note to the reader

The United Nations University Press series on the *Changing Nature of Democracy* addresses the debates and challenges that have arisen as "democratic" forms of governance have blossomed globally. The march of democracy has defined the close of the twentieth century; the fulfillment of individual and collective aspirations, good governance, and the nurturing of civil society form the benchmark of political organization. However, democracy defies a universal model, and the definition of democracy continues to be elusive. Moreover, the performance of democracy often fails to live up to its promise. This series explores two areas. First, it examines the theoretical discourse of democracy, such as the tension between procedure and substance, the dialectic between principles and institutions, the challenge of reconciliation and peace-building in democratic transition, the balance between universal and communitarian notions of democracy, between participation and efficiency, and between capital and welfare. Secondly, the series explores how these themes and others have been demonstrated, with varying effect, in a number of regional settings.

Titles currently available:

The Changing Nature of Democracy edited by Takashi Inoguchi, Edward Newman, and John Keane
The Democratic Process and the Market: Challenges of the Transition edited by Mihály Simai
Democracy, Governance and Economic Performance: East and Southeast Asia edited by Ian Marsh, Jean Blondel, and Takashi Inoguchi
Democracy in Latin America: (Re)Constructing Political Society edited by Manuel Antonio Garretón M. and Edward Newman
Democratization in the Middle East: Experiences, Struggles, Challenges edited by Amin Saikal and Albrecht Schnabel

Democratization in the Middle East: Experiences, struggles, challenges

Edited by Amin Saikal and Albrecht Schnabel

United Nations University Press

TOKYO · NEW YORK · PARIS

United Nations University Press
The United Nations University, 53-70, Jingumae 5-chome, Shibuya-ku, Tokyo, 150-8925, Japan
Tel: +81-3-3499-2811   Fax: +81-3-3406-7345
E-mail: sales@hq.unu.edu (general enquiries): press@hq.unu.edu
http://www.unu.edu

United Nations University Office in North America
2 United Nations Plaza, Room DC2-2062, New York, NY 10017, USA
Tel: +1-212-963-6387   Fax: +1-212-371-9454
E-mail: unuona@ony.unu.edu

United Nations University Press is the publishing division of the United Nations University.

Cover design by Joyce C. Weston

Printed in the United States of America

UNUP-1085
ISBN 92-808-1085-5

Library of Congress Cataloging-in-Publication Data

Democratization in the Middle East : experiences, struggles, challenges / edited by Amin Saikal and Albrecht Schnabel.
   p.   cm.
Includes bibliographical references and index.
ISBN 92-808-1085-5
1. Democratization—Middle East. 2. Democracy—Middle East. 3. Peace— Middle East. 4. Secularization—Middle East. I. Saikal, Amin, 1950– II. Schnabel, Albrecht.
JQ1758.A91   D466   2003
320.956—dc21
2002155283

Contents

v

To the innocent victims of conflicts in the Middle East

Acknowledgements

The idea for this book has its origin in a multi-year, multi-case-study project (and subsequently multi-volume book series) of the United Nations University's Peace and Governance Programme on the *Changing Nature of Democracy*. The overall project has so far produced one thematic volume, as well as case-study volumes on Central and Eastern Europe, East and Southeast Asia, and Latin America. Each volume features its own thematic focus, although in the context of evolving democratization trends within and between the countries of their respective regions.

This volume in the series, written by a group of scholars and scholar/practitioners, reports on democratization in the Middle East. The volume examines the role of a number of key issues in determining success and failure in introducing and solidifying democratization processes in the countries of the region. With this volume we hope to engage a broad audience – the general public, concerned citizens, policy and scholarly communities – in the academic and political analysis of democratization trends, challenges, and constraints in this culturally rich, yet conflict-ridden region of the world.

We are grateful to a number of individuals and institutions who have helped us carry this project to this stage. We acknowledge the financial and administrative assistance of the United Nations University (UNU) in Tokyo. Yoshie Sawada of the Peace and Governance Programme has provided invaluable assistance in administering the technical, organizational, and financial aspects of this project. We are indebted to the Jordan

Institute of Diplomacy, its then-President Kamel Abu S. Jaber, as well as his assistant, Raghda Quandour, for hosting an extremely fruitful planning meeting of the project's contributors in December 1999. We thank the UNU Press, particularly Gareth Johnston, for their patient and expert assistance throughout the preparation of this manuscript. We are grateful to Monica Blagescu and Nargiza Lukmanova for editorial assistance with the various revisions of the manuscript for submission to the UNU Press. We further express our gratitude to Liz Paton for copyediting the manuscript and to the book's three anonymous reviewers, whose comments and suggestions have been very helpful in finalizing the volume. We are grateful to our contributors for the thoughtful preparation of their chapters, their diligence in responding to feedback from the editors and peer reviewers, and their patience in updating their contributions in response to a rapidly changing situation in the Middle East. Finally, we thank our families for their encouragement and support throughout the preparation of this volume. Amin Saikal is also indebted to Carol Laslett for her support in looking after his office affairs while he has been involved in this and several other similar projects.

It is our hope that, in the long run, the peoples of the Middle East will be able to enjoy a life of peace, justice, and prosperity. We believe that this requires continued efforts towards genuine democratization. Although we are hopeful for a positive future, we are saddened by the violence and injustice that still ravage much of the region. Our volume is therefore dedicated to the many innocent victims of the current political environment throughout much of the Middle East.

Amin Saikal
Albrecht Schnabel
August 2002

1

A rough journey: Nascent democratization in the Middle East

Albrecht Schnabel

The tumultuous and frustrating escalation of violence between Israelis and Palestinians, particularly since 2000, the continuation of international sanctions against Iraq and its suffering population, the continuing violence in Algeria, and high levels of structural violence committed by authoritarian governments in virtually all states of the region – all these are constant reminders that the societies in the Middle East are still far removed from a condition of stable peace. Conflict, violence, and repression, particularly in this era of globalization, produce economic and social stagnation that will marginalize these countries, and the region overall, even further in an environment in which peace and political stability are the basic foundations for economic competitiveness in the global economy. This is not to speak of the immense human suffering produced by internally and externally initiated, supported, and manipulated violence and instability.[1]

There are many reasons for the region's political instability, economic plight, and human suffering. However, the lack of open political systems, heavy-handed authoritarian rule by autocratic governments, and most governments' violent and repressive struggles with opposition movements and groups are key factors in limiting these societies' potential for human, economic, and social development.[2] Genuine democratization, if successful and sustained, can produce accountable, transparent, participatory, inclusive governance, instead of exclusive and repressive rule. Liberalization of political and economic systems throughout the region

1

could support domestic peace and, by extension, strengthen regional peace and stability. Of course, a transition from autocratic and closed systems to open and democratic ones cannot be realized without pain. Thus, the contributors to this volume recognize and discuss the experiences of, and potentials for, instability created by political and economic transition processes. Transition pains, however, can be reduced if the society is in general receptive to political, economic, and cultural opening, and if it already displays a civic political culture that has been carefully promoted and groomed by civil society throughout the years and decades preceding the official initiation of a democratization process. Unfortunately, as several chapters in this volume show, few authoritarian governments in the region allow, let alone encourage, civil society to thrive and prepare the population, political parties, and movements to contribute constructively to eventual democratization.

Despite the acknowledged (and experienced) problems of intermittent democratization pains, this group of authors believes that, certainly in the long term, democratization is a positive and worthwhile endeavor for all societies of the region. What is required is not the immediate (or even eventual) adoption of full-fledged Western-style liberal democracy, but a gradual process toward more participation in the political and economic life and governance of the country, in harmony with religious norms and teachings respected throughout society. The question is not whether democracy would be an asset for peace and justice in the Middle East, but which path toward a more participatory and accountable political system should be embraced as one that would suit each society. Moreover, as Majid Tehranian argues in chapter 5, democratization is a journey, a process; it is not a condition. Each society's journey is, and should be, unique to its own historical, traditional, cultural, economic, and political environment. The vehicle, speed, and route taken to embark on the journey toward democratization are as individual as are the end results. Each society should have the right to take its individual journey. There is some agreement among the contributors to this volume that the journey is best started through gradual, controlled democratization. Democratic institution-building must match the (re)development of civil society, nourishing a political civic culture that helps all segments of society recognize the benefits of democratization – in the form of more equitable, accountable, transparent, and good governance by all and for all. The events of 11 September 2001 in particular, and the subsequent political, economic, and military campaign against terrorism, led by the United States but internationally supported, have taught us an important lesson: in the absence of justice, development, and responsible and good governance, "uncivil" society will thrive in the shadow of legitimate grievances that cannot be expressed through constructive and non-violent political channels. Although good governance and development will not eradicate the desire of a few to bring great havoc upon their own people and others, they will likely remove the explicit and implicit popular support that terrorist groups enjoy (and on which they depend as they search for combatants, funding, and places to hide and train).

There are only few or, as some would argue, no established democracies in the region, and, at best, some fledgling experimentation with democratization, driven – as well as hindered – by cautious steps toward political liberalization. In this context, discussions about the utility of democratization in preventing structural and direct violence within and between the societies of the Middle East can as yet be only an academic exercise. However, in the long run there is a possibility for democracy to unfold in the region. A number of main challenges need to be overcome to make this happen: Islamic fundamentalism; the negative role of external great powers; the Israeli–Palestinian conflict; the legacy of a long history of violence; and clashes between Western and local/regional political and spiritual norms and values.[3]

There is hope for progress if the countries in the region become more prosperous, more cooperative, less influenced by the preferences of external powers, and supported and assisted by the international community, which would in turn be represented by a restructured, reformed, and neutral United Nations. Of course, meeting these conditions represents a formidable, possibly insurmountable, challenge. However, some progress is taking place: there is evidence that secularization and religiosity can exist in harmony, that political leaders are able to balance tradition and modernity, and that both spirituality and physical life can prosper in the multi-ethnic, multi-cultural, and multi-religious societies of the Middle East. Democracy, if based on a solid civic culture, can provide the glue for the functioning of such multi-faceted societies. Democracy can provide opportunities to address and resolve inevitable frictions in non-violent and constructive ways. All the while, constructive problem-solving at the domestic level may then spill over to interstate relations as well.

There is reason to believe (however faint it may be) that the societies of the Middle East are not condemned or cursed to endure violence, injustice, and marginalization in the global economy forever. Solutions to these problems exist. Democratization is part and parcel of any serious strategy to liberate the region from the scourges of war and injustice and from the highly politicized interpretation and distortion of religious teachings that, in their original meaning, are meant to encourage, not undermine, the construction of tolerant, just, and inclusive societies.

This chapter outlines the background of this research project, its aims, and its main findings. It serves not only as an introduction to the chapters that follow but also as a summary and synthesis of the main arguments presented throughout the book.

Objectives

This book addresses a number of key issues that will determine failure or success in establishing sustainable democratization efforts in the region. Peace and stability, both domestic and interstate, and both negative and positive, are necessary for democratization processes to take hold. Simultaneously, democratization is necessary for peace and stability to unfold and, most importantly, to endure. Attempts to pursue peace without democratization, or democratization without peace, exacerbate instead of reduce the prospects of tension and war within and between the countries of the Middle East. The following issues are thus explored in one or more of the chapters in this volume, in the context either of the entire region or of a sub-region or an individual country: the relationship and interrelationship of peace and democracy;[4] the current state of democratic development in individual countries; and the roles played by international organizations and civil society actors in the democratization processes of individual countries as well as in the region in general.

Country analyses consider, among others, patterns of democratization (top–down versus bottom–up, or immediate versus gradual processes of democratization); costs and benefits of democratization; barriers to and support for democratization; the relationship between civil society and the state; internal and external factors of democratization; the relationship between Islam and Islamic movements and democratization; experiences of democratic transition processes and resulting national and regional peace dividends; and the interdependence of development, peace, and democratization and political and economic transition.

This volume considers trends toward genuine democratization. In that context, much discussion focuses on types and levels of political liberalization. The contributors are aware that political liberalization and political democratization are two processes that must be distinguished from each other. Whereas democratization, with a focus on popular political participation and elite accountability, requires political liberalization (the promotion of individual freedoms and rights), the latter can happen without the former. Although political liberalization can be witnessed throughout much of the Middle East, movement toward genuine democratization, enshrined and consolidated in both constitutional arrangements and political practices, is rare.[5] Yet, as one regional analyst argues, "[i]t is no longer possible to delay the establishment of the pluralistic, democratic state in our Arab world because we need the benefits that such a state provides – good governance, marked by transparency, accountability and participation at the grass-roots level in the march of the nations."[6] The following chapters explore the extent of genuine progress toward democratization and the degree to which it has in fact been eluding the region despite the urgency with which true change must be pursued if the countries of the region are to overcome the "tremendous challenges ... in achieving the levels of human development that only good governance, including its political aspects, can ensure."[7]

Defining democracy and democratization

Throughout the volume, varying definitions of the term "democracy" are used and discussed.[8] This reflects the diversity of approaches taken by different contributors to evaluate the progress made in the region toward democratization, and it explains why some contributors are more optimistic while others are less optimistic about the region's prospects for both democratization and resulting peace dividends. Such disagreement is of course not unique. As Schmitter argues, "[a]cross time and space – not to mention culture and class – opinions have differed concerning what institutions and rules are to be considered democratic ... [while] ... [t]he concrete institutions and rules which have been established in different 'democratic' countries have similarly differed."[9] Recognizing these differences in definition and expectation and accepting the fact that there is more than one "ideal" model of democracy – in a universal but also, much more significantly, in a regional context – are key to peaceful relations among nascent democracies and to relations between them and established democracies. As Schmitter further notes, "[g]iven the positive connotation which the term [democracy] has acquired, each country tends to claim that the way its institutions and rules are structured is the most democratic ... [while] ... [t]he 'others,' especially one's enemies and competitors, are accused of having some inferior type of democracy or another kind of regime altogether."[10] Such arrogance breeds resentment, which, in the long run, breeds violence. In particular, the application, experience, and debate surrounding the validity of the democratic peace are thus in no small measure highly dependent on the compatibility of definitions and expectations of what constitutes a democracy, as well as on a thorough understanding and appreciation of the vulnerabilities generated by the transition process from autocracy to democracy.[11]

The contributors to this volume utilize different interpretations and definitions of democracy. Tom Najem borrows David Potter et al.'s definition of democratization, describing it as a movement "from less accountable to more accountable government, from less competitive (or non-existent) elections to freer and fairer competitive elections; from severely restricted to better protected civil and political rights, and from weak (or non-existent) autonomous associations in civil society to more autonomous and more numerous associations."[12] Najem further defines democratization as progressive evolution of these components (account-ability, elections, civil and political rights, and autonomous associations) in the context of, and conditioned by, state and political institutions, economic development, social divisions, civil society, political culture and ideas, and transnational and international engagements. The end product is a minimalist definition of democracy, which, according to Bruce Russett, "[i]n the contemporary era ... denotes a country in which nearly everyone can vote, elections are freely contested, the chief executive is chosen by popular vote or by an elected parliament, and civil rights and civil liberties are substantially guaranteed."[13]

For Kamel Abu Jaber, universal suffrage and free elections are only rudimentary components of a democracy. These must be enhanced by constitutional limitations on the government, the rule of law, and the protection of human rights. Amin Saikal also argues that some forms of popular representation and electoral legitimacy are far from sufficient to proclaim democratic governance and are often simply used to practice what is no more than concealed authoritarianism. A minimalist definition of democracy, based on popular power and popular sovereignty, must be the beginning, not the end, of a democratization process. Only when supplemented with constitutionally enshrined separation of powers, political pluralism, and individual rights and freedoms can a minimalist concept serve as the basis for the development of a liberal, pluralist, tolerant, and stable society.

Etel Solingen uses Robert Dahl's more inclusive concept of "polyarchy," with the following seven pillars: elected officials; free and fair elections; inclusive suffrage; right to run for office; freedom of expression; alternative information protected by law; and associational autonomy.[14] This definition is still very limited and focuses mainly on structures. Moreover, these requirements are relatively easy to meet, even without significant loss of power for political leaders, and they also do not extend democracy to the economic, social, and cultural aspects of political life.

Majid Tehranian describes democratization as a journey, a journey toward, as Lincoln put it, "government of the people, by the people, and for the people." Tehranian points to four main elements of this advanced, and much more comprehensive, concept: political, economic, social, and cultural democracy. Political democracy consists of popular sovereignty; universal suffrage; protection of life, liberty, and the pursuit of happiness; majority rule and minority rights; fair representation and periodic elections; peaceful succession; direct voting (referenda) on critical issues such as rule of law, *habeas corpus*, bill of rights, and responsibilities of citizenship. Economic democracy features protection of property; free markets; free competition; government regulation of trade and investment to ensure the absence of monopolies and the presence of fair standards in trade, competition, health, and environment. Social democracy means social security for the unemployed, the retired, pregnant women, and children; and provision of public health, education, and welfare. Finally, cultural democracy requires universal education; access to means of communication; and freedom of identity, including speech, assembly, religion, language, privacy, and lifestyle. This is a very comprehensive, but also very demanding, slate of key components that must be met by true democracies to qualify as such.

Gerald Steinberg takes a different approach. He focuses on a socioreligious interpretation of democracy. Religious democracy recognizes the supremacy of religious teachings and writings. Leaders make rulings based on scriptures and receive authority from religious institutions, while the populace expects rulings and policies to be in harmony with religious principles. Although this approach seems to clash with the broader, seemingly more inclusive, definitions mentioned above, a number of contributors argue that most religious teachings, particularly those of Islam and Christianity, embrace, support, and in fact demand obedience to values and norms that resemble modern concepts of democracy. If properly interpreted, religious authority can be reconciled with secular democracy; on the other hand, narrow or abusive interpretations of religious teachings may create the perception of supposed incompatibility and conflict.

To return to Schmitter, "no single set of institutions and rules – and, above all, no single institution or rule – defines political democracy. Not even such fundamental characteristics as majority rule, territorial representation, competitive elections, parliamentary sovereignty, a popularly elected executive, or a 'responsible party system' can be taken as its distinctive hallmark."[15] Democracy is a composite of rules, freedoms, and relationships, in each and every case defining a certain stage of evolution in the relationship between the rulers and the ruled – gradually bringing both closer together in continuous evolution until they overlap in near-perfect congruence. This journey toward "good governance" inevitably takes different paths, at different speeds, in different political, economic, cultural, and social contexts.

Chapter summaries

The contributions in part I of this volume focus on the importance of conflict prevention and peacebuilding in promoting lasting intra- and interstate peace in the region. They discuss the role of democratization in an eventual (yet still largely hypothetical) democratic peace in the region and the evolving role of the United Nations in determining war and peace throughout the Middle East. Chapter 2, by Albrecht Schnabel, argues that peace management, conflict prevention, and post-conflict peacebuilding are key concepts that need to inform internal and external assistance in the long process toward building stability, security, and, eventually, prosperity in the region. The chapter presumes that only a working "security community," based on the provision of human security in domestic politics and of regional security in states' relations with their neighbors, can offer lasting regional peace and stability. The realization of both negative and positive peace must be the goals, as well as the driving forces, of transition processes throughout the region. This process must be fostered from outside and must embrace the assistance of benevolent external actors, including international organizations such as the United Nations. This requires the condemnation of peace spoilers – domestic (individuals or radical movements) as well as international (individual states and international organizations).

Sustainable democratization can be achieved only if the following conditions are met. Democratization has to come from below and from above. Although top–down gradualism is crucial in preventing abrupt dislocations and crises during transition periods, parallel efforts to support civil society are crucial in creating sustainable democracies that can withstand occasional regression from above. Moreover, democratization processes are sustainable only if minorities are protected; democratization will fail if the majority rules through the oppression of minority populations. In addition, successful democratization efforts have to go hand in hand with solid economic performance, political stability, and the unimpeded development of civil society.

Ultimately, the region as a whole will prosper in the age of increasing economic globalization only if it can rid itself of war and persistent violence. So far the region has not done well in bridging its differences and in coming to terms with post–World War II (let alone post–Cold War) realities. Even if domestic stability improves and democratization progresses, the countries of the region need to settle their differences and struggles over contested territories before interstate cooperation can succeed. Although contested borders and territories are at the moment the key issues of international conflict, they will eventually be superseded by competition over access to water and other scarce natural resources. The region must create a solid foundation for regional cooperation and trust before it can embark on solving such future problems. If current struggles over land and borders are not resolved, future problems will only compound regional instability, and further conflicts over old and new security issues will be unavoidable.

Major international actors in the region, such as the United States, must not dodge their responsibility for regional peace-making; American support for Israel's policies in the region and American and Soviet intervention in regional politics during the Cold War have in large part created or compounded many of today's problems. The Soviet Union has disappeared, but the United States survived the Cold War and has to confront its Cold War legacy in this, and other, regions of the world. Although the chapter makes some references to the application of its arguments in the Middle East, it remains largely at the theoretical level, leaving the practical application of the discussion to subsequent chapters that pick up on many of the main themes raised in Schnabel's examination.

In chapter 3, Etel Solingen examines the prospects of democratic peace pervading the Middle East. She discusses the theoretical assumption that democracy is an important prerequisite for international peace, because democratic regimes tend not to fight other democracies. According to this hypothesis, the presence of democratic regimes throughout the Middle East would be the guarantor of stable peace and would, in addition to creating more just and participatory states, effectively prevent interstate conflict in the future. However, democracies do fight non-democratic regimes, so the presence of only one "spoiler," one autocratic regime, would severely limit the opportunities for regional democratic peace and a regional security community of the type discussed in Schnabel's chapter. Solingen shows that, so far, the application of the democratic peace hypothesis in the Middle East can be little more than an academic exercise because few, if any, of the countries in the region are well-functioning, full-fledged democracies (with the possible exception of Israel).

Moreover, periods of peaceful relations between former antagonists in the region cannot be explained by successful democratization processes – democratization is in its nascent stage throughout much of the region. Other factors, such as economic liberalization or the unpredictable emergence of enlightened or moderate leaders, have so far been more potent factors in explaining why former foes have opted for cooperation instead of confrontation. Nevertheless, because democratization offers an avenue for more active participation in national decision-making processes, further entrenchment of popular participation in the political process and public demands for fair, legitimate, and representative governance will strengthen democracies. This will limit unpredictable and arbitrary rule, which triggers domestic and international instability and conflict. Solingen further shows that fear of violence and instability in transition processes clearly pose threats to regional stability. In fact, interaction between weak and battered transitional democracies may be more fragile and conflict prone than that between stable autocracies.

Solingen observes that democratization processes, where they have taken place, happened top down not bottom up. Although this process offers less opportunity for public initiative and participation, it prevents the dramatic (and traumatic) consequences of often violent struggles between the various groups competing for power, influence, and public support. Slower but gradual progress toward democratization, initiated and controlled from above, even if accompanied by undemocratic measures to neutralize spoilers of the democratization process (such as radical religious or nationalist movements), can in the long run lead to functioning democracies. Solingen sees reason to believe that Islamic forces may in the long run be "co-opted" or enticed into democratic processes. This is the case when governments successfully respond to the needs of minority populations, and when all political movements have opportunities to participate in the political process. When democratization is parallelled by economic development, rising standards of living, and increased domestic and international peace, rank-and-file allegiance to radical movements has proved to be quite volatile, further improving chances for successful transitions.

Democratization in individual countries would presumably benefit from the resolution of interstate conflicts in the region. What has the United Nations done, and what can it do, to facilitate solutions to the various violent conflicts plaguing the region to this day? In chapter 4, Amin Saikal examines the role of the United Nations in the Middle East, with a focus on the Iran–Iraq war, the post–Cold War confrontation with Iraq following its attack on Kuwait in 1990, and the evolution of the state of Israel since World War II. Saikal shows how the United Nations' key role in the creation of Israel, which alienated the Arab communities in the region, made it difficult for the organization to play a constructive part in the decades-long peace process between Israel and the Palestinians. Additionally, the increasingly pro-Palestinian stance of the General Assembly in the wake of decolonization and increasing membership of formerly colonized and disenfranchised communities throughout the developing world created distrust of the United Nations among Israel and its Western supporters (particularly the United States).

Successive wars in the region involved the United Nations not as a power broker but as a key agency in delivering humanitarian assistance and in implementing and monitoring peace agreements and cease-fires. The implementation of Security Council resolutions that offered opportunities for durable solutions depended largely on US support and initiative. Thus, little happens in the region without explicit encouragement or pressure by the United States, particularly when it concerns Israel's security status.

During the Cold War, many Arab countries were backed by either the

Soviet Union or the United States, and various autocratic governments were propped up and supported by one or other of the superpowers for purely strategic reasons. UN involvement in the region was stifled by America's veto power in the Security Council and its strong support of Israeli policies in the region. The United Nations was called upon to implement Security Council resolutions that would not be honored by Israel, or to clean up the post-war disorder created by externally incited and/or supported wars (UN Emergency Forces I and II). As Saikal puts it, the United States tended to act at the expense of the United Nations. Although ending the Iran–Iraq war was a success story for the United Nations, this was possible only because the United States endorsed UN mediation (it saw no strategic gain in taking the lead by itself), Gorbachev supported a stronger United Nations, and the warring parties had reached a stalemate. In contrast, the United Nations' role in the Gulf War was mainly driven by the United States. The United States needed and received a "vague conceptual endorsement" from the United Nations to pursue what it considered to be a necessary response by the remaining superpower in a unipolar post–Cold War international order. The United States acted under Chapter VII of the UN Charter in expelling Iraq from Kuwait. To this day it continues air strikes against Iraq and it enforces economic sanctions that have long been considered unnecessary and inhumane by large parts of the international community (including the United Nations itself).

Saikal's concluding comments do not hold much hope for a more effective role of the United Nations in stabilizing the Middle East. For this to happen, he argues, three steps have to be taken: Western powers have yet to agree on a post–Cold War international order (and the United States' role in it); the United Nations has to undergo structural reforms to adjust the organization and its activities to post–Cold War realities; and the United Nations has to be provided with adequate resources and mandates enabling it to perform the tasks currently performed by the United States. Unfortunately, these three points are at the heart of the United Nations' limited capacity, even in fulfilling the tasks entrusted to it by the Security Council. The United Nations is by design an instrument in the hands of the international community or, more accurately, in the hands of a few powerful actors that, in different constellations, at different times, dominate and determine international politics. These limitations apply to the United Nations' activities not only in the Middle East but anywhere in the world. New agreements on a post–Cold War order, UN reform, and increased funding are of course desirable and would alleviate some of the United Nations' current inadequacies, but in the short run they are unrealistic goals. The United Nations' role in the Middle East will likely continue to be muted by

American willingness (or absence thereof) to pressure Israel into cooperation with its Arab neighbors, the Palestinians in particular. In that
case, the United Nations will remain relegated to play second fiddle to
American regional strategic policies and preferences.

The chapters in part II examine the relationship between Islam, secularization, and prospects for democratization. Is the embrace of Islamic
religion and culture throughout the Arab nations of the Middle East an
obstacle to justice, stability, development, and democracy in the region,
as often assumed? In chapter 5, Majid Tehranian explores the uneasy
relationship between the mosque and the state throughout the Arab
Middle East. Islamic teachings originally envisioned the unity of state
and religion (whereas Christianity did not), but periods of unison eventually gave way to periods of separation between mosque and state. As
Tehranian shows, colonial powers' preference for top–down political rule
in their colonies limited democratization processes. Democratization and
liberalization were driven from above, by a small elite who had studied
abroad and decided that economic liberalization was inevitable if state
and nation were to survive in a competitive regional and international
industrial economy. However, little was done to create a broad-based
civic political culture. The results are now visible: with the recent advent
of modernity and the communications revolution, it is now the lower
strata of the population, marked by allegiance to traditional Islam, that
threaten to uproot the secularized elite.

The suppressed masses are the main force in slowing down, halting, or
even reversing secularization – by utilizing democratic processes. Moreover, top–down democratization has not resulted in the creation of a
broad-based civic culture and democratic political institutions and processes. As Tehranian argues, "although some Middle Eastern societies
have made halting progress toward political democracy, most of them
have failed to make any significant strides toward social or cultural democracy." In countries where rulers continue to buy the population's allegiance and loyalty by providing social services and low taxes (financed
through exports of mostly oil or gas), calls for further participation in
the political and economic life of the country become louder nevertheless. However, this does not necessarily mean that these societies embrace secularization, which has been tainted by former elites' embrace of
Western customs and cultural, political, and economic attitudes. In the
name of secularization and the search for pre-Islamic identities, these
societies have experienced a roller-coaster ride in their search for cultural
identity. Tehranian takes us through various stages of Islamization and/or
secularization: from periods of convergence between mosque and state;
to periods of secularization and the suppression of the mosque by the
state; to confessional systems; to examples of uneasy but successful coexistence of mosque and state.

Coexistence, along with confessional systems and constitutional regimes, seems most promising in the context of the multi-ethnic, multi-
religious, quasi-secularist societies of the region. Most importantly,
political democratization must give rise to economic and cultural democratization. Only then will democratic structures offer opportunities
to all for political, cultural, and economic participation, while preventing majority rule of either secularized or ultra-conservative groups. A
combination of the reforms implemented by Ataturk and Reza Shah
with more broad-based grassroots input, support, and strong constitutionalism could bring stability, peace, and justice to countries individu-
ally and to the region as a whole. '

Mark Tessler, in chapter 6, examines a crucial piece of the larger
puzzle examined in this book: what do public attitudes tell us about the
linkage between Islam and democracy? Are public attitudes toward more
democratization and political openness influenced by religiosity and adherence to Islamic belief? Popular perceptions in Western societies, often
resembling anecdotal stereotypes, hold that Islam and democracy are
mutually exclusive concepts, and that levels of piety and acceptance of
democratic principles are inversely correlated; that is, the more religious
a person is, the less likely it is that he or she will embrace democratic
principles. As Tessler reports, such perceptions of the relationship between piety and democracy in the region may be misinformed by Western experiences. In West European and American societies, more religious people indeed tend to hold more conservative views and attitudes
toward governance and domestic and foreign policies. Tessler's study
shows that, at least in Morocco and Algeria, this is not the case.

If one assumes that the embrace of and commitment to civic virtues
are key requirements for the creation and maintenance of stable democracies, it is crucially important to study, monitor, and access public
attitudes toward democratic principles and policies that support secularization and democratization. There have been very few attempts systematically to study the impact of Islamic religious attachments on individuals' attitudes toward democracy and governance. Tessler's original
study and conclusions show that, "despite some statistically significant
relationships, Islam appears to have less influence on political attitudes
and behavior than is frequently suggested by students of Arab and Islamic society." Moreover, in the context of his examination of the Moroccan and Algerian societies, Tessler shows that Islam is not necessarily
an obstacle to democracy. Islamic attachments do not seem to obstruct
the emergence of an open political culture, and thus eventually of sustainable democracy. Interestingly, the only significant correlation between piety and political conservatism was found among women, who
seem to fear greater economic inequality between the sexes as an indirect
consequence of a liberal political and economic order.

The third and final part of the book examines democratization processes and their contributions (or lack thereof) to domestic and regional peace in the context of a number of case studies: Syria, Lebanon, and Jordan; Israel; Iran and Iraq; Libya, Tunisia, Algeria, and Morocco. In chapter 7, Kamel Abu S. Jaber shows that Syria, Lebanon, and Jordan are all characterized by incomplete democratization processes, which have produced the requisite institutional arrangements yet with only limited powers and legitimacy vested in them. In fact, as Abu Jaber points out, the most significant political forces, those that make, break, and shape democratization processes, are individual leaders and their personalities. Abu Jaber demonstrates that democratization in the Arab world usually takes a top–down approach, is applied arbitrarily, and is hostage to internal and regional conflicts. The region is in need of more than purely symbolic democracy. However, a certain period of top–down rule in the democratization process is required to balance and stabilize the effects of economic, political, and cultural reforms. These reforms establish the foundations for a solid civic culture and instill faith in democracy and government among ordinary citizens. This will help overcome the frustrations that exist over persisting authoritarian rule of the state.

As Abu Jaber argues, Syria's democratization process has been characterized by several coups d'état, multiple constitutions, and the Ba'th party's tight and autocratic grip on power, but also by some limited economic liberalization. Lebanon is characterized by strong sectarianism and both coexistence and segregation of different religious groups. Lebanon enjoyed some autonomy under Ottoman rule, and its Christian population developed strong ties with Rome. The French "adoption" of Lebanon heralded an era of Westernization. In the wake of the 1926 liberal constitution, high political posts and parliamentary seats were divided among the four main religious groups. The remaining 14 groups, however, have been excluded from holding high office. Although the Lebanese enjoy some freedoms, democracy is still at a very rudimentary stage. Nevertheless, commitment to a free press, a functioning parliament, and growing civil society have helped build a relatively strong sense of identity among the Lebanese.

Jordanians enjoy similarly basic political freedoms. Jordan's Hashemite lineage has offered secular and religious legitimacy to the state, which supports an institutionalized, moderate political system. The country benefits from an almost homogeneous population, with political representation offered to minority groups. Even during periods of transition and heavy-handed rule from the top, only little violence has occurred. Under martial law, opposition parties continued to operate, suffering only limited repression. Many of their leaders were later brought into high-ranking government posts. Jordan's kings have managed to

lend legitimacy to a patriarchal monarchy with democratic characteristics. Abu Jaber concludes by discussing the merits of opting for the
Jordanian approach, especially given his preference for state-driven development. He argues for a relativist approach to defining and designing
democratization processes in the region, to allow for deviations from
idealized (Western) concepts of democracy.

In chapter 8, Gerald Steinberg examines the relationship between democracy and peace in the context of Jewish political tradition. In general,
he argues that the authority of democratic and secular institutions finds
widespread support among both religious and secular communities in
Israel. He identifies the biblical call for the protection of the land of
Israel as the key issue over which Israel's religious and secular leaders
struggle in their search for a common ground. Nevertheless, and particularly after Prime Minister Rabin's assassination in the wake of the implementation of the 1993 Oslo Peace Accords, support shifted away from
the insistence on the territorial integrity of Israel to an emphasis on the
preservation of life and peace, and thus – despite the recent escalation of
violence – the continuation of the peace process with the Palestinians
and other Arab neighbors.

Steinberg describes the difficulties and complexities involved in the
creation of the modern Jewish state – a mix of traditional religious
structures and norms with democratic institutions and principles of late
nineteenth-century Europe. The Jewish population inevitably became
divided between secular and religious groups. Secular institutions, including courts, often stood in stark contradiction to religious norms. The
"land for peace" approach taken by secular governments to pursue peace
talks with the Palestinian community is a particularly tricky issue: ultra-
orthodox religious leaders insist on the biblical right to all of Israel's
territories, to the point where they incite the army to reject government
orders that call for the removal of settlers who are in violation of the
government's peace agreements. Steinberg shows how the land for peace
approach has triggered violent antagonism between secular and ultra-
orthodox Jews, who clearly subjugate secular rule to biblical rule. Nevertheless, several groups within the religious community give priority to
democratic governance and the preservation of life over the call to
protect Jewish lands. Steinberg notes, however, that incomplete democratization in countries throughout the region may at this stage be beneficial to Israel, because popular support for negotiations with Israel
has been far weaker among Arab populations than among their political leaders. Democratic systems would give stronger voice and muscle
to pro-Palestinian sentiments, which would create further antagonism
against Israel and its current policies and actions vis-à-vis the Palestinian
population and state.

Balancing religious Zionists (who do not recognize the legitimacy of secular authorities and consider them a threat to the safety and integrity of the Jewish state of Israel) with both secular and moderate religious communities is a difficult and delicate task. Although moderate forces have been gaining strength in both government and religious circles, tensions between Jewish traditions and secular political structures and political preferences will continue. Steinberg notes that both secular and religious schools are engaging in campaigns to promote democratic values (and Israel's commitment to them) among the younger generation. In the long run, this will strengthen public support for peace agreements and for an independent Palestinian state and the willingness to support the dismantling of illegal settlements. External factors, however, do play an important role in this development, including democratization processes among neighboring Arab societies and the level of daily violence caused by ongoing hostilities.

In chapter 9, Amin Saikal explores the relationship between peace and democratization processes in Iran and Iraq. He shows that Western-style liberal democracy may not be suitable for many countries in the region. On the contrary, regional leaders have used Western models to create sham democracies that are in reality forms of veiled authoritarianism, created to maintain an appearance of commitment toward the democratization process and intended for internal and external consumption. Saikal argues that more recognition and credit should be granted to indigenous attempts to develop local versions of civil society and democracy, based on the conditions and traditions of each country. Iran's attempts to create an Islamic version of civil society and democracy, with the participation and protection of minority groups, may serve as a model for other local attempts to develop democracies that go beyond minimalist definitions of democratic governance (popular power and popular sovereignty) and facilitate gradual and non-violent reforms of internal and external political processes. The Ijtihadis' approach outlined by Saikal closely resembles efforts by moderate Jewish religious leaders to reconcile biblical norms with socio-political realities, discussed in the preceding chapter.

Saikal calls for commitment to move beyond minimalist forms of democracy. Systems that are democratic in form and authoritarian in substance produce violence through the exclusion of some parts of the population. Overly enthusiastic attempts to embark on Western-style democratization, as experienced during the Shah's reign in Iran, will lead to violence if no effort is made to integrate religious forces that have for a long time defined a society's political, social, and cultural life. If radical religious and secular groups are persecuted rather than integrated in the transition process, counter-revolutions and violence will result, particularly when reform processes (as has been the case in Iran) fail to produce the economic gains expected by the public.

The war with Iraq successfully deflected the public's attention from the lack of reform dividends and improvements over the previous regime. Khomeini's ability to appease both Jihadis and Ijtihadis created a basic level of coexistence between modernizers and traditionalists. After the war, however, continuing socio-economic problems and efforts by Ijtihadis to portray Islam as compatible with democracy, along with a solid electoral process, brought Khatami to power in July 1997. Khatami's embrace of Islamic civil society and democracy and his commitment to dialogue between civilizations have produced a version of democracy that is different from, but not necessarily in opposition to, Western concepts and expectations. An inclusive approach that pursues progress in the context of freedom of thought and expression (and thus supports a vibrant civil society) offers opportunities to respect Islamic traditions within a more open, participatory society. Jihadis feel that the principles and aims of the revolution are being undermined. Balancing their interests with reforms certainly slows down the democratization process, but it keeps it on track and – most importantly – non-violent.

In contrast to Iran, Iraq has experienced nothing but violence and autocratic rule under the 30-year dictatorial regime of Saddam Hussein. Saddam's preference for a violent and repressive culture, backed during the Cold War with petro-dollars and some American support, offers no scope for democratic reform or the evolution of a functioning civil society. His tragic and misguided decision to attack Kuwait, and the subsequent Gulf War, robbed Iraq of most of its sovereignty, weakened its domestic structures, and is still continuing to impose great pain on Iraq's population. Even if Saddam is removed from power, the prospects for democratic reform are scant after decades of suppression and the virtual extinction of Iraq's former middle class.

In chapter 10, Tom Najem examines democratization processes in Morocco, Algeria, Tunisia, and Libya. In all four states, he argues, overwhelming state power has inhibited the development of civil society and a solid democratic political culture that could serve as the foundation of democratic processes once the current regimes leave power. Najem argues that Islamist forces are not, as modernization theorists would have it, responsible for the lack of democratization processes in otherwise semi-modern, semi-developed societies. Rather, structural issues, internal as well as external, have served as obstacles to political, economic, and cultural opening. It is here that the four states differ from each other: different combinations of structural forces created or supported strong authoritarian states that are vehemently opposed to political, cultural, and economic liberalization. Najem argues that under such conditions only intense external pressure or internal pressure from powerful and widely supported civil society organizations could trigger movement toward real democratization. He examines a number of key factors in the progress (or lack thereof) of each country's democratization process: the role of the state and political institutions; economic development; social divisions; civil society; political culture and ideas; and transnational and international engagements.

Morocco features some rudimentary democratic characteristics, including a limited pluralist system and civil society, although they are tightly controlled by the monarchy. Islamist groups and others who question the legitimacy and policies of the monarchy are excluded from the political process. There is some limited inclusion of opposition forces, but only to the extent that the king's authority is not threatened. Although Morocco has no significant oil resources, the state still uses economic "carrots and sticks" to control powerful economic and urban classes. Civil society enjoys only limited autonomy. The monarchy's link to Islamic tradition effectively curtails the strength of Islamist opposition groups. Algeria's struggle with Islamist political forces helps the monarchy in solidifying support for the status quo. While the IMF and the World Bank pressure the state to liberalize, fears of Algerian-style violence contain external pressure for political reforms. The new king's actions to reform the political system and promote human rights are positive steps but are not indicative of any limitation of the king's powers.

Algeria's authoritarian military state is at war with strong and popular Islamist forces that show little commitment to democratic ideals. Najem shows that the consequences of Algeria's liberal reforms in the early 1990s served as an example of the danger posed by political reforms in a society that lacks a broad-based democratic political culture. Free elections brought Islamist groups with anti-democratic platforms to power, triggering the state's refusal to hand over political control. This was the precursor to a decade of violence and internal conflict and military rule. International fears of the prospect of an Islamist state have so far fueled external support for the military regime.

Also in reaction to Algeria's experience, Tunisia's government refuses to allow Islamist groups to participate in the political process. Whereas the 1970s had brought some liberalization, economic decline and social inequities led to opposition to the regime throughout the 1980s, culminating in a coup. The new government embarked on a reform process to open up the political system, effect a reconciliation with opposition groups, and revive the country's political, economic, and cultural life. Nonetheless, it marginalized the strongest Islamist group (Mouvement de la tendance islamique), which became progressively more radical, triggering increasingly repressive policies by the state. The gains of initial liberalization were lost and the stand-off between the repressive regime and the Islamist opposition continues to this day.

Libya is ruled by an authoritarian state, with no immediate chances for democratization or the evolution of a functioning civil society. Qaddafi's rentier state uses oil money to buy off political opposition, to appease the population, and to strengthen the state's grip on the political, economic, and social life of the entire society. Although the regime's legitimacy and authority were under threat in the wake of international sanctions, declining oil prices, tribal instability, and Islamist opposition, the lifting of UN sanctions and an increase in oil revenues have stabilized Qaddafi's grip on power. Without a democratic political culture or civil society, there is little hope for political liberalization, even should Qaddafi's rule come to an end.

Najem shows that, for a variety of reasons not directly related to the influence of Islam, a number of countries in the region are cursed with authoritarian governments that are in full control of political, economic, and social life, with no or little intention of allowing civil society and democratic political processes to flourish. With no pro-democratic forces waiting in the wings, even a crisis or the collapse of current regimes will not necessarily lead to improved prospects for democratization. Continued violence and the instability of political transitions would hinder positive reforms and increased prospects for domestic and regional peace.

Lessons

Despite the differences and difficulties in defining minimally acceptable features of a democracy, all authors agree on at least the following: none of the constituent states in the region, with the exception of Israel in certain specific ways, has reached a level of democratization that would guarantee a path toward sustainable democracy and prevent a future return to non-democratic governance and de-secularization and de-liberalization of the economy and society. Moreover, the absence of stable democracies increases actual and potential instability throughout the region. Repression of opposition forces and suppression of civil society development are but a few examples of the structural violence created by authoritarian or quasi-democratic regimes. Although many factors contribute to the propensity of nations to wage either war or peace against their own populations and their neighbors, socially, politically, and economically stable systems certainly raise the odds that peace prevails over war. We are undoubtedly many years away from reaping peace dividends from sustained democratization processes in the Middle East. In addition, most contributions to this volume show that, if anything, reform processes toward political, economic, and cultural liberalization have so far brought much instability and violence to the region, as traditional (often religious) values continue to clash with secular ethics, norms, and practices.

Four issues are particularly important in preventing transitional violence and in neutralizing threats to nascent democratization processes. First, broad sectors of the population need to be familiar with, and ideally fully embrace, civic virtues and a democratic political culture, manifested through the presence of a healthy, functioning, and influential civil society. Second, political leaders must be fully committed to reform processes, to the extent that they are prepared to relinquish some of their own powers to strengthen democratic governance. Third, regional conditions must be favorable – including the resolution of grave problems that divide the region and pitch individual states or groups of states against each other (such as the Israeli–Palestinian conflict, the ongoing military campaign against Iraq, or the support by some, and objection by others, of America's continued "war on terrorism"). Fourth, external conditions must be conducive to conflict resolution and peace, including the absence of manipulative external powers' involvement in regional politics and the presence of international economic conditions that will allow Middle Eastern countries to bear the cost of democratic governance and the provision of social and other services that are necessary to maintain popular support during the inevitable ups and downs of transition and reform periods.

Transitions to democracy can be violent – more violent than the structural violence that is ever-present under authoritarian rule. On the one hand, democratization processes are stifled because of fears that an opening of the system might trigger the rise of democratically elected, but anti-democratically inclined, political parties and movements. On the other hand, commitment to democratization is necessary to establish, it is to be hoped at some not too distant point in the future, a more accountable, just, and transparent political order. Most contributors agree that, in order to push forward democratization processes while advancing internal and regional peace, reforms must be gradual and monitored and controlled from the top, and they must be supplemented by a similarly gradual process toward the establishment of a broad-based and broadly supported civil society. Only such gradual reform processes will be successful in the end. Democratization is, as described so aptly by Majid Tehranian, a "journey" that takes time to be completed, not an event that can be planned and executed at will.

Notes

1. For an estimate of the human and material costs of the various armed interstate and intrastate conflicts in the Middle East between 1948 and 1992, see Saad Eddin Ibrahim, "Liberalization and Democratization in the Arab World: An Overview," in Baghat Korany, Rex Brynen, and Paul Noble, eds., *Political Liberalization and Democratization in the Arab World: Theoretical Perspectives*, Boulder, CO: Lynne Rienner, 1995, p. 35, Table 2.1.
2. See the United Nations Development Programme (UNDP), *Arab Human Development Report 2002*, New York: UNDP, 2002, for a strong call for Arab societies to further human development through, among others, education, economic growth, poverty reduction, democratization, and regional cooperation.
3. For previous studies on prospects for, trends in, and obstacles to democratization in the Middle East, see the two-volume series edited by Baghat Korany, Rex Brynen, and Paul Noble, *Political Liberalization and Democratization in the Arab World: Theoretical Perspectives*, and *Political Liberalization and Democratization in the Arab World: Comparative Experiences*, Boulder, CO: Lynne Rienner, 1998.
4. Although democratic peace theory is mentioned by a number of contributions to this volume, and discussed more prominently in chapter 3, the volume will deal only marginally with it. For democratic peace theory to be tested in a regional context, a minimum of two (and preferably more) established democracies would be required before a meaningful examination of the results of the propositions of the theory is possible. This is not currently the case in the Middle East.
5. See UNDP, *Arab Human Development Report 2002*, particularly chapter 7 on "Liberating Human Capabilities: Governance, Human Development and the Arab World," pp. 105–20.
6. Leila Sharaf, as quoted in UNDP, *Arab Human Development Report 2002*, p. 115.
7. UNDP, *Arab Human Development Report 2002*, p. 106.
8. For some seminal writings on the processes of democratization, see Robert A. Dahl, *Polyarchy: Participation and Opposition*, New Haven, CT: Yale University Press, 1971; Guillermo O'Donnell, Philippe C. Schmitter, and Laurence Whitehead, eds., *Transitions from Authoritarian Rule: Prospects for Democracy*, Baltimore, MD: Johns Hopkins University Press, 1986; Robert A. Dahl, *Democracy and Its Critics*, New Haven, CT: Yale University Press, 1989; Larry Diamond, Juan J. Linz, and Seymour Martin Lipset, eds., *Politics in Developing Countries: Comparing Experiences with Democracy*, Boulder, CO: Lynne Rienner Publishers, 1990; Samuel Huntington, *The Third Wave: Democratization in the Late Twentieth Century*, Norman, OK: University of Oklahoma Press, 1991; Juan J. Linz and Alfred Stepan, *Problems of Democratic Transition and Consolidation*, Baltimore, MD: Johns Hopkins University Press, 1996; and Larry Diamond, *Developing Democracy: Toward Consolidation*, Baltimore, MD: Johns Hopkins University Press, 1999. For a very recent discussion, see *Journal of Democracy*, vol. 13, no. 3, July 2002, on the theme of "Debating the Transition Paradigm."
9. Philippe C. Schmitter, "Some Basic Assumptions about the Consolidation of Democracy," in Takashi Inoguchi, Edward Newman, and John Keane, eds., *The Changing Nature of Democracy*, Tokyo: United Nations University Press, 1998, p. 32. *The Changing Nature of Democracy* was the first book in a series of studies on democracy and democratization undertaken by the United Nations University. The present book is part of this series.
10. Ibid.
11. On this discussion, see, for instance, Rudolph J. Rummel, "Democracies Don't Fight Democracies," available at http://www.peacemagazine.org/9905/rummel.htm; Miriam

Fendius Elman, ed., *Paths to Peace: Is Democracy the Answer?* Cambridge, MA.: MIT Press, 1997; Thomas Schwartz and Kiran Skinner, "The Myth of Democratic Pacifism," *Hoover Digest*, No. 2, 1999; Spencer R. Weart, *Never at War: Why Democracies Will Not Fight One Another*, New Haven, CT: Yale University Press, 1997; Michael E. Brown, Sean M. Lynn-Jones, and Steven E. Miller, eds., *Debating the Democratic Peace*, Cambridge, MA: MIT Press, 1996; Torak Barkawi and Mark Laffey, eds., *Democracy, Liberalism, and War: Rethinking the Democratic Peace Debate*, Boulder, CO: Lynne Rienner Publishers, 2001; and Paul H. Huth, *The Democratic Peace and Territorial Conflict in the Twentieth Century*, Cambridge: Cambridge University Press, forthcoming in 2003.

12. David Potter, David Goldblatt, Margaret Kiloh, and Paul Lewis, eds., *Democratization*, Cambridge: Polity Press, 1997, p. 6.

13. Bruce Russett, "A Structure for Peace: A Democratic, Interdependent, and Institutionalized Order," in Inoguchi, Newman, and Keane, eds., *The Changing Nature of Democracy*, p. 160.

14. Dahl, *Democracy and Its Critics*, p. 221.

15. Schmitter, "Some Basic Assumptions," p. 33.

Part I

Democratic peace, conflict prevention, and the United Nations

2

Democratization and peacebuilding

Albrecht Schnabel

Successful democratization is essential to bring peace to the countries of the Middle East. Internal stability, development, justice, reconciliation, minority protection, and popular participation in the political process – all hallmarks of a stable, inclusive democracy – will in the long run help the region move beyond its many protracted intra- and interstate conflicts. The process of democratization cannot be either purely just or purely pragmatic: it facilitates the rebuilding of society by merging society- and institution-building, thus creating the foundations for intergroup trust and non-violent interaction and competition.

Of course, the ultimate goal would be, as in any other region, to reach a state of "positive peace" – the absence of inequality, injustice, and oppression, and the maintenance of political, social, and economic conditions that assure the well-being of individuals and communities. Positive peace results from the provision of, and investment in, human security – the satisfaction of human needs, from the most basic survival needs to needs for self-expression, general welfare, and freedom of choice and expression.[1]

The satisfaction of human security,[2] the foremost task and responsibility of states vis-à-vis their citizens, is necessary to maintain the inner peace of the individual and peace between individuals, between communities, and, in extension, between states. Unfulfilled human needs cause frustration, resistance, and, eventually, violent conflict. The provision of human security requires action in response to many non-traditional security threats, ranging from economic to environmental to societal security. Often referred to as "structural violence," structural inequalities in social, economic, and political systems result in poverty, malnutrition, lack of health care, crime, and many other social illnesses that threaten the lives and livelihoods of many more people than does direct violence by one's own state or outside attackers. The costs of non-traditional security threats (such as environmental degradation, human rights violations, or poverty) can be as devastating for human beings as those of traditional security threats (such as military threats or armed domestic violence), and they always bear the potential of escalation to armed violence and war. The provision of human security assures sustainable, positive peace. The liberalization of political, economic, and social systems and the protection of minorities from the risks associated with majority rule are key components of a state's efforts to offer human security to its population.

However, we are far from a state of positive peace in the Middle East. Armed conflict pervades the region, in various types and shades: regional conflicts; resource wars; separatist and nationalist conflicts; irredentist conflicts; ethnic, religious, and tribal power struggles; revolutionary and fundamentalist struggles; and pro-democracy and anti-colonial struggles.[3] The peoples and governments throughout the Middle East are thus facing a tall order: the first task is to secure a state of "negative peace" and to settle current wars and violent conflicts. Although even negative peace cannot be secured for long unless peacebuilding strategies resolve the underlying root causes of violence, these causes cannot be resolved and positive peace cannot be initiated in the presence of violence. The difficulties in pursuing the Middle East peace process in the presence of daily violence between Israelis and Palestinians speak for themselves. Improving peaceful relations in the region is a complex task, involving the simultaneous pursuit of both negative and positive peace, of peacekeeping and peacebuilding, and of the settlement of current disputes and the simultaneous prevention of future ones.

Can democratization help rebuild violently divided societies and prevent the emergence – or resurgence – of conflict? What needs to be done, and by whom? What are the roles of international organizations, states, and civil society? Successful democratization is a crucial component of structural, early, prevention of violent conflict. Stable democratic regimes usually do not go to war against their own people. This guarantees internal peace and stability. Democratic regimes also tend not to go to war against other democracies. This enhances regional peace and stability. Together, internal and regional security are the prerequisites for political stability and economic development and the eventual evolution of what Karl Deutsch[4] and, more recently, Barnett and Adler[5] have described as security communities.

The chapter begins with a discussion of the challenges of rebuilding war-torn, divided societies. It then examines the role of democratization in peacebuilding and conflict prevention. It outlines the pitfalls of democratization and points to ways in which this process can be made less conflict prone, divisive, and threatening to indigenous cultural and political histories and preferences. This discussion will then continue in the context of democratization processes throughout the Middle East, where the forces of secularization, religion, tradition, and radicalization often clash with the need for peace, development, and regional cooperation. The chapter concludes with a look at the chances of democratization as a peace management tool throughout the region, and the requirements and opportunities for early conflict detection and prevention through (and throughout) the democratization process.

Divided societies: Challenges, problems, dangers, requirements

Divided and conflict-torn societies are marked by a traumatic impoverishment of economic, political, and social relations between groups and individual citizens. Intergroup violence compounds existing divisions within society, and new divisions are added. The political, economic, and socio-cultural breakdown of (multi)national communities makes it extremely difficult to rebuild a sense of identity and communal belonging once violence has ceased. Whereas it may be possible to impose a sense of *Gesellschaft* from outside, the sense of *Gemeinschaft* has to grow from within. Democratization processes serve both of these goals.

Violently divided societies are characterized by institutional breakdown: weak or non-existent political institutions; a power vacuum; vigorous competition for power; weak or non-existent civil society institutions; and limited government legitimacy and authority. In the absence of legitimate governments, power vacuums create fierce competition for influence and access to territory and economic resources. In this environment, appeals to nationalist or religious identities, as the primary common denominators and sources of communal pride and power, lead to fear and retaliatory moves by other ethnic or religious groups within multi-communal states. Intergroup conflicts can quickly escalate into violence. In many countries, civil war along ideological lines and against repressive governments, often propped up by one of the Cold War superpowers, has pitched different sections of society against each other, or against their own governments.

Governments that oppress all or portions of their population, that eradicate civil society institutions and limit people's access to self-rule and free expression, are in a very weak position once the instruments of oppression are gone, external support is denied, or a viable opposition begins to question the oppressor's self-declared legitimacy. Such is the situation when societies emerge from civil wars. Without strong institutions (judicial, political, economic, cultural) states cannot be rebuilt, and international actors will not be able to locate legitimate partners with whom to negotiate and cooperate. A weak society needs strong and legitimate institutions to help rebuild trust, confidence, and a more stable future. However, a weak and divided society cannot produce a strong and legitimate government. International organizations have helped societies build their own institutions (such as by organizing and monitoring democratic elections in Bosnia, Kosovo, East Timor, or El Salvador), or have replaced those institutions with trusteeships until the political environment is safe enough – and the domestic civic culture is mature enough – to sustain a peaceful political process.

Democratization attempts are caught in a difficult situation. True democratization cannot happen without a strong, established, well-functioning, and broadly supported civil society – which produces potential leaders at all levels of governance and socializes and mobilizes the general public around democratic and civic duties and responsibilities. However, such organizations can prosper only in an environment characterized by order, stability, and freedom of expression. That environment, in turn, requires the existence of a viable democratic process.

If domestic capacities are lacking, external support may be required. Externally supported creation of fragile, yet somewhat functioning institutions is meant to trigger the momentum needed to encourage the evolution of a functioning civil society. The latter will, after a few years of consolidation and post-conflict stability, produce the first wholly internally crafted government. At that time, external involvement, if still provided at that point, can cede.

Democratization and peacebuilding in violently divided societies

"Democracy" describes a political system; "democratization" describes a process. The political system can be created, even imposed, on a war-torn society almost overnight. However, the process of democratization is a long-term commitment by internal and external actors to the consolidation of a democratic culture that must, at some point, become self-sustaining.

In more general terms, a democratic government "must combine three essential conditions: meaningful *competition* for political power amongst individuals and organized groups; inclusive *participation* in the selection of leaders and policies, at least through free and fair elections; and a level of *civil and political liberties* sufficient to ensure the integrity of political competition and participation."[6] Both "[p]articipation and contestation are crucial: while democracy can take many forms, no system can be called democratic without a meaningful level of both."[7] Only if citizens feel that their government is accountable, representative of all groups and individuals, theirs to control, and responsive to civil society concerns will a government enjoy the authority – yet rarely the appreciation – to steer society through the difficult and painful waters of post-conflict transition.

Democratization allows a divided society to rebuild a sense of community – a prerequisite for overcoming a culture of violence and developing a culture of peace and cooperation. It is moreover necessary to pursue this not only in a local and national context but also within the region at large. Democratization processes in post-conflict societies are based on compromise and cooperation between and among former foes. They require forgiveness, reconciliation, and pragmatic, yet non-violent, political maneuvering to be effective and successful. They operate between justice and pragmatism in seeking the most effective approaches to peacebuilding, and thus a return to relations in which competition and disputes are solved non-violently, within the context of legal and moral guidelines that regulate peaceful interactions between individuals and groups. However, the creation of a post-conflict democratic system of governance and social interaction (accountable governments and a flourishing civil society) requires the assistance and support of the international community and its various intergovernmental organizations.

Unfortunately, long-term commitment is difficult to secure from international organizations. Although all regional organizations and the United Nations possess the ability to contribute to peacebuilding and democratization where they have a comparative advantage (political, economic, or military assistance), few have the resources and standing power to remain engaged on a long-term basis. Thus, peacebuilding has to employ the tools of the possible. Successes have to be visible and relatively quickly achieved, justice has to be served to an acceptable degree, and the foundation for long-term stability has to be – again visibly – laid. Pragmatic decisions have to be made and the advantages of peacebuilding must be recognizable for those waiting to benefit from it (societies previously at war) and those supporting it (international community).

Democratization allows all that: the imposition of new structures to serve at least partial justice, input from outside, and visible progress and means to monitor the success or failure, progress or breakdown, of social reconstruction. Democratization efforts, first from above and simultaneously and subsequently from below, provide the tools for peace-building and social reconstruction that can be monitored from the outside. Such monitoring (together with assessment and evaluation) is done not only by those in power and those studying a post-conflict society, but also by the media and, thus, by ordinary people who lend support to (or withdraw it from) their government's international peacebuilding efforts in places that are far away and, at first sight, of marginal significance to their own national security.

Democratization: Where democratizers meet conflict managers

According to Bloomfield and Reilly, "[d]emocratic systems have a degree of legitimacy, inclusiveness, flexibility and capacity for constant adaptation that enables deep-rooted conflicts to be managed peacefully. Moreover, by building norms of behavior or negotiation, compromise, and cooperation amongst political actors, democracy itself has a pacifying effect on the nature of political relations between people and between governments."[8] In post-conflict societies, externally facilitated democratization often merges justice with pragmatic approaches to conflict management, conflict resolution, and society-building.

However, conflict management and conflict resolution are not necessarily synonymous terms. Democracy is an instrument of conflict management: differences between various actors are transformed by peaceful means into cooperation and mutual compromise. After all, conflict can be a positive and crucial element of social and economic enhancement; in essence, conflict denotes competition – the competition of ideas and practices that drive intellectual, artistic, and economic progress. But the same competition can have negative and destructive consequences if competing interests are not reconciled and are seen as mutually exclusive. Even if such conflicts are settled, they are far from being resolved. Competing/conflicting parties may have reached a point where no party expects to gain considerably from the prolongation of conflict, or where external actors provide incentives for ending the conflict; but this does not mean that the root causes of conflict are addressed, let alone resolved.[9]

The democratization process offers divided populations peaceful alternatives to violent competition. In essence, similar battles over similar issues (political power, territory, economic access, or claims to cultural supremacy) can now be carried out at the non-violent level of democratic political interaction. The polling office and legislative assembly replace the battlefield, and the ballot and the speaker's podium replace the gun as the principal weapon in intergroup competition. This interaction does not by itself re-establish justice, but it requires forgiveness when the recent past takes long to forget. It is conceivable that justice simply cannot be served fully – at any time, in any context, in any circumstance. Divided societies will never be the same as they were before violence broke out. However, over time they can grow again into new societies, ideally ones that are able to use the lessons from the past to prevent future conflicts.

International organizations play an important part in creating a working balance between justice and pragmatism in post-war peacebuilding efforts. They can provide both the "carrots" and the "sticks" to nurture successful transition processes. International organizations have a key role in economic and technical assistance, the organization and supervision of elections (and the fair implementation of their results), assistance in security sector transformation (such as arms conversion, disarmament, demobilization, the establishment of civilian control over military forces), assistance in the repatriation of refugees, rebuilding infrastructure and educational and health systems, among many other crucial post-conflict rebuilding efforts.[10]

A number of issues are crucial in this context. Is the international community committed to principled peacebuilding processes in post-conflict or post–civil war situations? Who is the international community – a global society of states and individuals represented by the United Nations, a number of globally operating non-governmental organizations, or regional organizations that have the political will and the means to invest in the stability of neighboring states, or some combination of these? Is it possible to enforce peacebuilding efforts and, if so, which external actors are able to and can be entrusted with this task? What is the role of the United Nations – does it play a central role or simply a subsidiary monitoring and legitimizing role in regional efforts toward post-conflict peacebuilding?

The sustainability of outside commitment and political will is a crucial factor in determining the long-term success of peacebuilding efforts. As Crocker and Hampson note, "[a]s in law or business, statecraft illustrates the maxim that the real negotiation begins only *after* the agreement is signed. Outsiders who orphan the settlements they have helped to produce, by getting out too early due to lost interest or political will, will watch the agreements collapse."[11] Peacebuilding and democratization efforts that go beyond symbolic elections or refugee resettlements (both of which can be decisively counterproductive if not pursued as part of a well-planned greater peacebuilding strategy) have to be matched with cooperation by the people and leaders in post-war societies if the momentum for external assistance is to be maintained. Post-conflict peacebuilding is a costly exercise, and those paying for it (the citizens of the countries involved in assisting these efforts) need to be assured that their investment in regional peace and security will pay off eventually.

The democratization process is – and should be – a key component of peacebuilding efforts in violently divided societies. Civil war destroys the very political, economic, and social fabric that serves as the foundation for secure and peaceful relations within a community. The culture of violence, prevalent particularly during and after civil wars, has to give way to a culture of peace, grounded in a representative and accountable government and a free and influential civil society. This is already difficult in the context of a society that has not been torn apart by intergroup war, and is all the more difficult to achieve in a post-conflict political and social environment.

Without peacebuilding there can be no social healing, and without social healing there can be no effective peacebuilding. Democratization presents a practicable compromise: it serves the immediate, short-term need for institution-building and governance, required for the reconstruction of basic stability and order. Legitimate and representative governing structures can be removed, altered, and reinforced peacefully, without resort to violence. Democratization efforts stabilize a society to the point where badly needed outside economic assistance will enter the rebuilding process. Although absolute justice may initially take the back seat to pragmatic rebuilding efforts, democratization processes will, in the long run, allow for reconciliation and social healing.[12]

The pitfalls of democratization

Democratization in violently divided societies nonetheless bears its risks. Rapid economic and political transition can lead to intolerable displacement of those who suffered most during the war – those whose property has been destroyed, the internally displaced, the elderly, children, and women. Post-war transition has to be gradual and sustainable, and it has to offer justice for those (on all sides of a conflict) who have to overcome grave psychological traumas before they can grasp the opportunities offered by political and economic transition.

It is moreover important to nurture civil society, to assure a democratization process from below and not solely from above. If democratization is purely elite driven, even if these are counter-elites from the pre-war era, democracy may not take hold where it is most important – among the citizens of the divided post-war society. Thus, although the cooperation of elites is clearly instrumental in solidifying democratic institution-building, an effort also has to be made to incorporate civil society in this process. Only then will we achieve "democratic *consolidation*: that democratic practices become so deeply internalized by political actors that acting outside the institutional 'rules of the game' becomes unthinkable."[13] Civil society needs to be engaged in translating constitutional norms into a widely accepted and practiced political, social, and economic way of life.

Although intergroup conflict may now be carried out in polling stations and not on battlefields, the end result may still be an elected government divided along ethnic lines.[14] Depending on the personal character and war-time roles of the candidates elected for political office, early elections may freeze intergroup rivalries beyond the society's aptitude for intergroup and post-war healing. Indeed, "poorly designed democratic institutions can also inflame communal conflicts rather than ameliorate them ... [T]he introduction of 'democratic' politics can easily be used to mobilize ethnicity, turning elections into 'us' versus 'them' conflict."[15] There is a great danger that old elites will be the elites of tomorrow. This is of course counterproductive to reconciliation and post-war society-building. Democratization efforts allow all groups to compete for power, including those perceived as the aggressors and main protagonists of war.

However, each group may well consider the other groups as the villains to be blamed for the destruction and displacement caused by the war, and find it difficult to share political power (let alone social relations) with their former foes. Because democracy is based on compromise, cooperation, and power-sharing, justice may have to be served through symbolic acts of reconciliation and blaming – through truth commissions, criminal tribunals, and other symbolic means of social healing. Justice nevertheless does not have to be sacrificed, allowing the old state to re-emerge in the guise of a new one. Again, international organizations play an important role in "guiding" the speed and application of peace-building efforts, to assure that this will not happen.

"Sustainable democratization" is the key approach to violently divided societies. This implies that democratization processes are part of, and indeed central to, the post-conflict peacebuilding effort. Citizens of a society that has learned to engage freely and openly on a political level are also able to trade and live peacefully with each other – and with others beyond its borders. A well-functioning civil society, alongside a representative and accountable government, allows for the social healing that is necessary to recreate a functioning social fabric. The political, social, economic, environmental, and security breakdown of divided societies can then be successfully addressed. However, in the absence of sustained democratization efforts, social healing and society-building are greatly impeded and may not happen at all, paving the way for a return to violence and national and regional instability. Democratization allows for a maximum of pragmatic change and conflict resolution without abandoning justice and hopes for eventual reconciliation.

Violent conflicts can be prevented only by internal and external stabilization efforts. Individual societies and the region need to be stabilized, in part through democratization efforts and the benefits of what the democratic peace theory argues – the positive spillover for interstate relations from functioning democracies. That entails both crisis diplomacy and the prevention of escalating crises, as well as measures to address the political, economic, and social root causes of instability and violence, and the stabilization of long-term political and economic development. Economic development is particularly important for a democracy to prosper, and for leaders to secure and maintain the support of their people and undermine calls by extremist groups for alternative routes. Both internal actors (civil society, non-state actors, political parties) and external actors (regional and international organizations, other states, international non-governmental organizations, diaspora communities) can be productive, but also disruptive, in this process.

Democratization, regional peace, and the Middle East

As the UN Development Programme's *Arab Human Development Report 2002* notes,

[t]he wave of democracy that transformed governance in most of Latin America and East Asia in the 1980s and Eastern Europe and much of Central Asia in the late 1980s and early 1990s has barely reached the Arab states. This freedom deficit undermines human development and is one of the most painful manifestations of lagging political development. While de jure acceptance of democracy and human rights is enshrined in constitutions, legal codes and government pronouncements, de facto implementation is often neglected and, in some cases, deliberately disregarded. In most cases, the governance pattern is characterized by a powerful executive branch that exerts significant control over all other branches of the state, being in some cases free from institutional checks and balances. Representative democracy is not always genuine and sometimes absent. Freedoms of expression and association are frequently curtailed. Obsolete norms of legitimacy prevail.[16]

Indeed, the prospects for genuine democratization appear to be bleak. Sustainable democratization in the Middle East can thus be achieved only if a number of conditions are met. First, democratization comes from below as well as from above. Pressure from below will simply evaporate if the political leadership is not receptive to the ideals of democratic governance and is unwilling to open up the political process, for fear of having to share, or potentially surrender, political power. On the other hand, top–down democratization will not fall on fertile ground if the requisite political culture has not developed and society is unfamiliar with, and possibly alienated by, the freedoms as well as responsibilities that accompany political liberalization and participation. Democratization supported only by the leadership or only by society is at best weak and fragile, at worst doomed to failure. So far, top–down democratization has been the rule throughout the Middle East.

Secondly, democratization will not be sustainable if the majority rules without giving adequate protection to minorities, and if minority ethnic groups and religious fringe groups are marginalized, alienated, driven to extinction, and, as a last resort, driven to radical actions to make themselves heard. Throughout the Middle East, states have so far found it difficult to reconcile majority interests with minority concerns.

Finally, successful democratization efforts have to be linked with solid economic performance and political stability and, as much as possible, the unimpeded growth and maturity of civil society. The Middle East does not score high on this last point either. The evolution of civil society depends largely on decisions made by governments, including the willingness to consider civil society as a partner in improving governance and to engage them in a dialogue about both the pace and path of democratization. Eventually, democratization will benefit all: political, economic, and social liberalization will reduce tensions, which will increase political stability, investor confidence, and, as a result, economic performance and development.

Opportunities for democratization

What are the advantages of and opportunities for successful democratization efforts throughout the region? Democratization adds legitimacy to multi-cultural governments in multi-cultural societies. It allows for the representation of and participation in the political process of all ethnic and religious groups, social classes, and genders. It allows for the governance of the majority, while minorities are respected and protected. It supports the promotion of positive peace and the strengthening of social and political structures to support justice, equality, and access to and participation in the political and economic life for all of the population. It increases the chances for regional cooperation on traditional (military–strategic) and non-traditional (all other threats to people's lives and well-being) security issues.

It emancipates and empowers the people of the region, thus removing opportunities for external powers to "rule the rulers" and meddle freely in regional affairs. This will result in greater independence from what is widely perceived as cultural and political imperialism – and the local resentment this causes. It will help eliminate popular tolerance of, and in some countries overt support for, government-sponsored terrorism used to intimidate external powers into retreating from the region. Eventual inter-religious peace and reconciliation in the Middle East could even serve as an example for other parts of the world.

Difficulties of the democratization process

Certain pitfalls of democratization have already been mentioned. In its nascent stages, and particularly if pursued too fast and as a carbon-copy of Western political experiences, democratization can empower anti-democratic elements in society. Nationalists or religious or ethnic fanatics may be elected to power and office, upon which they might derail democratization processes that have already begun. Poorly planned democratization efforts can thus allow the rise of those who will disband them.

In contrast to "honest" democratization efforts, "dishonest" democratization takes place when leaders pursue political liberalization as a façade for veiled authoritarianism. This does not lead to true political opening, instead providing cover for the continuation of repressive policies by equally repressive regimes, and does nothing to promote sustainable peace, human rights, and the corresponding social and economic policies. Top–down, elite-driven democratization, accompanied by the suppression of civil society, is similarly counterproductive to real democratization. Leaders do not need to suppress civil society formation and input if they are serious about opening the political process. If they do suppress civil society, they are not seriously interested in democratization. Nevertheless, gradual, top–down democratization may be the safest approach to assure eventual democratic consolidation. Thus, there is a great need for enlightened, moderate, and pro-democracy political and religious leaders whose aim is to transfer power gradually to maturing civic societies and, eventually, to release authority to a popularly elected and supported representative government.

Democracy may not be able to accommodate dramatically different, possibly opposing, views of intergroup and interstate relations that are too strong to allow for compromise and reconciliation. However, democracy will not support the continuation of oppression and discrimination by a few against the many. The promotion of democracy in the Middle East does not have to focus on an "imported" Western, quite possibly inappropriate, model of political, economic, and social order. The promotion of an open and just society is desirable by all humans, irrespective of their heritage, history, or ethnic or religious affiliation. Let us recall

Dahl's main criteria for a democratic political system: elected officials; free and fair elections; inclusive suffrage; the right to run for office; freedom of expression; alternative information protected by law; and associational autonomy.[17] These can be considered among a number of universal trademarks of a true democracy, nascent or well established. According to these criteria not a single country in the Middle East is a true democracy, although some are more or less firmly set on the path toward a more open, participatory and just society.

So far, Israel comes the closest to what one could consider a base-line democracy. Other countries are moving closer to those universal ideals. Morocco displays impressive tolerance for freedom of press and association, as well as a vibrant civil society. Prior to the civil war, Lebanon exhibited a high degree of pluralism; this environment must be recreated. In Egypt, multiparty politics are in place, but they are restricted by electoral laws and procedures that favor one major party – the National Democratic Party. Jordan has seen successful multiparty elections and a relatively free press debate on domestic and foreign policy. Saudi Arabia and the smaller Gulf states experiment cautiously with democratization and shared power.

Syria, Iraq, Iran, Sudan, and Libya are very resistant to democratization. In Syria, democratization efforts are suppressed. In Iran, only those fully committed to Islamic ideals are allowed to participate in elections; women and non-Muslims do not enjoy full political rights. There is no attempt at democratization in Iraq and Libya, where authoritarian rulers (Saddam and Qaddafi) cling to power. Sudan's military regime has reversed democratization trends.[18]

Ideally, democratization throughout a region would eventually create what Karl Deutsch described as a "security community."[19] For this to happen the countries of the region must feature similar regime types (preferably all democratic regimes). This is not the case in the Middle East. The countries should also have similar economic systems, with comparable performance (free market economies with positive economic growth). The Middle East is far from reaching that goal. The countries would ideally have similar and shared cultures, ethnicity, religion, and history. Although this might be the case for a majority of countries in the Middle East (Islamic religion, Arab culture), opposition to the state of Israel and Zionism is highly explosive.

Further, members of a security community should enjoy a common history of cooperation or war. Clearly, the Middle East has seen its share of war, but that has not yet been translated into a common desire to dedicate regional cooperation to the promotion of peace (as has been the case in, for example, post–World War II Western Europe). The region ranks high on war, embodying the antithesis of a security community.

Moreover, a security community should not be burdened with unresolved antagonisms. However, interstate and, indeed, intercommunal relations in the Middle East are characterized by complex and numerous antagonisms. Members of a security community respect each other's sovereignty and borders. Unfortunately, borders are contested throughout the region, and some states are virtually governed by other states, or to a great deal depend on, or are influenced by, other countries from the region or abroad. A security community grows closer if there are frameworks for functional cooperation on various issues. So far the region scores low on this point, although there is great potential for functional cooperation on economic or environmental issues, and its capacity to facilitate mutual confidence and security-building. Cooperation across a security community is facilitated by easy and frequent exchange of people, goods, and services, which does not occur in the Middle East. Finally, a functioning security community depends, at least during its nascent period, on the presence and commitment of a benevolent and mutually respected hegemon. No country in the region enjoys the trust of all or most countries in the region – although Jordan came close to playing that role under the rule of the late King Hussein.

Successful democratization throughout the region could be instrumental in creating many of the conditions that allow a region to move toward a security community. In turn these conditions would foster the consolidation of democratic rule and participation. The key elements of these domestic and regional reconciliation processes are economic liberalization, increased prosperity, and bottom–up democratization. All presuppose the primacy of secular politics over religious extremist politics. Several scenarios can be envisioned:[20]

1. Democratization could lead to a radical Islamic take-over and the creation of regime types seen in Iran or Sudan. This would be counterproductive to peace in the region.
2. Democratization could allow for the expression of the Islamic voice, its deflation, and possible internal disintegration. This has already been seen in Jordan and Palestine. This would benefit the peace and integration process in the region.
3. Cooperation between secular groups and a reduction of the influence of extremist Islamic and Zionist forces could lead to a cross-religious bargain.
4. Reconciliation between secular and religious parties could pave the way for the transition from competition to cooperation. This is a difficult but ideal scenario.
5. Following renewed competition for a dominant political culture, civil wars could emerge, similar to the long struggle in Algeria, possibly expanding on a region-wide scale.

Concluding thoughts: Democratization and regional peace management

The end of the Cold War has brought changes that could have been instrumental in greater internal democratization and regional integration in the Middle East. During the Gulf War, Saudi Arabia and the other Gulf states aligned with the United States and, indirectly, with Israel. This undermined Arab states' solidarity with Saddam Hussein (and, among others, gave rise to terrorist movements such as Osama bin Laden's al-Qaida). Then, at least in the early to mid-1990s, the United States became more critical of Israel's policy toward Palestine, and slow progress was made in Israel's reconciliation with the Palestinian state. Finally, improving relations with Iran and, to a certain degree, Libya have offered opportunities for regional stabilization. However, continuing international sanctions against Iraq and ongoing bombardments by the United States and the United Kingdom have had destabilizing effects on the region, as do American pro-Israeli policies under the Bush administration, particularly in the context of sharply renewed violence since late 2001.

Tensions have been high following the terrorist attacks on the World Trade Center in New York and the Pentagon in Washington DC on 11 September 2001. These events could stabilize or destabilize the region – the newly declared war on terrorism unites many previously antagonistic countries, but it also pitches moderate Islamic countries (which support the United States) against fundamentalist Islamic countries (which consider the war on terrorism a pretext for the West to wage war on Islam).

All these challenges create a dynamic political environment throughout the region. The status quo will be replaced by a reordering of the region's international relations – among regional states and between them and the larger international community. This dynamism gives rise to hopes and worries at the same time. The region may open up even further, or it could become more introverted. Much will depend on US foreign policy toward the region, in the context of three issues: terrorism, Iraq, and Israel. These may well be the linchpins of regional security for years to come. Basic stability and the absence of violent conflict may bring opportunities for individual countries to build peace and manage conflict without resorting to violence, thus creating the proper environment for domestic political change in support of the long process toward democratic consolidation. Further unrest and instability, however, will strengthen autocratic rule and hamper transition efforts and processes toward economic, social, and political opening.

We can identify several stumbling blocks on the way to true democratization, domestic and regional security, and development: the possible further consolidation of historical, traditional, and religious ways of life that appear incompatible with bottom–up democratization; fears of Israeli, American-backed, hegemony; fears of an escalation of America's war against terrorism and a possible crackdown on Iraq. Although political and economic priorities are currently pitched against regional, historical, and religious loyalties, these loyalties (and the reasons behind them) are continuously subject to re-evaluation.

The role of democracy in rebuilding war-torn societies in the Middle East and in preventing renewed or continuing outbreaks of violence is crucial. Understanding the prerequisites and necessity for successful democratization may lead to early warning and early efforts to stabilize the democratization process throughout the region. External actors should apply fewer sticks and more carrots – sticks antagonize the population, radicalize some segments, trigger violence, and make it all the more difficult for governments committed to gradual democratization to keep the process on track. Eventually, a working democracy and a regional community that values security, justice, and peace over historical claims and grievances will offer structures and processes for peaceful resolution of disputes and conflict. The management of (eventual) peace and stability in the Middle East must be founded on a firm commitment to democratization throughout the region and the consolidation of democratic systems supported by strong civic cultures.

Notes

1. For an excellent examination of human needs theory, see John Burton, ed., *Conflict: Human Needs Theory*, New York: St. Martin's Press, 1990.
2. For a recent discussion of human security, see Majid Tehranian, ed., *Worlds Apart: Human Security and Global Governance*, New York: I. B. Tauris, 1999.
3. For this classification of conflict types, see Michael Klare, "War, Conflict, and Peace in the Post–Cold War Era," in Michael Klare, ed., *Peace & World Security Studies*, Boulder, CO: Lynne Rienner, 1994, pp. 101–2.
4. Karl Deutsch et al., *Political Community and the North Atlantic Area: International Organization in the Light of Historical Experience*, Princeton, NJ: Princeton University Press, 1957.
5. Emanuel Adler and Michael N. Barnett, eds., *Security Communities*, Cambridge: Cambridge University Press, 1998.
6. David Bloomfield and Ben Reilly, "The Changing Nature of Conflict and Conflict Management," in Peter Harris and Ben Reilly, *Democracy and Deep-Rooted Conflict: Options for Negotiators*, Stockholm: International Institute for Democracy and Electoral Assistance, 1998, p. 19.
7. Ibid.
8. Ibid, p. 17. See Immanuel Kant, *Perpetual Peace*, reprinted in Hans Reiss, ed., *Kant: Political Writings*, Cambridge: Cambridge University Press, 1991; William J. Dixon, "Democracy and the Peaceful Settlement of International Conflict," *American Political Science Review*, vol. 88, March 1994, pp. 14–32; Michael D. Ward and Kristian S. Gle-

ditsch, "Democratizing for Peace," *American Political Science Review*, vol. 92, March 1998.

9. See Pauline Baker, "Conflict Resolution versus Democratic Governance: Divergent Paths to Peace?" in Chester A. Crocker, Fen Osler Hampson, with Pamela Aall, eds., *Managing Global Chaos: Sources and Responses to International Conflict*, Washington, DC: United States Institute of Peace Press, 1996, pp. 563–71; and Nika Strazisar, "Rethinking the Concept of Peacebuilding: Bosnia and the Lessons for Kosovo," in Albrecht Schnabel, ed., *Southeast European Security: Threats, Responses, Challenges*, Huntington, NY: Nova Science Publishers, 2001, pp. 205–26.

10. See Hans-Georg Ehrhart and Albrecht Schnabel, eds., *The Southeast European Challenge: Ethnic Conflict and the International Response*, Baden-Baden: Nomos, 1999.

11. Chester A. Crocker and Fen Osler Hampson, "Making Peace Settlements Work," *Foreign Policy*, no. 104, Fall 1996, p. 57.

12. Baker, "Conflict Resolution versus Democratic Governance," pp. 563–71.

13. Ben Reilly, "Democratic Levers for Conflict Management," in Harris and Reilly, *Democracy and Deep-Rooted Conflict*, p. 137.

14. Albrecht Schnabel, "When the Cure Turns into Poison – The Federal State and Ethnicity: From the Nigerian to the Canadian Experience," in Wladislaw T. Kinastowski and Peter J. Misiaszek, eds., *Options for a Renewed Canada*, Waterloo: Department of Political Science, University of Waterloo, and Department of Political Science, Wilfrid Laurier University, 1993, pp. 133–46.

15. Bloomfield and Reilly, "The Changing Nature of Conflict and Conflict Management," p. 17. For an example of the literature on the difficulties and dangers of democratization processes, see Guillermo O'Donnell and Philippe Schmitter, *Transitions from Authoritarian Rule*, vol. 4, *Tentative Conclusions about Uncertain Democracies*, Baltimore, MD: Johns Hopkins University Press, 1986; Edward D. Mansfield and Jack Snyder, "Democratization and the Danger of War," *International Security*, vol. 20, Summer 1995, pp. 5–38; Larry Diamond, Marc F. Plattner, Yun-han Chu, and Hung-mao Tien, eds., *Consolidating Third Wave Democracies*, Baltimore, MD: Johns Hopkins University Press, 1977; Axel Hadenius, ed., *Democracy's Victory and Crisis*, Cambridge: Cambridge University Press, 1997.

16. UNDP, *Arab Human Development Report 2002*, New York: United Nations Development Programme, 2002, p. 2.

17. Robert A. Dahl, *Democracy and Its Critics*, New Haven, CT: Yale University Press, 1989, p. 221.

18. Etel Solingen, "Democratization in the Middle East: Quandaries of the Peace Process," *Journal of Democracy*, vol. 7, no. 3, July 1996, pp. 139–53. See also Saad Eddin Ibrahim, "Liberalization and Democratization in the Arab World: An Overview," in Baghat Korany, Rex Brynen, and Paul Noble, eds., *Political Liberalization and Democratization in the Arab World: Theoretical Perspectives*, Boulder, CO: Lynne Rienner, 1998, pp. 29–57. For a recent analysis of the impact of, among others, the lack of genuine democratization on the region's poor comparative level of human development, see UNDP, *Arab Human Development Report 2002*.

19. Deutsch et al., *Political Community and the North Atlantic Area*, p. 5.

20. The first three scenarios have been discussed by Solingen, "Democratization in the Middle East."

3

Toward a democratic peace in the Middle East

Etel Solingen

The 1990s witnessed a revival of the hypothesis that the democratic nature of states has important implications for war and peace. In particular, students of international relations have associated democracy with a reluctance to wage wars against other democracies. This chapter examines the relationship between democracy and peace primarily in the context of the Arab–Israeli conflict, but also in the Middle East more broadly defined. Clearly, the democratic peace hypothesis cannot explain the trend away from war in the early and mid-1990s in this democracy-deprived region. Furthermore, this trend was superseded by a return to convulsive violence in the Palestinian–Israeli conflict by the end of the decade. Yet democratization as a process may have something to say about the prospects for stable peace. This chapter provides a profile of democratization throughout the region, highlighting the central dilemmas it faces and distilling some preliminary lessons from the 1990s regarding the impact of democratization on both furthering and inhibiting war and peace in the region. The region-wide political crisis triggered by the tragic terrorist attacks of 11 September 2001 (9/11) brings into relief the importance of taking stock of earlier experiences with democratization and peace.

The democratic peace hypothesis: Hindsights and foresights

A diverse menu of alternative hypotheses emerged in the 1990s, designed to explain why democratic states are not likely to wage wars amongst themselves.[1] One hypothesis builds on a Kantian conception of citizens' consent, according to which the legitimacy granted by the domestic public of one liberal democracy to the elected representatives of another is expected to have a moderating effect away from violent solutions. Disagreements and conflict may remain between democratic dyads but are not resolved through military means. In facing authoritarian adversaries, however, democracies perceive no barriers to the use of violent means.

A second set of hypotheses holds that free speech, electoral cycles, and the public policy process restrain democratic leaders from extreme responses toward fellow democracies. In turn, when facing authoritarian and praetorian adversaries, democracies rescind the moderating effects of institutional checks and balances.

A third brand of conjectures expects the reciprocal transparency and abundant information (on the internal evaluations of a policy) available to democratic dyads to improve the chances of cooperation. Transparency allows a democratic dyad to embrace mutual concessions because both parties assume there is a low risk of the other side defecting or abandoning its commitments. The public nature of the political process is expected to raise the costs of reversing obligations undertaken toward a fellow democracy. Maximizing information is of particular importance in the creation of security arrangements, where the risks of error and deception can be catastrophic. Asymmetric levels of transparency, in contrast, lower the incentives for democracies to embrace cooperation with non-democracies. The latter's surreptitious procedures presumably make it harder to foresee potential assaults on the stipulations of cooperative arrangements.

A fourth approach focuses on the assumption that democracies are respectful of the rule of law and appear to undertake more credible and durable international commitments. These features presumably strengthen their reputation as predictable partners, allowing democratic dyads to rely on diffuse reciprocity (rather than on a quid pro quo basis).[2] Nondemocratic regimes might be replaced by challengers capable of reshuffling international commitments to maintain legitimacy at home. In fact, in the absence of serious domestic constraints, non-democratic rulers may enter into an agreement and soon after renege on it. A democratic dyad would thus arguably operate under conditions of strong mutual credibility, whereas problems of uncertainty over ratification and implementation would be exacerbated for asymmetric or non-democratic dyads.

Finally, citizens of liberal democracies are assumed to be particularly wary of wars because these often exact heavy losses of life and property. This general aversion to losses – when shared by democratic adversaries – induces caution in the management of conflict among them. Nondemocracies, in contrast, are suspected of seeking total, rather than limited, objectives and are far less sensitive to costs. The asymmetries in

sensitivity to loss for mixed (or non-democratic) dyads hinder cooperation, leaving the door open for violent resolution of conflicts.

In sum, for all these normative, institutional, and instrumental reasons,
the absence of war and the ability to cooperate are considered to be robust for democratic dyads but feeble for mixed (and for non-democratic)
dyads. The democratic peace is said to induce mutual restraint because of
the combined effects of symmetrical trust, accountability, institutional
checks and balances, transparency, and credibility that inspire relations
within democratic dyads or clusters.

These hypotheses could, *prima facie*, explain the absence of peace between Israel and its Arab neighbors for many decades, given a common
characterization of the asymmetry between Israel as a democracy, on the
one hand, and the dearth of democratic institutions in the Arab world, on
the other. Presumably, had there been interactive democracies, peace
might have come about.[3] Instead, the absence of democratic dyads has
correlated with military conflict and war since 1948.[4] Nonetheless, the
same dyads that waged wars for decades also transcended them: first
Egypt and Israel after Camp David, later Israel and the Palestine Liberation Organization (PLO) after Oslo, and then Israel and Jordan. These
dramatic developments did not take place in the domain specified by
democratic peace thinking: in no instance can these peace breakthroughs
be traced to democratic dyads in action. Moreover, given non-democratic
continuity in the Arab world for many decades, the small variance in the
independent or explanatory variable (the democratic nature of regimes)
hinders our ability to estimate the effects on the dependent variable
(conflict or cooperation), the outcome we would like to explain. In general terms, although with some caveats and new developments analyzed
below, Arab–Israeli relations in war and peace have unfolded against a
constant – a single democracy (Israel) interacting with an array of non-
democratic regimes.

Two points should be clear at the outset. First, the democratic peace
hypothesis suggests only that joint democracy (in a dyad or cluster) is a
sufficient condition for the avoidance of war. Democracy is thus not a
necessary condition; other factors, according to different alternative
theories, may account for the emergence of peace.[5] Secondly, the inade-
quacy of the democratic peace argument for explaining significant past
shifts in the Middle East should not obscure its potential utility in identifying prospects for stable peace in the future. Whatever other independent variables may account for the initiation of cooperative relations, the
eventual establishment of democratic states is often expected to contribute to the absence of war. This remains only a prospect in the midst of a
reality of slow and open-ended transitions toward more democratic forms
in the region.

Democratization in the Middle East: A profile

Despite the common uneven, slow, and tentative process of democratization, some differences among regimes throughout the region have become evident. These distinctions partially alleviate the problem of little variance in the independent variable and allow a preliminary assessment of how very incipient changes toward democracy have affected regional outcomes. For our purposes here, change toward democracy involves a process geared to the eventual operation of what Robert Dahl[6] has characterized as a "polyarchy," although in this chapter the concept of "democracy" will be retained even while relying on Dahl's definition. Dahl describes seven institutions of polyarchy: elected officials, free and fair elections, inclusive suffrage, right to run for office, freedom of expression, alternative information protected by law, and associational autonomy. These institutional characteristics of democracy are universal (even if the strength and mix are not) and cannot be modified by relativist and exceptionalist concepts derived from different religious, cultural, or other doctrinal sources. Democratization involves the incremental attainment of these characteristics. The more elements of this formula are present in a given polity, and the fuller their operational content and implementation, the more advanced that polity can be said to be on the path toward democracy. Throughout this chapter the terms "non-democratic" and "authoritarian" are used to indicate a state that has not yet attained such characteristics, even if it is undergoing some of the transitional phases.

By these standards only Israel can be considered democratic, except for its rule over Palestinians in the West Bank since 1967. Within Israel proper, radical religious groups have worked to challenge democratic principles directly, while the politics of coalitional formation have progressively enhanced the bargaining power of more moderate religious parties whose agendas sometimes dilute democratic values.[7] For instance, the intrusion of religion into Israel's civil law has had undemocratic consequences for the presumably equal status of women, who are subject to some of the discriminatory rules applicable within their respective confessional jurisdictions (Jewish, Muslim, and others). Neither have Arab citizens of Israel enjoyed the same legal status as Jews, insofar as the Law of Return does not apply to them nor are they called upon to serve in the Israeli Defense Forces. Even with these caveats, Israel is widely considered to be a vibrant democracy with no equivalents in the 22 Arab states or Iran.

Yet in the 1990s there was some movement toward at least some of the institutions of democracy and political liberalization throughout the region, a movement that was tentative, piecemeal, and marked by significant reversals. In January 1996, Palestinians went to the polls to elect their president and Legislative Council in their first free, internationally supervised, elections. Morocco pioneered in its tolerance for freedom of the press and association, and a relatively strong (in regional terms) civil society placed some barriers on the monarchy. The 1990s witnessed further advances, particularly a government led by the traditional opposition (although appointed by the late King Hassan) and the ascent of young King Mohammed VI to the throne in 1999. Until the 1970s Lebanon embodied elements of pluralistic competition that were rare elsewhere in the neighborhood. In a context of highly fragmented communal representation, the first parliamentary elections in 20 years were held in 1992, although Syria's complete control over the country has stymied democratization. Egypt returned to multiparty politics in 1976 but has restricted political participation through electoral laws and procedures that favor the ruling National Democratic Party.[8] Despite some steps to grant amnesties to jailed Islamist activists in the late 1990s, the Egyptian government launched an offensive against human rights and pro-democracy organizations. In 2000, a noted scholar and activist, Saad Eddin Ibrahim, was convicted on trumped-up charges of defaming Egypt's reputation and receiving foreign funding without governmental permission, in a process symptomatic of a broader setback in liberalization. Jordan has experienced competitive parliamentary elections since 1989 and a lively press debate over domestic and foreign policy. Liberalization has suffered some setbacks, particularly after 9/11; at the same time, a governmental human rights commission recommended changes in Jordanian law that yielded the first court decision granting a woman a divorce (not an insignificant event in this region) in 2002. In October 1992, elections for the National Assembly (suspended since 1986) were held in Kuwait, launching political reform.[9] The 1999 elections yielded a parliament heavily controlled by the opposition, Islamist and liberal. There have been some steps to widen political participation in Qatar and Oman. Qatar, host to the unprecedented Al-Gezira TV network, held its first elections (for municipal councils) in 1999, allowing women participation. Embryonic liberalization in Bahrain in the late 1990s created new space for an eventual restoration of the 1973 constitution and possible parliamentary elections in October 2002, the first in nearly three decades. In the 2002 elections for municipal councils, women were allowed to vote and run for office for the first time, although Islamist parties, which won all 50 seats on the five councils, also pressured the population to vote only for male candidates.[10]

In many of the countries cited in this brief overview, the aftermath of 9/11 and the Israeli military incursion into the West Bank in early 2002 triggered some setbacks. However, these cannot universally be characterized as "reversals" of democratic transitions. For a reversal to take place, specific democratizing steps must have been suspended (such as the postponement of elections in Jordan) or slowed down. Instead, in some cases, the events of late 2001 to early 2002 triggered significant pressures for democratization, as with the Palestinian Authority. Such pressures for democratization from below in the aftermath of a war are not unusual, as the Greek and Argentine *juntas* experienced in other contexts. In yet other cases, little movement toward democratization was taking place prior to these events anyway, so their effects changed the *status quo ante* only marginally, as we shall see next.

Liberalization in Saudi Arabia has been fairly narrow, although some regard the inception of the Majlis Al-Shura (Consultative Council) as an important step for an otherwise extremely cautious kingdom. Iran's elections since 1992 have progressively reflected a trend toward liberalization, culminating in the 2000 parliamentary elections, which placed the Islamist *ancien régime* on the defense. The 2001 presidential elections returned strong support for President Khatemi's efforts to liberalize what is still a polity strongly controlled by the more militant Islamist faction headed by Khamenei. Even in Sudan, General Omar al-Beshir has removed Hassan Tourabi's stranglehold over the country, albeit retaining centralizing power himself. Most resistant to liberalization have been Iraq, Syria, and Libya. Saddam Hussein has entrenched his brutal rule even further through complete command over the fewer resources flowing to Iraq, which has been under sanctions since its invasion of Kuwait in 1990. Syria and Libya remain highly personalistic authoritarian states forcefully battling demands for liberalization.

Two main features have characterized the incipient transitions wherever they have taken place. First, liberalization has been managed from above, launched by regimes in power and state elites with varying degrees of support from, and co-optation of, societal actors, always while retaining control over the expansion of political rights. From Egypt to Tunisia and Jordan, elites designed national pacts and rules of procedure limiting oppositional activity and keeping control over political programs, party policies, and political meetings. Manipulation from the top continues to yield approval rates of over 95 percent, as in Egypt.[11] Developments in the Palestinian territories under Palestinian Authority control since 1994 are an exception to this general trend of democratization from above. Palestinians have resisted the centralizing leadership of Yasser Arafat, who was elected president in 1996 under the freest elections held in the Arab world in recent history. This pressure from below (and from the elite as well) accelerated after Israel's military incursion into the West Bank in 2002.

Systematic comparative research on democratic transitions across regions suggests that, in principle, the implications of democratization from above are less damning than might be expected. This literature depicts

political pacts designed to manage transitions as a fairly successful formula for peaceful evolution into stable democracies.[12] Peaceful mass
mobilization had similarly promising results, whereas violent turmoil and
uprisings have rarely led to stable democratic outcomes. Yet aggregate
evidence should not be taken as a firm basis for predicting democratic
stability everywhere. Furthermore, clear-cut transitions to democracy
from below in the 1980s and 1990s have also enjoyed significant durabil-
ity, as in South Korea, the Philippines, and Central Europe.

A second aspect of incipient democratization throughout the region
relates to the dilemma posed by the rise of Islamist movements. Transitions have created uncertainty over whether democratization would lead
to democracy or to fundamentalist Islamic theocracies.[13] Islamic doctrine
may well be compatible with democracy, although a wide expert scholar-
ship and exegesis on Islamic doctrine has not reached any measure of
consensus on this issue.[14] However, at the dawn of the twenty-first century the actual record of Islamist regimes had reassured very few of that
compatibility. Ruling Islamist regimes in Iran, Sudan, and Afghanistan
resisted and reversed democratization for two decades, engaged in widespread violations of basic human rights, and furthered the physical elimination of ethnic and religious minorities and/or political adversaries. As
argued earlier, liberalizing forces from within the regime in Iran have not
yet succeeded in overcoming resistance from the hard-line Islamist wing.

As for the platform of extreme Islamist movements challenging ruling
coalitions, the establishment of an Islamist state has been their central
declared objective. Most Islamist groups have dismissed democracy as
"a Western concept with no place in a Muslim society,"[15] leading Jihad
Al-Khazen to argue that "Muslim fundamentalist parties are undemocratic, no matter what they say."[16] In Algeria, many preachers from the
Front Islamique du Salut (FIS), not just the Armed Islamic Group, were
openly disdainful of Western democracy and unwilling to guarantee
elections beyond 1992.[17] The record in the 1990s spoke overwhelmingly
against the existence of a strong democratic current among Islamist
groups – at least by the standards spelled out above – beyond tactical
reliance on elections as a springboard to power. At the same time, more
recent developments suggest that democratic currents may be gaining
strength. In Iran and elsewhere, the emergence of moderate Islamist
groups would bode well for the potential of a democratic Islamist alternative.[18] This battle between moderate and extremist versions of Islam
acquires particular relevance in the aftermath of the terrorist attacks on
New York's World Trade Center.

Democratic inclusion can strengthen more judicious Islamist movements and moderate them at the same time.[19] This seems to have been
the outcome of electoral inclusion in Jordan since 1989. There and elsewhere in the region, Islamist parties have had relatively limited success at

the polls. Even in Algeria the FIS obtained 25 percent of eligible votes in the December 1991 elections. Sudan's National Islamic Front (NIF) never won more than 20 percent (Tourabi himself was never able to get himself elected under real elections). Tunisia's MTI (Mouvement de la tendance islamique, renamed Hizb al-Nahdha, or Renaissance Party) captured about 14 percent of the vote in 1989.[20] The strength of Islamist parties in Palestine declined from about 16 percent in December 1995, on the eve of the first (and only) Palestinian elections, to about 14 percent in June 1996.[21] Al-Najah and Bi'r Zayt professor Basim al-Zubaydi suggested that Hamas (Islamic Resistance Movement) would be politically threatened if it continued to rally round the old tune, ignoring the masses' demand for a new tune that creates a movement for the middle classes.[22] Both the peak levels of electoral strength for Islamist movements and their subsequent decline are compatible with what might be labeled the "balloon theory" of radical Islamist movements, premised on the view that rank-and-file supporters of such movements are "remarkably mobile in terms of granting and withdrawing their allegiance."[23] Moreover, these few instances suggest that political inclusion appears to lead to diminishing political returns for Islamist movements, with stable – and at times declining – electoral strength. Finally, strong institutional arrangements protecting the integrity of the democratic system may help prevent a small plurality of votes (Islamist or otherwise) from undermining democratic continuity. The prospects for establishing such arrangements remain uncertain.

In some cases co-optation of moderates has been accompanied by the forcible eradication of violent groups, as in Egypt, Algeria, Yemen, Bahrain, and Oman. In Jordan, a new government under King Abdullah reached an agreement with political parties in 1999 on overhauling the Elections Law. Some members of parliament regarded these changes as aiming at appeasing the mainstream Muslim Brotherhood – the effective power behind the Islamic Action Front – and at compensating for the government's crackdown on Hamas and the expulsion of Hamas leaders to Qatar. In Palestine, learning from its mistake of boycotting the first Palestinian elections, Hamas started a political party in March 1996, the Islamic National Salvation Party, later formally approved by the Palestinian National Authority (PNA). At the same time, the PNA has resorted to arrests and intimidation to control the activities of Islamist leaders and activists.

Implications of democratic transitions for the peace process

What do we know about the general relationship between democratization and peace, and what are the implications of what we know for the Arab–Israeli peace process? Plunging into that vacuum, a study by Mansfield and Snyder[24] suggests that former authoritarian states where democratic participation is on the rise are more likely to engage in wars than are stable democracies or stable autocracies. Furthermore, states that make the biggest leap from autocracy to extensive mass democracy are about twice as likely to fight wars in the decade after democratization as are states that remain autocracies.[25] Although the implications of these findings seem unpromising for the case under consideration, certain alleviating conditions must be considered.

Nationalism, theocracy, and war

Mansfield and Snyder's association between democratization, belligerent nationalism, and war has deep historical roots. A certain "conventional wisdom" echoing that association for the case of the Middle East has emerged in the past two decades, particularly among those concerned about the potential hijacking of democratization by radical Islamist movements. Rouleau dissected the affinity between nationalism and religious fundamentalism, asserting that Islamist movements are quintessentially political.[26] The Charter of the Islamic Resistance Movement (Hamas) clearly reflects that affinity: "Nationalism, from the point of view of the Islamic Resistance Movement, is part and parcel of religious ideology. There is not a higher peak in nationalism or depth in devotion than *Jihad* when an enemy lands on the Muslim territories."[27] And, in Hassan Tourabi's own words, "[t]he only nationalism that is available to us, if we want to assert indigenous values, originality and independence of the West, is Islam ... It is the only doctrine that can serve as the national doctrine of today."[28]

The operational content of this old–new nationalism is outright opposition to the Arab–Israeli peace process,[29] rendering some credibility to the association between democratization, belligerent nationalism, and war.[30] Ahmad Husayn Mustafa 'Ujayzah, leader of Egypt's militant group Vanguards of Conquest, declares: "We support all the Islamic and national forces and reject normalization with the Zionist enemy. We demand the abrogation of the Camp David accord and its annexes ... We believe that 'Abd-al-Nasir's regime did make national achievements that could not be ignored ... We believe that the Nasirite current is at present a nationalist one that has many positive points."[31] Even Jordan's Muslim Brotherhood, a beneficiary of Jordan's liberalizing process, rejected Oslo at the outset, as well as the Palestinian National Authority and the notion of an independent Palestinian state. Khalid Mish'al, head of Jordan's Hamas Political Bureau, has consistently declared that "political agreements cannot end the Zionist threat to our nation."[32] The same views were expressed by leaders of Hamas and Islamic Jihad in the West Bank and Gaza, before and after the 2002 Israeli military incursion. Radical Islam has also fueled regional conflict within the Arab world and beyond. Until recently, the Islamic Republic of Iran exacerbated conflict, incited subversion and terrorism, and built up conventional and unconventional weapons.[33] The Beshir–Tourabi regime in Sudan funded violent opposition to the peace process, launched a deadly campaign against Sudanese Christian and animist dissidents in the south, escalated conflict with Egypt in the north (over Halayeb), and armed a resistance guerrilla group fighting the Ugandan government.[34] The record of Afghanistan's Taliban allied with the Bin Laden terrorist network is now well documented. In sum, according to this school of thought, the actual performance of Islamist regimes in Sudan, Afghanistan, and Iran and of radical Islamist movements throughout the region fits the hypothesized organic connection between democratization, fundamentalist theocracy and nationalism, and external violent behavior.

Proponents of the "conventional wisdom" school do not necessarily challenge the theoretical compatibility of Islam and peace. Rather, they associate Islamist recalcitrance against peace overtures with the amply exploited political opportunities such a strategy offers. *Jihad* evokes a promise of redemption from both dreadful material conditions and unfulfilled spiritual aspirations through scapegoating and rejection of "the alien." Bin Laden's terrorist attacks in Yemen, Nairobi, and New York are clear instances of this pattern, which externalizes the blame through *jihad*. Yet the record of Islamist regimes in power does not support expectations that Islamist strategies – political and economic – would result in more just, more equal, more productive, or more innovative societies.[35]

The "conventional wisdom" that Islamist movements invariably subsume religious and other ethical considerations to political payoffs has not gone unchallenged. Esposito, for instance, rejects the instrumentalist perspective while interpreting Islamist movements as advocates of virtuous lifestyles and religious tolerance.[36] Since peace with Israel falls largely outside this vision, as interpreted by Esposito, even this more benign perspective does not undermine the potential association between democratization, nationalism, and war. Far more promising are Tessler and Grobschmidt's empirical findings reflecting less friction between democratization, Islamic inclusion, and the Arab–Israeli peace process than is commonly assumed.[37] The triumph of moderates and reformists in the February 2000 elections in Iran was celebrated by neighboring Gulf states as the prelude to a more cooperative relationship. It may be premature, but not completely far-fetched, to herald the dawn of a new age in Iran's approach to the Arab–Israeli conflict, once moderates prevail.

This could begin to erode the links between democratization, Islam, and violent conflict.

Focus: Israel and Palestine

How has the association between democratization, belligerent national-ism, and war played out in the specific context that constitutes the crux of the Arab–Israeli conflict? Eric Rouleau's "balloon theory" of radical Islamist movements advanced that Hamas is "like a balloon that will de-flate the moment the PLO gets something significant from the Israelis."[38] This view was validated in the aftermath of the Oslo agreements, which led to the emergence of a Palestinian National Authority under President Yasser Arafat. The Islamist camp – including Hamas, Islamic Jihad, and independent Islamists – was estimated to control about 23 percent of the vote shortly after Oslo. In January 1994, opposition groups could count on 39 percent of the votes, against 38 percent favoring Fatah and its allies.[39] Fatah's approval rate rose to 49.5 percent in early 1995, while Hamas's dropped from 16.6 to 14.4 percent. By late 2000, in the wake of the second *intifada* launched in September that year, support for Fatah had declined below 33 percent and Hamas's had risen to 19 percent.[40] After the difficult events of April 2002, Fatah's popularity was 32 percent (compared with 28 percent in December 2001), whereas Islamist groups retained a December 2001 approval of 25 percent, higher than the 17 percent they had in July 2000.

Clearly, the Islamists' popularity decreased with the perception of a viable peace process in the mid-1990s and increased with the return of violent tactics by 2000. On the one hand, the rise in oppositional strength to Yasser Arafat can be traced to the slow pace of the peace process, particularly delays in Israel's withdrawals from the West Bank after Benjamin Netanyahu's victory in Israel's 1996 elections. No less impor-tant, on the other hand, was the rise of a secular opposition that decries the stalled process of democratization since 1996.[41] Many in this camp demanded greater personal freedoms and less concentration of power around Yasser Arafat, but were not inherently against the overall peace process (as most Islamist groups have been). Neither was this group uni-formly supportive of the Oslo process. Challenges to Arafat emerged even within Fatah, the virtual ruling party, and within the PNA, de-manding an end to corruption and repression.

Were such forces to prevail politically in the aftermath of Arafat's era, it is possible to envisage a positive relationship between Palestinian de-mocratization and future regional cooperation. However, as Palestinian–Israeli relations have reached new lows throughout 2002, it is hard to gauge the current, let alone future, strength of a democratically oriented alternative that also advocates reconciliation with Israel. According to a May 2002 poll by the Palestinian Center for Policy and Survey Research (PCPSR), 66 percent of Palestinians support the Saudi peace plan calling for the establishment of two states, Palestine and Israel, although it is unclear what precise arrangement is assumed here regarding refugee issues. As for democratization, an overwhelming majority of 91 percent supports fundamental changes in the Palestinian Authority, including dismissal of ministers (95 percent), holding elections soon (83 percent), and the unification of the security services (85 percent).[42]

In Israel itself, extreme ultra-nationalist messianic movements constitute not merely a danger to peace but a threat to the stability of its own democratic institutions.[43] As Liebman argues, "one can identify a mainstream within religious Jewry in Israel, whose core assumptions, attitudes, and values are in many cases in conflict with the system of assumptions, attitudes, and values that undergird a stable democratic polity."[44] Such assumptions are no less in conflict with the most basic requirements for a peaceful settlement of the Israeli–Palestinian question. Netanyahu's coalition (1996–99) gave new life to this political bloc, which helped undermine much of the progress achieved by the Labor–Meretz coalition (1992–96) regarding democratizing reforms within Israel and reconciliation with Palestinians. Likud's political tent was stretched far enough toward this camp to accept the political embrace of some of the most radical religious and nationalist groups, including settlers whose allegiance to Greater Israel overtakes any allegiance to the State of Israel, to its elected leaders, or to democracy.

A new Labor-led coalition under Ehud Barak replaced Netanyahu in 1999, including Meretz and its commitment to further democratization and the peace process as well as religious parties (Agudat Israel, Shas) opposed to both, albeit in different degrees. As with at least some of its Palestinian neighbors, here too there is a clear association between political forces demanding a deepening of Israel's democracy and those committed to the peaceful establishment of a Palestinian state. The peace camp within Israel absorbed a severe blow following the rejection of Barak's proposals by Arafat at Camp David. The launching of the second *intifada* reduced this camp's political influence even more dramatically, helping Ariel Sharon become prime minister. By early 2002, the Palestinian population's overwhelming support for terrorist attacks against civilians within 1967 Israel destroyed Israel's peace camp completely, leading to overwhelming Israeli support for the military incursion in April 2002, designed to undermine the terrorist infrastructure. This is nothing new: the threat of war can lead to national unity governments that often narrow the margins of democratic debate. Yet it would seem premature, given the past trajectory of Israeli democracy (see below), to dismiss the future role of embattled opponents of the Sharon government's policies, such as Yossi Beilin. The nature and direction of democratization in the Palestinian camp will have much to do with this future.

Democratization from above, peace from above

As argued above, democratization from above has been the norm wherever democratization has taken place throughout the Middle East. Furthermore, the peace process itself (Madrid 1991, Oslo 1993, the 1994 Israeli–Jordanian peace agreement, the 1991–96 multilateral negotiations) was a result of decisions taken by ruling elites – with greater or lesser popular support – to shift gear and marshal peacetime resources for socio-economic renewal. This renewal was expected to secure the leaders' own political survival, but did not go far enough to achieve that objective. The effort to construct "peace from above" was not restricted to the Arab world. Israel's Labor–Meretz coalition presented the Israeli public with a *fait accompli* – the September 1993 Declaration of Principles – and, literally the day after, the coalition amassed a 65 percent rate of approval.[45] Although public support faded later in response to violent Islamist terror, yielding a rejectionist coalition under Benjamin Netanyahu, electoral approval for the peace process became evident from the election of Ehud Barak in 1999. As argued, Arafat's rejection of Barak's Camp David proposal returned a hard-line government to Israel in 2001. "Peace from above" does not make peace undemocratic when incumbents eventually face the electoral consequences of their foreign policy decisions, as Israel's Labor Party did twice in the 1990s.

The gradual and controlled pace of democratization in the Arab Middle East is certainly lacking from a normative democratic standpoint, but it has at least one redeeming advantage. Mansfield and Snyder point to the unwanted consequences of sharp leaps from authoritarianism to democracy, assumed to increase the likelihood of war. Gradualism may not merely mitigate the possible effects of such leaps for regional stability but also guarantee more stable democratic outcomes. As the literature on democratic transitions suggests, piecemeal democratization through progressive political pacts is well suited to usher in a strong and irreversible democracy. Stable democracies, in turn, are the foundation of democratic zones of peace. Few consider the prospects that full autocracies such as Syria, Iraq, and Sudan might turn fully democratic in rapid sequence to be significant.[46] This low probability could, in principle, put to rest concerns about a heightened likelihood of belligerent behavior among states undergoing swift shifts. At the same time, today's autocracies do not appear to be viable and stable partners in the creation of a stable, peaceful regional order.

Democratization from above, however, does have the potential for progressing too slowly, and even reversing. Mansfield and Snyder found autocratization (including regressing to autocracy after failed experiments with democracy) to increase the probability of war. The link between autocratization and war reflects the successful use of nationalist or militant Islamist formulas and of democratic openings for the sake of developing populist legitimacy while dismantling the democratic process itself. This pattern resonates with the prevalent political use of Islam throughout the region. We are still under the fog of 11 September 2001 and the war in Afghanistan, which make any predictions about the prospects for genuine democratization from above highly contingent. These prospects are heavily conditional on the outcome of another process: the economic transformation of the region.[47] Economic liberalization is central to the connection between democratization and peace in the Middle East, as elsewhere.

On the one hand, if democratization from above succeeds in consolidating a genuine democratic opening among Arab states participating in the peace process, the leaders are not likely to emerge discredited on account of their accommodating regional policies. King Hussein of Jordan was the model here. Growing democratization could continue, hand in hand with efforts to construct a regional order compatible with socio-economic and political reconstruction (i.e. a peaceful order). On the other hand, if democratization stalls (as in post-1996 Palestine) and leaders fall short of delivering on broadened civil, political, human, and economic rights, such failure can undermine – and has undermined – other potential achievements.[48] Under those conditions, political challengers might find it helpful to trap their opposition to peace negotiations in pro-democracy rhetoric, affecting the peace process in adverse ways, as Hamas is beginning to do in the aftermath of the war of 2002. However, it is questionable that a return to the "remote" past (pre-1990s) is feasible for any political regime aspiring to survive the political demands for an improved present and future. President Khatemi's camp has driven this point home to the Iranian people. This point leads, once again, to the centrality of economic performance to both democratization and peace.

Preliminary conclusions and suggestions for further research

The disjointedness between the literatures on the democratic peace (in international relations), on the one hand, and on democratic transitions (in comparative politics), on the other, has had detrimental effects for both fields. Peace is an important requirement for the effective implementation of political reforms, and democratization affects the proclivity and political wherewithal to pursue peaceful regional arrangements. Building on this chapter's efforts to conceptualize transitions to democracy and their impact on war and peace, we can distill some preliminary conclusions of relevance to the Arab–Israeli conflict and the Middle East more broadly defined.

On the democratic peace theory

The good news is that incipient democratization throughout the region has increased the variability in the independent variable somewhat, albeit quite marginally, allowing preliminary observations of a possible impact of democratization on peace. On this account, one finds some evidence of a fit between embryonic efforts to democratize the polity and to embrace the peace process in the Palestinian elections of 1996 and the trends in Jordan and some of the Gulf states.[49] Much of this trend was reversed in the aftermath of Islamist terrorist attacks on Israel in 1996 and the subsequent ascent of hard-line coalitions there. The most autocratic regimes in the region also remain the most opposed to Arab–Israeli cooperation. The bad news is that the definitional debates affecting the democratic peace theory are compounded when dealing with a process rather than an end-product. At what levels of democratization do we observe changes in the direction of either conflict or cooperation?

Given the presumed connections between domestic political institutions and foreign policy embedded in the democratic peace, the argument that Israel can reach peace with its Arab neighbors only when they become democratic has some *prima facie* appeal. Undoubtedly, leaders of a democratic state face difficulties when promoting a peace agenda in conjunction with authoritarian leaders across the border, insofar as the subjects of the neighboring non-democracy regard the imposed peace as an autocrat's *diktat*. This leads them at best to accept a "cold peace," and at worst to resist the peace, as part of overall resistance to authoritarianism.

However, arguments that make peace contingent on symmetric democratic institutions have three main problems. First, they are not a logical corollary of the democratic peace theory, which allows for alternative paths to peace that do not require democracy. Secondly, such arguments are sometimes conveniently used by those who oppose Israeli concessions on other grounds, including Likud leaders such as Benjamin Netanyahu and Ariel Sharon, and their coalition ally Natan Sharansky. Thirdly, the absence of concessions may help strengthen the authoritarian nature of Arab states, including Palestine. Having said that, it is important to remember that the belated outbreak of democracy in parts of the Arab world has a deeply rooted internal logic. Any attempt to trace the fate of Arab democracy merely to Arab–Israeli relations not only is misleading but likely only perpetuates both authoritarianism and conflict.

On democratization and the peace process

The threats to peace hypothesized by Snyder and Mansfield, stemming from the eventual transition of mixed regimes (which exhibit features of both democracies and autocracies) into full democracies, cannot be dismissed. However, it is important to remember that mixed regimes have been in the vanguard of peacemaking in the Arab Middle East, with Jordan, Palestine (in 1996), and Egypt advancing furthest in the process of normalization with Israel, and with Morocco, Tunisia, and some Gulf states providing a regional supportive network.[50] Thus far, gradual and controlled democratization has provided a safety valve against the unwanted consequences hypothesized by Snyder and Mansfield. Democratization from above may help secure a stable democratic outcome but also has the potential for progressing too slowly or even reversing.[51] Neither of these two prospects bodes well for the peace process. The ideal sequence of a peaceful transition to fully democratic polities in the near future, as has occurred in Latin America and much of Eastern Europe and East Asia, does not appear to be very probable.

On radical Islam, democracy, and the peace process

Anticipating whether democratization will lead to democracy or theocracy is burdened by "the predictability of unpredictability," a phenomenon described by Timur Kuran that may be only marginally different for the Middle East today than it was for the Soviet Union and Eastern Europe in the 1980s.[52] Predictions are hindered by the imperfect observability of private preferences in a region where both state and societal coercion encourage preference falsification, an effect that can conceal "bandwagons in formation." Some analysts have predicted bandwagons forming along Islamist tracks, expecting them both to emasculate democracy and to shelve peace overtures. Others – including Kuran himself – have warned against assuming a conquering Islamist revolution, particularly given a partial window into private preferences. This warning is compatible with the "balloon theory" on the volatility of political commitment to Islamist parties, which, in turn, enables democratization and political inclusion to subsume, and transcend, opposition to the peace process. The affinity between Islamist regimes, democracy, and peaceful overtures has not yet been backed by any empirical referents (Sudan, Saudi Arabia, Libya, Afghanistan), but events in Iran could yet unfold in that direction.

On economic liberalization, democratization, and peace

A more complete understanding of the relationship between democratization and peace will require spelling out the mutual effects of another variable – economic liberalization – on both democratization and peace. The brittle foundations of peace in the region have sources other than the brittle foundations of democracy. As I have maintained elsewhere,[53] domestic political coalitions advancing internationalization and economic liberalization have proven more often than not to embrace the peace process, arguably as the most efficient regional order, for both domestic political and global implications. In contrast, backlash coalitions more resistant to internationalization have also forcibly opposed the peace process, in both its bilateral and multilateral contexts. The political-economic makeup of ruling coalitions steering democratization may thus help illuminate the conditions under which democratization favors peace. However, neither lagging economic reforms nor the scant attention paid to domestic distributive issues bode well for democracy, economic liberalization, or peace.

In sum, even a minimalist, relaxed version of the democratic peace hypothesis cannot explain the big strides toward a more peaceful region made in the early 1990s. In the future, the Middle East could become a critical testing ground for this theory if – in a historically highly belligerent regional context – peace takes root in tandem with democratic political structures. Alas, whereas the theory must await full democracies to bloom in the region, those negotiating for peace cannot afford to do so. The slow pace of both democratization and economic liberalization, and some of their unintended effects (extremist Islamist ascendancy and socio-economic upheaval), pose serious dilemmas for ruling coalitions and endanger any cooperative strategies.[54] The consolidation of a genuine democratic opening, and one sensitive to the distributional impact of economic liberalization, may be a necessary condition for sustaining a peace negotiated from above. A stable peace (*salaam* rather than *hudna*[55]) may be a long way off, but it may be helped by today's efforts to untangle how we – and, most of all, the peoples of that region – are likely to get there.

Notes

Research was assisted by an award from the Social Science Research Council (SSRC) of an SSRC–McArthur Foundation Fellowship on Peace and Security in a Changing World (1998–1999). Interviews in the region were supported by funding from the United States Institute of Peace. I thank Marie-Joelle Zahar, Jack Snyder, Edy Kaufman, Mark Tessler, and the editors of this volume for their useful comments. This chapter incorporates events and processes since 1996, introducing some new issues while modifying and updating some of the arguments that first appeared in "Democratization in the Middle East: Quandaries of the Peace Process," published in the *Journal of Democracy*, vol. 7, no. 3, July 1996. I acknowledge the journal's permission to reprint segments of that earlier version.

1. For a more thorough overview of alternative hypotheses about democracy and peace, see Etel Solingen, "Democracy, Economic Reform, and Regional Cooperation," *Journal of Theoretical Politics*, vol. 8, no. 1, January 1996; Etel Solingen, *Regional Orders at Century's Dawn*, Princeton, NJ: Princeton University Press, 1998.

2. Reciprocity can be generalized – indefinite (diffuse), involving more trust – or specific and applicable to a discrete, even isolated, context. See Robert O. Keohane, "Reciprocity in International Relations," *International Organization*, vol. 40, no. 1, 1985, pp. 4–5.

3. Hudson rejects this counterfactual; see Michael Hudson, "Democracy and Foreign Policy in the Arab World," in David Garnham and Mark Tessler, eds., *Democracy, War, and Peace in the Middle East*, Bloomington, IN: Indiana University Press, 1995, pp. 195–221.

4. As Russett argues, placing the Lebanese–Israeli encounters of 1948 and 1967 in the "war between democracies" category stretches the definition of democracy (and war), as does Hudson's analysis of "imperfectly representative" Arab regimes in the late 1940s; see Bruce Russett, *Grasping the Democratic Peace: Principles for a Post–Cold War World*, Princeton, NJ: Princeton University Press, 1993, p. 18.

5. See, for instance, the relevance of coalitions forming in response to internationalization, and their role in regional war and peace (Solingen, *Regional Orders at Century's Dawn*).

6. Robert A. Dahl, *Democracy and Its Critics*, New Haven, CT: Yale University Press, 1989, p. 221.

7. Ehud Sprinzak and Larry Diamond, eds., *Israeli Democracy under Stress*, Boulder, CO: Lynne Rienner, 1993; Edy Kaufman, Shukri B. Abed, and Robert L. Rothstein, eds., *Democracy, Peace, and the Israeli–Palestinian Conflict*, Boulder, CO: Lynne Rienner, 1993.

8. Iliya Harik, "Pluralism in the Arab World," *Journal of Democracy*, vol. 5, no. 3, July 1994, p. 51; Farid El-Khazen, "Lebanon's First Postwar Parliamentary Elections, 1993," *Middle East Policy*, vol. 3, no. 1, 1994; Cassandra, "The Impending Crisis in Egypt," *The Middle East Journal*, vol. 49, no. 1, Winter 1995; Baghat Korany, Rex Brynen, and Paul Noble, eds., *Political Liberalization and Democratization in the Arab World*, vol. 2, Boulder, CO: Lynne Rienner, 1998.

9. Shafeeq Ghabra, "Democratization in a Middle Eastern State: Kuwait, 1993," *Middle East Policy*, vol. 3, no. 1, 1994.

10. Neil Macfarquhar, "In Bahrain, Women Run, Women Vote, Women Lose," *New York Times*, 22 May 2002, p. A3.

11. See, for instance, Susan Sachs, "Writer Joins Growing Ranks of Egypt's Accused," *New York Times*, 4 August 2000, p. 3.

12. Guillermo O'Donnell, Philippe C. Schmitter, and Laurence Whitehead, eds., *Transitions from Authoritarian Rule: Tentative Conclusions about Uncertain Democracies*, Baltimore, MD: Johns Hopkins University Press, 1986; Terry Lynn Karl and Philippe C. Schmitter, "Modes of Transition in Latin America, Southern and Eastern Europe," *International Social Science Journal*, no. 53, May 1991.

13. As'ad AbuKhalil defines "Islamic fundamentalism" to refer to "all those movements and groups that aspire to the complete application of Islamic laws, as interpreted by leaders of the movements, in society and the body politic." The generic applicability of the concept of fundamentalism invalidates the critique of this term as ethnocentric by

apologists of Islamic fundamentalism. In the Middle East context, Islamic and Jewish fundamentalists are equally characterized by efforts to build theocratic states, whether they accept democracy as the appropriate means or not. See As'ad AbuKhalil, "The Incoherence of Islamic Fundamentalism: Arab Islamic Thought at the End of the 20th Century," *Middle East Journal*, vol. 48, no. 4, Autumn 1994, p. 677.

14. For a sample of arguments on both sides, see Shukri B. Abed, "Democracy and the Arab World," in Kaufman et al., eds., *Democracy, Peace, and the Israeli–Palestinian Conflict*; John O. Voll and John L. Esposito, "Islam's Democratic Essence," *Middle East Quarterly*, vol. 1, no. 3, September 1994; AbuKhalil, "The Incoherence of Islamic Fundamentalism." On Islamic liberals and their affinity with democracy, see Nazih Ayubi, *Political Islam: Religion and Politics in the Arab World*, London: Routledge, 1991, pp. 201–13. See also Tessler, chapter 6 in this volume.

15. Ziad Abu-Amr, "Hamas: A Historical and Political Background," *Journal of Palestine Studies*, vol. 22, no. 4, Summer 1993, p. 18.

16. Jihad Al-Khazen, "Interview: Editor of Al Hayat," *Middle East Policy*, vol. 3, no. 4, April 1995, p. 71.

17. Michael C. Dunn, "Algeria's Agony: The Drama So Far, the Prospects for Peace," *Middle East Policy*, vol. 3, no. 3, 1994; William B. Quandt, "The Urge for Democracy," *Foreign Affairs*, vol. 73, no. 4, 1994. On the explicit and fierce condemnation of democracy by the most popular Muslim preachers throughout the Middle East, see Emmanuel Sivan, "Eavesdropping on Radical Islam," *Middle East Quarterly*, vol. 2, no. 1, March 1995.

18. See, for instance, Charles Kurzman, "Liberal Islam: Prospects and Challenges," *Middle East Review of International Affairs (MERIA) Journal*, vol. 3, no. 3, September 1999; and Dale Eickelman, "The Coming Transformation of the Muslim World," reprinted from FPRI Wire, *Middle East Review of International Affairs (MERIA) Journal*, vol. 3, no. 3, September 1999.

19. Mottahedeh has made that case. See Roy P. Mottahedeh, "The Islamic Movement: The Case for Democratic Inclusion," *Contention*, vol. 4, no. 3, Spring 1995. In contrast, Salame argued that, in practice, moderates and militants alike play a political game that mutually reinforces their bargaining power. See Ghassan Salame, "Islam and the West," *Foreign Policy*, vol. 90, Spring 1993. See also G. Hossein. Razi, "Legitimacy, Religion, and Nationalism in the Middle East," *American Political Science Review*, vol. 84, no. 1, March 1990.

20. Dirk Vandewalle, "Ben-Ali's New Era: Pluralism and Economic Privatization in Tunisia," in Henri Barkey, ed., *The Politics of Economic Reform in the Middle East*, New York: St. Martin's Press, 1992, p. 113; Mohammed Abdelbeki Hermassi, "Islam, Democracy, and the Challenge of Political Change," in Yehudah Mirsky and Matt Ahrens, eds., *Democracy in the Middle East*, Washington DC: Washington Institute for Near East Policy, 1993, p. 47; Laurie Mylroie, "Promoting Democracy as a Principle of U.S. Middle East Policy," in Mirsky and Ahrens, p. 16; Graham Fuller, "A Phased Introduction of Islamists," in Mirsky and Ahrens, p. 25; Milton Viorst, "Sudan's Islamic Experiment," *Foreign Affairs*, vol. 74, no. 3, 1995, p. 58; Mottahedeh, "The Islamic Movement," p. 124.

21. Center for Palestine Research and Studies, "Results of Public Opinion Poll #23, 28–30 June 1996," Nablus, Palestine, p. 13.

22. Muhammad Daraghimah, "Hamas Facing the Difficult Questions of Whether to Change or Not," *Al-Ayyam*, no. 4, July 1999, pp. 1, 19, cited in FBIS-NES-04 Jul 1999.

23. Augustus R. Norton, "The Challenge of Inclusion in the Middle East," *Current History*, vol. 94, no. 588, January 1995, p. 2. On the need to avoid basing policies on inflated claims of fundamentalist support, see Timur Kuran, "Fundamentalist Economics and

the Economic Roots of Fundamentalism: Policy Prescriptions for a Liberal Society," in Martin Marty and R. Scott Appleby, eds., *Fundamentalism and Public Policy*, Chicago: University of Chicago Press, 1995.

24. Edward Mansfield and Jack Snyder, "The Dangers of Democratization," *International Security*, vol. 20, no. 1, Summer 1995; Edward Mansfield and Jack Snyder, "Democratization and War," *Foreign Affairs*, vol. 74, no. 3, 1995.

25. Ibid.

26. Eric Rouleau (interview), "Eric Rouleau Talks about the Peace Process and Political Islam," *Journal of Palestine Studies*, vol. 22, no. 4, Summer 1993, p. 55.

27. "Charter of the Islamic Resistance Movement (Hamas) of Palestine, Special Document," *Journal of Palestine Studies*, vol. 22, no. 4, Summer 1993, p. 125.

28. Quoted in Viorst, "Sudan's Islamic Experiment."

29. Hudson, "Democracy and Foreign Policy in the Arab World."

30. Mustafa Mashhur, deputy general guide of Egypt's brotherhood, urged confrontation with the "enemy" in his "freedom, elections, and enemies" (Aal-sha'b, in FBIS, 16 March 1995, p. 11).

31. Interview by Abd-al-latif Al-manawi, *Al-sharq Al-awsat*, 9 September 1999, p. 3.

32. Interview by Muhammad Shuraydah, *Al-safir*, 24 January 2000, p. 5.

33. Geoffrey Kemp, *Forever Enemies?: American Policy & the Islamic Republic of Iran*, Washington, DC: Carnegie Endowment for International Peace, 1994.

34. On Sudan's virtual state of war against all its neighbors and its mobilization of 500,000 volunteers, see Saad Eddin Ibrahim, "Arab Elites and Societies after the Gulf Crisis," in Dan Tschirgi, ed., *The Arab World Today*, Boulder, CO: Lynne Rienner, 1994. Eritrea (which broke off diplomatic relations with Sudan) and Uganda have brought complaints against Sudan to the UN Security Council.

35. On the failure of Islamist regimes to provide genuine economic alternatives and to achieve redistribution, see Kuran, "Fundamentalist Economics and the Economic Roots of Fundamentalism," and Olivier Roy, *The Failure of Political Islam*, Cambridge, MA: Harvard University Press, 1994.

36. Voll and Esposito, "Islam's Democratic Essence."

37. Mark Tessler and Marilyn Grobschmidt, "Democracy in the Arab World and the Arab–Israeli Conflict," in Garnham and Tessler, eds., *Democracy, War, and Peace in the Middle East*.

38. Rouleau, "Eric Rouleau Talks about the Peace Process and Political Islam," p. 45.

39. Khalil Shikaki, "Current Trends in Palestinian Public Opinion," paper presented at a Friedrich Naumann Foundation Workshop on "Monitoring Change in the Israeli and Palestinian Social and Political Systems," Jerusalem, 3–5 October 1994; Leila Dabdoub, "Palestinian Public Opinion Polls on the Peace Process," *Palestine-Israel Journal*, no. 5, Winter 1995.

40. Poll of Palestinians by the Jerusalem Media and Communication Centre (JMCC), 21–24 December 2000, reported in *Paldev Digest*, 9–10 January 2001, Special Issue (#2001-8), at paldev@lists.mcgill.ca. Data for 2002 are from the Palestinian Center for Policy and Survey Research, http://www.pcpsr.org/survey/polls.

41. The Palestinian National Authority banned and suppressed the emergence of new parties such as *al-'ahd* (the pledge) and several other independent parties, sometimes through arrests and threats. On the democratic opposition to Arafat, see *Al-majallah*, 5–11 September 1999, pp. 28–31, cited in FBIS-NES, 5 September 1999.

42. PCPSR, Survey Research Unit, Poll no. 4, 2002, http://www.pcpsr.org/survey/polls/2002.

43. Ehud Sprinzak, *The Ascendance of Israel's Radical Right*, New York: Oxford University Press, 1991; Ian S. Lustick, "Lessons from Ireland and Algeria," *Middle East Policy*, vol. 3, no. 3, 1994.

44. Charles S. Liebman, "Religion and Democracy in Israel," in Ehud Sprinzak and Larry Diamond, eds., *Israeli Democracy under Stress*, Boulder, CO: Lynne Rienner, 1993, p. 283.
45. Galia Golan, "A Palestinian State from an Israeli Point of View," *Middle East Policy*, vol. 3, no. 1, 1994, p. 62. Support for the Oslo agreement among Palestinians in the Occupied Territories in September 1993 was virtually identical: about 65 percent favored it. See Dabdoub, "Palestinian Public Opinion Polls on the Peace Process," p. 61.
46. Fred H. Lawson, "Domestic Transformation and Foreign Steadfastness in Contemporary Syria," *The Middle East Journal*, vol. 48, no. 1, Winter 1994; Raymond A. Hinnebusch, "Syria: The Politics of Peace and Regime Survival," *Middle East Policy*, vol. 3, no. 4, April 1995; David E. Sanger, "Fear, Inflation, and Graft Feed Disillusion among Iranians," *New York Times*, 30 May 1995, pp. A1, A6.
47. Robert L. Rothstein, "Cooperation across the Lines: Constraints and Opportunities," in Kaufman et al., eds., *Democracy, Peace, and the Israeli–Palestinian Conflict*.
48. On the legitimating potential of making the provision of human rights central to the process of democratization, see Nancy Bermeo, ed., *Liberalization and Democratization: Change in the Soviet Union and Eastern Europe*, Baltimore, MD: Johns Hopkins University Press, 1992, p. 194.
49. At times the perceived requirements of the peace process have narrowed democratic openings, as in Jordan and Palestine. See, for instance, Laurie A. Brand, "Effects of the Peace Process on Liberalization in Jordan," *Journal of Palestine Studies*, vol. 28, no. 2, Winter 1999.
50. As Korany has argued, Sadat accelerated the demise of a one-party system in Egypt in the 1970s, at which time he was also hatching a peace initiative toward Israel which culminated in the Camp David Accords of 1979. Bahgat Korany, "Restricted Democratization from Above: Egypt," in Korany, Brynen, and Noble, eds., *Political Liberalization and Democratization in the Arab World*, pp. 47–50.
51. Larry Diamond, Juan J. Linz, and Seymour M. Lipset, eds., *Democracy in Developing Countries: Latin America*, Boulder, CO: Lynne Rienner, 1989; Giacomo Luciani, ed., *The Arab State*, Berkeley, CA: University of California Press, 1990, p. xxiv; Mustapha K. El Sayyid, "The Third Wave of Democratization in the Arab World," in Dan Tschirgi, ed., *The Arab World Today*, Boulder, CO: Lynne Rienner, 1994; and, dissenting, Heather Deegan, *Middle East and Problems of Democracy*, Boulder, CO: Lynne Rienner, 1994.
52. Timur Kuran, "Now out of Never: The Element of Surprise in the East European Revolution of 1989," *World Politics*, vol. 44, no. 1, October 1991.
53. Solingen, *Regional Orders at Century's Dawn*, particularly chapter 6.
54. Most advanced in liberalizing their economies are Jordan (the first Arab state to enjoy a free-trade agreement with the United States), Morocco and Tunisia (both with free-trade agreements with the European Union), and to some extent Qatar and Bahrain.
55. The first connotes a more durable form of peace than the latter, which amounts to no more than a "cease-fire."

4

The United Nations and the Middle East

Amin Saikal

The United Nations' involvement in the Middle East has been extensive, complex, and wide-ranging. Ever since shortly after its establishment in 1945, the United Nations has been called upon to engage in political mediation, conflict resolution, peacekeeping, and human rights violation monitoring, as well as a variety of humanitarian relief activities. In the process, it has had more successes in the humanitarian areas than in the political field. A number of factors have been responsible for this, ranging from the fact that the Middle East has been a region of enormous complexity, underlined by its growing geostrategic importance and a high level of political volatility; to the United Nations' functioning for most of its life as a Cold War institution, reflecting mainly the rival interests of the United States and the Soviet Union; to the United States' concerted efforts, especially since the 1967 Arab–Israeli War, to limit the United Nations' political role in favor of its own in the Middle East. Although the Soviet Union has gone and the Cold War has ended, there has been no reduction in America's efforts to maintain its political dominance in the region, given its continuing deep economic and strategic interests in the area.

This chapter has three main objectives. The first is to look at the historical role of the United Nations in the Middle East. The second is to assess the United Nations' successes and failures in both political and non-political terms. The third is to focus on the opportunities and challenges that have confronted the United Nations' peacekeeping and peacemaking role in the region since the Gulf War of 1991 over Kuwait and the collapse of the Soviet Union in the same year.

The new state of Israel

The United Nations' involvement in the Middle East began in 1947 when the organization itself was in its infancy. It had a very difficult and precarious start, immediately attracting the distrust of the Arabs, who viewed it as a pro-Zionist and pro-Western organization. This was subsequently to be matched by a parallel development on the part of Israel and its main ally, the United States, which found the United Nations, or more specifically the General Assembly, taking an increasingly pro-Arab stand. This laid the basis for the United Nations to have no more than a spasmodic political role – a role that the United States sought to marginalize by augmenting its own interventionist diplomacy in a region of vital importance to it. To appreciate the force of this view, it is important, first, to look at some of the most relevant historical developments.

The UN involvement in the Middle East commenced against the backdrop of a bitter conflict brewing between the majority Arab population and minority Jewish inhabitants, most of whom were recent settlers, of what was then the British mandated territory of Palestine. When the British government finally found the conflict too taxing and decided in February 1947 to unload its burden, it turned the problem over to the newly created United Nations for resolution. This was the first major conflict-resolution role thrust upon the United Nations. It was clear from the outset that the United Nations lacked the necessary experience and mechanisms for handling a problem as complex as that of Palestine. However, in the highly charged atmosphere of international guilt and sympathy for the Jews that the Holocaust had created, which the Zionist movement was able to use to pressure the West to support its cause, the United Nations was expected to discharge this new responsibility with blistering speed.

Driven by the permanent members of the Security Council – especially the United States, which Britain wanted to involve in finding a resolution to the Palestine problem – the General Assembly resolved in a special session on 15 May 1947 to establish an 11-member Special Committee on Palestine (UNSCOP) to investigate the problem and make recommendations. Although the Arab Palestinian leadership refused to participate in UNSCOP's consultation process on the grounds that it was irrelevant, the Committee produced a majority report and a minority one: the majority report recommended a clear partition of Palestine into separate Jewish and Arab states, with Jerusalem to be put under International

Trusteeship; the minority report called for a single federal state, with Jerusalem as its capital.

The majority report, which was put to a vote in the Special Committee of the General Assembly on 25 November, at first fell short of the two-thirds majority required for adoption. However, after much lobbying and arm-twisting by the supporters of the majority report, especially the United States, the report was adopted on 29 November. All the Arab and Muslim delegates walked out in disgust, and even the Mandate Power, the United Kingdom, abstained, "making it clear that it would not assist in the implementation of a plan which could only be put into effect by force."[1]

This decision by the United Nations indeed proved to be one of the organization's most controversial and momentous decisions. The Jewish leadership promptly accepted the outcome as the most important foundation of legitimacy for the creation of an independent state of Israel, but the Arabs, the depth of whose aspirations and feelings had not been gauged, rejected it with disbelief and shock. They had not expected a resolution of this kind in their wildest imaginings. They quickly condemned the UN action, losing faith in the organization's ability to be impartial, fair, and just to them.[2]

The Zionists prompted the British to end their rule sooner than anybody could have anticipated and Israel declared independence, securing immediate recognition from the United States, and the regular armies of the neighboring Arab states joined their Palestinian counterparts for the first time to reverse this development, with disastrous consequences for Arabs on all fronts. They not only lost the war but also most of the territories allocated to the Arab Palestinians under the UN partition plan, which caused massive dislocation and human misery for the Palestinians, 700,000 of whom became refugees in neighboring Arab countries. This could only reinforce the Arabs' resentment of the United Nations as primarily responsible for legitimating the creation of Israel and creating what they saw as an uncontrollable force of destruction for them. Thus the United Nations' management of the problem laid an important foundation for an erosion of the organization's political credibility in the region over the next decade.

Of course, the United Nations quickly realized that it had made a major contribution to the creation of an explosive situation, producing real prospects for lingering bloodshed and instability in the region. This was reflected in the process of damage control that it set out to achieve. As well as disbanding UNSCOP, it adopted a series of measures that were in one form or another to shape the character of its future peacekeeping, peace mediation, and humanitarian operations not only in the Middle East but also around the world. These measures included the General

Assembly's appointment (immediately following Israel's declaration of independence) of a Mediator "to promote a peaceful adjustment of the future situation in Palestine," and the Security Council's authorizing, in the wake of the first Arab–Israeli war, of the deployment of unarmed UN military observers, who formed the base for the Truce Supervision Organization (UNTSO), which to the present day supervises truces arising from a number of other resolutions pertinent to the situation. Of these resolutions, perhaps the most important was Resolution 194 (III), which established a three-nation Conciliation Commission, re-emphasized the need for the internationalization of Jerusalem, and resolved that the refugees should be allowed to return to their homes and that compensation should be paid to those who did not want to return. The General Assembly also set up a special fund and a special organization, which led to the creation in 1949 of the UN Relief and Works Agency (UNRWA) to look after the destitute Palestinian refugees.[3]

However, although they addressed some of the humanitarian aspects of the conflict, these measures resulted in no major political shifts in the situation. Israel's refusal to give up anything that it now considered as imperative for its existence as a sovereign state, and the United States' growing reluctance to bring pressure to bear on Israel to accept a substantive compromise, halted any resolution of the conflict in its tracks. The United Nations' one salient positive achievement was its provision of humanitarian help to the Palestinian refugees – something UNRWA continues to perform by supporting what has now grown to about 2 million refugees in the Occupied Territories and neighboring states. However, the effect of this humanitarian achievement was overshadowed from the beginning by the United Nations' lack of progress in the political arena, giving the Palestinians in particular and Arabs in general little reason to overcome their distrust of the United Nations arising from its initial partition decision.

As time passed, the Israeli–Palestinian dispute only deepened and widened, with a growing entanglement in regional complexities and American–Soviet rivalry. Whereas the forces of radical Arab nationalism under Gamal Abdul-Nasser from 1952 called for regional changes in pursuit of a united Arab front against Zionism, colonialism, and imperialism, the United States hardened its support for Israel as a strategic asset in a zone of increasing political turbulence but economic significance, and the Soviet Union turned its back on Israel to support the radical Arab cause as the best way to undermine the US position in the region. As for the Palestinians, they found a source of salvation in Arab radicalism – a factor that led many of them to come together by the mid-1960s in support of a national liberation movement of their own, namely the Palestine Liberation Organization (PLO) under Yasser Arafat, but did not enable them ultimately to regain any of what they had lost to Israel.

Even so, the 1956 Suez conflict, the 1967 and 1973 Arab–Israeli wars, and the civil war between King Hussein and the PLO in Jordan in 1970, which essentially enlarged and complicated the Palestinian problem and conflated it with a wider Arab–Israeli conflict, created a series of intermittent but fresh opportunities for more decisive UN political interventions in pursuit of a favorable resolution. However, each time these opportunities failed to be taken. The United Nations intervened rather to provide face-saving measures for the local parties (to disengage) and for the major powers (to move away from a direct confrontation) as well as to put in place mechanisms and undertake activities to maintain peace for as long as the parties involved found it beneficial and tolerable. In this respect, it is important to recall some of the most important instances.

UNEF I

Having secured the first armistice agreements between the parties in the war of 1948 through the efforts of its Acting Mediator, Ralph Bunche, and building on this to monitor peace in the region, in the wake of the Suez War of 1956 the United Nations set out to consolidate its peacekeeping efforts. For the first and last time until the end of the Cold War, the Suez War caused the United States and the Soviet Union to embrace a united position against the aggressors, although for different purposes. The UN General Assembly adopted a number of resolutions calling not only for a cease-fire and withdrawal of Israeli forces from Egyptian territory, but also for the establishment of a United Nations Emergency Force (UNEF I), to replace the invading Anglo-French forces in the Canal Zone and Sinai. UNEF I was the United Nations' first armed peacekeeping force and proved to be quite effective in maintaining peace between Israel and Egypt for a decade.[4]

However, UNEF I could function only as long as the belligerent states allowed its stationing on their soils. When President Nasser demanded its withdrawal in mid-1967, the then UN Secretary-General, U Thant, promptly complied. This development, which was followed by the June 1967 War, has generated some disquiet, because some have argued that, if the Secretary-General had not acted so quickly, there would have been more time either to delay or to prevent the war. However, the counter-argument is that, if he had not acted, he not only would have violated the right of a sovereign state to choose whether or not it wanted the UN peacekeeping force, but also would have seriously risked the lives of the peacekeepers in the event that hostilities broke out.

Even so, in addition to new challenges, the 1967 War created an unprecedented opportunity for the United Nations to make a serious effort to find a resolution to the Palestinian problem in particular, and to the Arab–Israeli conflict in general. For the first time, the Arabs had been defeated so decisively that they could not but edge toward the possibility of a negotiated settlement. This fact was reflected in the warring Arab states' consent to the famous UN Security Council Resolution 242, which was adopted on 22 November 1967, as well as in President Nasser's overtures toward the United States for a negotiated settlement.

Resolution 242 was undoubtedly historic.[5] It constituted a serious attempt by the United Nations at conflict resolution, giving Arabs, at least initially, a degree of faith in the United Nations. Despite deliberately vague wording here and there, the resolution set the necessary foundation for a negotiated settlement. It called not only on the Arabs to respect the existence of Israel within secure borders, but also on Israel to withdraw from territories that it had occupied and to facilitate the return of the refugees. Although no mention of the Palestinians was made, this was implicit in the word "refugees." It is also important to note that, as part of conflict-resolution efforts, the UN Secretary-General augmented the use of his Good Offices by appointing a Special Representative, Gunnar Jarring, whose mission in support of mediating between the belligerent parties for a resolution lasted from early 1968 to early 1971.

UNEF II

The United Nations had a further opportunity to build on its post–1967 War efforts in the wake of the October 1973 Yom Kippur War, during which the superpowers came as close as they ever did to a direct confrontation in the Middle East. To circumvent a US–Soviet clash, the United Nations moved swiftly to adopt two further landmark decisions: the Security Council adopted Resolution 338, which called for an immediate cease-fire and implementation of Resolution 242; and it set up UNEF II, which was to fill the gap created by the abrupt departure of UNEF I six years earlier and to keep the belligerents apart and monitor the cease-fire.[6]

However, these measures largely went down the same path as the United Nations' previous efforts. They essentially provided a respectable way for the superpowers to avoid a direct confrontation and for their regional clients to limit their operations and accept an unconditional cease-fire, although the United Nations could do little to stop Israel from achieving its basic military objectives between the time of the Security Council's adoption of a resolution for the cease-fire and the point when Israel actually stopped fighting. As for the implementation of Resolution 338, it remained very much on paper in a way similar to 242, and gave the

United Nations little scope to make any serious inroads into a resolution of the conflict. Of course, a variety of factors contributed to the lack of progress, of which three were especially important.

The first concerned the fact that Israel's initial honeymoon with the United Nations did not last beyond the 1950s. As the era of post–World War II decolonization accelerated, the membership of the United Nations rapidly swelled with predominantly third world states. These new members tipped the balance in the General Assembly decisively in favor of the Palestinian/Arab cause and the Soviet Union. Consequently, from the late 1960s, the General Assembly passed a number of resolutions supporting the right of Palestinian people to self-determination (in some cases as a prelude to an independent homeland) and condemning Israeli treatment of the Palestinians under its occupation and its non-compliance with most of the relevant UN resolutions. It was this transformation of the General Assembly that eventually led to its inviting Yasser Arafat to address the Assembly in 1974, granting the PLO observer status, and finally adopting Resolution 3379 in November 1975 equating Zionism with racism.

Although the General Assembly's decisions are not mandatory and the United States continued to protect Israel's interests at the Security Council level, predominantly with its veto power, and although Resolution 3379 was revoked by Resolution 46/86 in December 1991, the growing pro-Arab attitude of the General Assembly eroded Israel's confidence in the United Nations. This meant that Israeli governments became increasingly uncooperative, as had earlier been the case with the Palestinians – a development that peaked with the election to power in 1975 of the right-wing Likud Party under Menachem Begin. Prime Minister Begin took exceptional dislike to the United Nations, treating it with considerable contempt.

The second factor was that, following the 1967 War, Israel was in a much stronger bargaining position. Occupying the West Bank, East Jerusalem, the Gaza, the Golan Heights, and Sinai, Israel not only secured a sizable territorial security belt for itself but also gained the necessary psychological strength to resist any proposed compromise that did not meet its terms. The 1973 War dented Israel's image of invincibility to an appreciable extent, pressuring it to become somewhat more obliging in diplomatic negotiations, but this development was not enough to force Israel to accept Resolution 242 as a basis for a "land for peace" settlement, with the Palestinians in particular and the Arabs in general. Israel was still in a position to bargain only for the kinds of deals most favorable to it.

The third factor is related to the United States' growing desire to be the paramount player in the Middle East. Washington made its first major intervention in this respect in Iran in 1953. In one of the Central Intelligence Agency's most successful covert operations of the Cold War, in the wake of an oil nationalization crisis between Iran and Britain, the CIA engineered the overthrow of the Iranian reformist, nationalist government of Muhammad Mossadeq, transforming Iran into a US client under the country's pro-Western conservative monarch, Muhammad Reza Pahlavi. The United States quickly complemented this development with the conclusion of bilateral and multilateral economic and military pacts with Turkey and Pakistan. The objective was to widen America's interests and protect them against the spread of Soviet communism and radical Arab nationalism and British influence in the region.[7] In a similar vein, the United States could not be benevolent toward the United Nations, or any other force for that matter, if their activities proved to frustrate its goal of regional dominance.

In this respect, however, the crunch came with the Suez conflict. Although the United States and the Soviet Union adopted a common approach to the crisis, it was clear that there was going to be little superpower cooperation from then on. Moscow's severance of its ties with Israel and development of close military relations with the radical Arab nationalist forces under President Nasser placed it firmly opposed to Washington in the Middle East. This, together with the decolonization rapidly enlarging the global support at the United Nations for the Arab cause and the Soviet position, caused not only Israel but also the United States to grow disenchanted with the United Nations. As the Soviet Union repeatedly backed the Arab cause, the United States became more determined than ever to reduce the role of the United Nations in the Middle East. Despite American–Soviet cooperation in the coming years over a number of UN resolutions, especially 242 and 338 as well as 425, which called for an end to the 1982 Israeli invasion of southern Lebanon and withdrawal of Israeli troops from the country, the United States precipitously unfolded a campaign to monopolize diplomatic initiatives with regard to the Arab–Israeli conflict and the region as a whole.

The United States versus the United Nations in the Middle East

The major US initiatives began with the Rogers Plan, launched following the 1967 War by the US Secretary of State, William Rogers, for a ceasefire to end the war of attrition between Egypt and Israel as a precondition for a settlement. The plan did not achieve much in terms of conflict resolution, largely because President Nixon's National Security Advisor,

Henry Kissinger, undermined Rogers' efforts as part of a power rivalry between the two. However, the plan produced a renewable six-monthly cease-fire, which remained in place until the October 1973 War, raising the credentials of the United States as the only power capable of making a key contribution to the fostering of peace in the region.

The second initiative was the "shuttle diplomacy" launched in the wake of the 1973 War by Kissinger, who had by then replaced Rogers as Secretary of State. Kissinger's approach to building peace block by block not only led to the disengagement of forces between Israel and Egypt, and Israel and Syria, but also established the first face-to-face contacts between Israel and two of its warring neighbors. This development generated much optimism about a possible resolution of the conflict, helping the United States to assume a more center-stage position in the peace-making process. The failure of the first American–Soviet-sponsored Middle East Peace Conference, held under UN auspices in 1974, simply enhanced the position of the United States as the only force with the necessary clout to find a resolution of the conflict.

Of course, given the deep-seated political differences and psychological barriers between Israel and the Arabs, there was little progress on the peace front until Egyptian President Anwar al-Sadat's dramatic visit to Jerusalem in November 1977. Although nothing can diminish the importance of Sadat's visit and Begin's desire to take Egypt out of the regional military equation – considerations instrumental in terms of creating more space for American involvement and accelerating the pace of a settlement on the Egyptian–Israeli front – if it had not been for American diplomacy, the visit might not ultimately have produced the desired results. It required President Jimmy Carter's personal mediation and extra American security and economic support for Israel, as well as sizable financial assistance to Egypt, to produce the 1978 Camp David Accords. These resulted in a peace deal between Egypt and Israel and the return of Sinai by Israel to Egypt in 1982.

Whatever the subsequent American initiatives and their outcomes – leading to the Madrid Middle East peace talks, which opened in November 1991, and to the Oslo peace process, which commenced in September 1993 between Israel and the PLO as the representative of the Palestinian people, and a number of associated agreements – US activities always aimed at establishing American centrality to any resolution of the Middle East conflict. From 1967 the United States succeeded in progressively reducing, for all practical purposes, the roles of the Soviet Union (and its successor, the Russian Federation) and the United Nations to those of fringe players in the region. Although the United States welcomed Russia to co-chair the Madrid talks, this plainly was just a diplomatic nicety. It came as no surprise that, despite the fact that the Israeli–PLO Declaration of Principles was formulated in secret negotiations between the two parties in Oslo, it was formally signed on the lawns of the White House in Washington on 14 September 1993 rather than at the United Nations or elsewhere.

The United States immediately seized the opportunity to have an exclusive role as a peacemaker in the Oslo process. While renewing its commitment to the defense of Israel's sovereignty and territorial integrity within the framework of its strategic alliance with the Jewish state, the Clinton administration set out to promote itself as an impartial broker and to claim whatever political kudos it could from the Oslo process. It set up a Middle East policy team, most of whose members had well-known emotional attachments to Israel, in order to reassure Israel that whatever the consequences of the Oslo process the United States was behind it all the way. For the next seven years, when the peace process experienced a very turbulent journey, the United States unquestioningly embraced Israel's demand that the United States remain the only outside power involved in the process. It rebuffed repeated Palestinian calls for wider outside mediation in the process, especially after the Oslo process faced increasingly serious difficulties following the assassination of Israel's Prime Minister Yitzchak Rabin by a fellow Jew in late 1995 in response to his commitment to the peace process. The United States actively discouraged any substantial role for the United Nations and the European Union, with a clear aim of maintaining a full monopoly on managing the process and avoiding pressure on Israel.

The only time that the United States allowed the United Nations and the European Union to play a somewhat substantial mediatory role was in early 2001, when the Oslo process had been derailed and the Palestinians had launched their second *intifada* (uprising) against the Israeli occupation, resulting in a bloody open conflict between the protagonists. It did so under mounting pressure from the failure of its own role and the need to avoid an international backlash. However, UN and EU involvement could not amount to much because it came too late and under conditions of conflict that could not be conducive to success. By now it was clear that what the Israelis and Palestinians required in terms of ending their hostilities and returning to the negotiation table was beyond the United Nations and European Union. The only power that could pressure both Israel and the Palestinians and meet their political and pecuniary needs to negotiate a successful final settlement was the United States – a factor that forced the new US Republican administration of President George W. Bush, which took office in January 2001, to maintain the United States' close involvement in mediation despite its initial reluctance. Thus the United States continued to be the central player in the

Arab–Israeli conflict, with the United Nations playing no more than a marginal political role in finding a resolution to the conflict.

The Gulf War

The end of the Cold War, with the collapse of the Berlin Wall in 1989 and the subsequent disintegration of the Soviet Union two years later, helped the United States to continue to strengthen its hold, at the expense of the United Nations and for that matter other international actors, on those parts of the Middle East that really mattered and where it had the required leverage. It was against this background that the United States successfully mounted first the Desert Shield operation and then, in January–February 1991, Operation Desert Storm – the largest American combat operation since the Viet Nam War – to reverse the 2 August 1990 Iraqi invasion of Kuwait. Since the Soviet Union's role and stature in world politics had dramatically weakened and the country was itself in need of some American aid to sustain its recently initiated program of democratic and capitalist transformation, Washington was left as the only superpower to assume world leadership. In combining its military might with checkbook diplomacy to oppose what was widely held to be an unjust invasion by a "demonic" regime, the United States rapidly managed to dominate the UN Security Council, stimulating and cajoling it to act in support of what American interests dictated. The United Nations simply served as a legitimizing body for US policy interests.

All the resolutions adopted by the Security Council – from those condemning the Iraqi invasion and calling for Iraq's immediate and unconditional withdrawal from Kuwait, to those authorizing the use of all means, including force, to repulse that invasion – were US driven. The resolutions were carefully coordinated to be in step with the US military build-up for the final confrontation.[8] At the end, the terms for the Iraqi defeat were also dictated, signed, and sealed by the United States. Even in the creation and enforcement of a "safe haven" for the Kurds in northern Iraq and an "air exclusion zone" for the Shi'ites in the south of the country in the face of Saddam Hussein's reprisals against those opposing his rule – an opposition that was mounted largely at the urging of President George Bush – the United States needed no more than a vague conceptual endorsement by the United Nations.

However, as has been largely true in the case of the Arab–Israeli conflict, the United States was happy to let the United Nations take over responsibility for monitoring and implementing the terms of the Iraqi defeat and catering for humanitarian needs generated in the wake of Desert

Storm, as long as the UN activities remained in line with US interests. In the final analysis, however, even in the humanitarian field, the United States has not always been supportive of the United Nations against operations that could be conducive to its pursuit of regional dominance. This has been further illustrated, for example, by the US position on repeated Turkish military incursions since late March 1995 into northern Iraq (and therefore the "safe haven") against the alleged armed operations of the Kurdistan Workers Party (PKK), fighting for the independence of the Turkish Kurds. The main reason that the United States and its Gulf War Western allies originally enforced the "safe haven" in northern Iraq was to enable relief agencies, most importantly the UN High Commissioner for Refugees, to cater for the Iraqi Kurds with a necessary degree of impunity. But when it has come to the Turkish invasions, the United States has not been prepared to condemn, let alone stop, the Turkish action, despite protests by humanitarian agencies that it had hindered their relief operations. This has made a mockery of the concept of "safe haven" and has implied that the United States is content to use force against its enemy, the Saddam Hussein regime, but does not want to use force against its ally, Turkey, because the latter's alliance is more important to US maintenance of its regional dominance than the United Nations' humanitarian operations.

The Iran–Iraq war

The case where perhaps the United Nations could claim a degree of success in peace mediation was in the Iran–Iraq conflict. In this conflict – the longest (1980–8), bloodiest, and costliest war ever fought in the history of the modern Middle East – the United States was largely content to support UN efforts toward a cease-fire, which came into force from mid-1988. What contributed substantially to the UN success in this instance was that: (1) the combatants had reached the point of total exhaustion; (2) Mikhail Gorbachev had embarked on his process of ending the Cold War and supporting the United Nations to become a more effective body; and (3) Washington had finally failed in its attempts to cultivate Iraqi President Saddam Hussein as an Arab bulwark against the United States' main enemy, Ayatollah Khomeini's Islamic regime, and ultimately could not rely on any of the combatants for important strategic gains in the region. It was therefore in the interest of the United States to act through rather than at the expense of the United Nations.

The history of UN involvement in the Middle East can be characterized more by its political failures than by its humanitarian services, which have brought much kudos to the organization. Having said this, it is important to be reminded that essentially the United Nations is the reflection of its members, especially its permanent Security Council members. For a long time it was paralyzed by the conflict between its rival superpower members. Since the end of the Cold War and the collapse of the Soviet Union, it has functioned more or less at the mercy of its most powerful member, the United States. However, the situation is changing, with demand for UN services sky-rocketing and some rifts developing within the Western alliance, for example over sanctions against Iraq. This could cause the United States to act more in concert with other permanent members of the Security Council than before. The future of the United Nations – in terms of direction, functions, and effectiveness – will depend very much on the achievement of three things: a consensus among the Western powers over a post–Cold War order; structural reform of the United Nations so that it truly mirrors the transition from a Cold War to a post–Cold War global situation; and the availability of resources and mandates to the United Nations so that it can take on the tasks that at present the United States performs in its name. Without achievement in these areas, the United Nations may not be able to play an effective political role in the Middle East for the foreseeable future.

Notes

An earlier version of this chapter originally appeared as "The Role of the United Nations in the Middle East," in Tom Woodhouse, Robert Bruce, and Malcolm Dando, eds., *Peacekeeping and Peacemaking: Towards Effective Intervention in Post–Cold War Conflicts*, London: Macmillan, 1998. Portions of this earlier version are reproduced with permission of Palgrave Macmillan.

1. Anthony Parsons, *From Cold War to Hot Peace: UN Interventions 1947–1994*, London: Michael Joseph, 1995, p. 7.
2. For a detailed discussion, see Avi Shlaim, *The Iron Wall: Israel and the Arab World*, London: Penguin Books, 2000, chapter 1.
3. See Parsons, *From Cold War to Hot Peace*, pp. 8–9.
4. For a detailed discussion, see Arthur L. Burns and Nina Heathcote, *Peace-Keeping by the U.N.: From Suez to the Congo*, New York: Frederick A. Praeger, 1963, chapter 2.
5. For a comprehensive discussion, see Arthur Lall, *The UN and the Middle East Crisis, 1967*, New York: Columbia University Press, 1968.
6. Arthur Lall, "UNEF and Its Withdrawal," in John N. Moor, ed., *The Arab–Israeli Conflict: Readings and Documents*, Princeton, NJ: Princeton University Press, 1977, pp. 597–607.
7. For a view of American diplomacy with regard to the Suez crisis, see Henry Kissinger, *Diplomacy*, New York: Simon & Schuster, 1994, chapter 21.
8 See Amin Saikal, "Iraq, UNSCOM and the US: A UN Debacle?" *Australian Journal of International Affairs*, vol. 53, no. 3, 1999, pp. 283–94.

Part II
Secularization and democracy

5

Disenchanted worlds: Secularization and democratization in the Middle East

Majid Tehranian

[M]odernization involves a process of secularization; that is, it systematically displaces religious institutions, beliefs, and practices, substituting for them those of reason and science ... [Max Weber called this process] "the disenchantment of the world." It eliminates all the superhuman and supernatural forces, the gods and spirits, with which nonindustrial cultures populate the universe and to which they attribute responsibility for the phenomena of the natural and social worlds. In their place it substitutes as the sole cosmology the modern scientific interpretation of nature. Only the laws and regularities discovered by the scientific method are admitted as valid explanations of phenomena. If it rains, or does not rain, it is not because the gods are angry but because of atmospheric conditions, as measured by the barometer and photographed by satellites.

"Modernization," *Encyclopedia Britannica Online.*[1]

This chapter considers secularization and democratization in the context of a diversity of Middle Eastern societies. It argues that relations between secularization and democratization in the Middle East are far more complex than those experienced by the West.[2] Islam and democracy have been allies in some contexts and adversaries in others. Historically, relations between mosque and state in Islamic societies have been significantly different from the relations between church and state in Christendom. In contrast to the Christian doctrine of separation of spiritual and temporal realms, Islam generally sees them as united. Politically, absolutist monarchies in the Middle East were not transformed into enlightened despotism as in Europe but, rather, became Western colonial satrapies. They could not therefore pursue an effective policy of modernization and secularization. In the anti-imperialist struggles, the Islamic ulama tended to make common cause with secular nationalists and liberals. Such alliances often led to nationalist and constitutional revolts, as in Egypt (1881), Iran (1905–9), and Ottoman Turkey (1908). However, as secularization gained momentum, it also led to a sense of betrayal by the religious elements, resulting in militant Islamic movements such as the al-Ikhwan al-Muslimun (Muslim Brotherhood) in Egypt (1928). Economically, most modern Middle Eastern states became directly or indirectly recipients of large oil revenues in the form of windfall "rents," which allowed them to avoid taxing their population while extending some social benefits and resisting the pressures for political participation. Thus, democratization and political accountability were not urgent demands from the population. Culturally, the transition from orality to literacy, print, and electronic media systems has led to accelerating mobilization of the tradition-bound lower strata of society with Islamic rather than secular ideological orientations.

A pathology of transition to modernity has characterized Middle Eastern development no less than it had plagued prior industrialization experiences in the world. The passage to modernity requires mobilization of human and natural resources, which in turn fosters ideologies of disciplined puritanism requiring mobilization, dedication, hard work, and abstinence from consumption. In past historical experiences, the Puritan, Nazi, Fascist, and Communist revolutions have performed that function. Faced with colonial domination, Middle Eastern societies have resorted to the more indigenous varieties of purist ideologies, including "pure" nationalism and Islamism. Such ideologies clearly hamper democratic development, which requires coexistence and compromise among political adversaries.

Following a brief discussion of the comparative aspects of secularization and democratization, the chapter takes a historical approach. It reviews the ebb and flow of secularization and democratization under the rubric of three historical phases: (1) incremental secularization and democratization in the nineteenth century, (2) radical secularization without democratization in the inter-war period (1918–40), and (3) radical Islamization with or without democratization in the post-war period. In conclusion, the problems and prospects for an emerging democratic coexistence between mosque and state, and the consequence of this uneasy relationship for peace and stability in the region, will be examined.

Secularization and democratization in comparative perspective

In modernization theories, secularization and democratization have been often considered mutually reinforcing processes. In the Marxist tradition, religion is considered the opium of the masses that blunts class-consciousness and revolutionary fervor. In the liberal tradition, traditional religious values are considered obstacles to modernity and modernization. In both traditions, secularization is considered an essential component of democratization.

This orthodox view may be generally valid for the Western historical experience. The rise of the modern world in Western Europe and North America was accompanied by a decline of religious authority and monarchical power. It also led to a rise of secular nation-states and a succession of liberal democratic revolutions that laid the foundations of the modern democratic states. One feature of this transition was the separation of church and state, as exemplified by the United States constitution. In Western countries with an official church, such as the Church of England in Britain, secular laws eventually prevailed. Moreover, the transition from orality and writing to print and electronic cultures generally led to a diffusion of knowledge. This, in turn, reduced the authority of the Roman Catholic Church as the custodian of revealed knowledge. Secularization in the West was thus the result of increasing democratization of knowledge and power. Jesus' injunction "render to Caesar the things that are Caesar's, and to God the things that are God's"[3] provided the theological legitimation for the separation of church and state.

By contrast to the early history of Christianity, temporal and spiritual authorities were united for the first 40 years of Islamic history (622–61). Under the leadership of Prophet Muhammad and his Rightly-Guided Caliphs (*khulaf al-rashidun*), the nascent Islamic community was led by political leaders who were at the same time considered vicars of God on earth. Following the assassination of the fourth Caliph Ali, the Prophet's son-in-law, political power passed to two dynasties that did not enjoy as much religious legitimacy. Although the Ummayed and Abbasid Caliphs continued to call themselves *amir al-mu'minin*, Commander of the Faithful, they were not universally respected or followed. Except for its first 40 years, therefore, Islamic history was characterized by a de facto separation of mosque and state.

But historical memories of pristine Islam have persisted to give rise to several different tendencies, including Islamic conservatism, messianism, reformism, mysticism, separatism, and revolution (see table 5.1). The most militant of these tendencies is an effort to return to the purity

Table 5.1 Islamic religious responses to secular regimes

Regime	Islamic tendency					
	Conservatism	Messianism	Reformism	Mysticism	Separatism	Revolution
Absolute monarchy or emirate	Saudi Arabia, 1932–present	Sudan, 1844–85	United Arab Emirates, 1971–present; Bahrain, 1971–present; Oman, 1741–present; Qatar, 1971–present			
Constitutional monarchy			Afghanistan, 1926–73; Iran, 1905–79; Egypt, 1937–52; Iraq, 1932–58; Jordan, 1946–present			
Republic	Iran, 1989–present		Iran, 1989–present; Egypt, 1952–present; Turkey, 1923–present; Lebanon, 1945–present; Syria, 1944–present		Takfir wa-Hijra (Condemnation and Migration), and al-Uzlat al-Shu'uriyya (Emotional Seclusion)	Iran, 1979–89; Sudan, 1986–present; Afghanistan, 1989–present
Military dictatorship			Iraq, 1958–present; Afghanistan, 1973–89			Iraq, 1958–present

of pristine Islam by unifying mosque and state power. This tendency has expressed itself in both conservative and revolutionary politics. The earliest of such movements was the nineteenth-century Wahhabi movement in the Arabian Peninsula that finally underlined the creation of the Saudi regime in 1932. The movement was and continues to be a puritanical doctrine that tries to re-establish pristine Islam. So was Ayatollah Khomeini's call for the establishment of an Islamic Republic. Both calls are fundamentally against secular regimes. They have reverberated throughout the Islamic world. However, the revolutionary tendency also contains within itself reformist secular potentials that have led in Iran to a struggle between the conservatives, liberals, and pragmatists.

The other three tendencies (messianism, mysticism, and separatism) may be considered strategies of resistance. By reliance on the messianic notions of the return of the Mahdi (in Arabic, he who is divinely guided), for centuries Muslims have risen against their oppressive governments. The latest such incidence took place in Sudan in 1885 when, by declaring himself Mahdi, Muhammad Ahmad successfully defeated the British forces.[4] In the mid-nineteenth century, the Babi movement in Iran led a less successful revolt. It merged with the constitutional revolutionary movement as well as the Bahai Faith founded by Mirza Hussein Ali, who had declared himself Mahdi in 1863 just before he was exiled.

Sufism, or Islamic mysticism, is arguably as old as Islam. In later centuries, it turned into a formidable movement of folk Islam organized in a variety of Sufi orders or brotherhoods (*ukhuwwat*). As a reaction against Islamic positivism, Sufism emphasized the Way (*Tariqa*) vis-à-vis the Law (*Shari'a*). It established a constellation of saints and places of Sufi gathering and worship other than the mosque, including *khaneqah*, *zawiya*, and *tekya*. A few Sufi orders, such as the Sanusis in Libya[5] and the Safavids in Iran, also achieved positions of state power by establishing dynastic rule. Official Islam considered Sufism a religious deviance until the eleventh century, when Imam Ghazali (1058–1111) reconciled its principles with those of the Shari'a. Sufi orders subsequently helped to propagate Islam into South and Southeast Asia. To this day, Sufism continues to be a source of religious inspiration for millions of Muslims. It provides a worldview that often shuns state power in favor of personal spiritual pursuits. It is largely quietist and, except for a few historical instances, it does not directly confront state power.

By contrast, as typified by *khawarij* in early Islam and Shi'ism in much of Islamic history, Islamic separatism challenges the legitimacy of the state on religious grounds. Today, many separatist groups in the Islamic world wish to set themselves apart from a dominant secular society that is perceived as depraved and beyond salvation.[6] In contemporary Egypt, such groups are exemplified by Jama'at al-Muslimin, later dubbed by authorities Takfir wa-Hijra (Condemnation and Migration), and al-Uzlat al-Shu'uriyya (Emotional Seclusion).

The six tendencies under discussion are not mutually exclusive. As table 5.1 shows, the conservative, reformist, and revolutionary tendencies can be readily identified in terms of historical periods and movements. But the religious tendencies toward messianism, mysticism, and separatism cannot be as readily identified and dated. The latter tendencies may be considered as strategies of resistance that have a long and sometimes secret history.

Secularization and democratization in the modern Middle East can be analyzed in terms of the ebbs and flows of the transition to modernity. As prismatic societies,[7] Middle Eastern countries present almost every color in the complex prism of mosque–state relations. However, patterns seem to have shifted from incremental to radical secularization and democratization followed by radical Islamization with or without democratization. Although it is too early to judge, the last period may be followed again by a period of incremental secularization and democratization. As in the Western transition to modernity during which Christianity was transformed through Renaissance and Reformation, Islam too is currently undergoing profound changes in its belief systems and practices. The transition from orality and literacy to print and electronic cultures in the Middle East, as elsewhere, is leading to democratization and secularization of knowledge and power.[8]

Before we discuss this evolutionary process, a few caveats on democratization and secularization are in order. First, as the preceding discussion has shown, Islam is not a monolith. There are enormous variations in beliefs and practices with respect to mosque–state relations. Secondly, in the processes of broadening and deepening of political participation, democratization is a journey *not* a destination. No country in the world can claim to have achieved perfect democracy, which in Lincoln's apt words means "government of the people, by the people, and for the people." However, elements of that ideal can be summarized as follows:

- political democracy: popular sovereignty; universal suffrage; protection of life, liberty, and pursuit of happiness; majority rule, minority rights; fair representation and periodic elections; peaceful succession; direct voting such as referenda on critical issues; rule of law, *habeas corpus*, bill of rights; and responsibilities of citizenship;
- economic democracy: protection of property; free markets; free competition; government regulation of trade and investment to ensure the absence of monopolies and fair standards in trade, exchange, competition, health, and environment;

- social democracy: social security for the unemployed, the retired, pregnant women, and children; the provision of public health, education, and welfare;
- cultural democracy: universal education; access to means of communication; freedom of identity, including speech, assembly, religion, language, privacy, and lifestyle.

As for secularization, the fundamental principle is a separation of religion and state. This does not, however, mean a separation of religion and politics. In a secular society, religious institutions, like other social institutions, are free to compete and express their political views in the marketplace of ideas. In contrast to theocracies, secular regimes do not allow a clerical class to monopolize political power in the name of God without reference to popular will. In this sense, democratization and secularization must be considered as two sides of the same coin.

One last caveat: significant differences in Sunni and Shi'a theologies and religious organizations have led to different consequences in Iran, Turkey, and the Arab world. Whereas the unity of temporal and spiritual authority continued to be a tenet of Sunni Islam, Shi'ism from the beginning was a minority sect upholding the legitimacy of the House of Ali against the temporal rulers. From time to time, Shi'a dynasties came to power, as in the cases of the Fatimids in Egypt (973–1171), the Buyids in Iran and Iraq (945–1055), and the Safavids (1501–1722) in Iran. But the majority sect continued to be Sunni, even in Iran until the Safavids brought Shi'a missionaries from Lebanon to convert the population to Shi'ism vis-à-vis the Ottoman Sunnis. For this reason, some scholars have argued that Shi'a Islam is an Iranian cultural creation that has grafted the Divine Rights of Kings onto Islamic theology by vesting spiritual and temporal authority exclusively in the House of Ali. Whatever its origins, Shi'ism in modern Iran and Iraq, where it is followed by majorities, has generally assumed an oppositionist posture against secular governments. According to Twelver Shi'ites, dominant in Iran and Iraq, legitimate power belongs to the Twelfth Imam Mahdi, who disappeared into occultation in 878 and who will reappear some day to restore peace and justice in the world. By virtue of their spiritual authority as custodians of the Inmate, the Shi'a ulama often succeeded in creating a state within the state. Collection of religious taxes (*khoms, zakat,* and *sahm-i-Imam*) and control of religious endowments (*waqf*) also gave them some financial independence. Although modern secular states have tried time and again to turn the ulama into state pensioners, the Shi'a ulama have often succeeded in maintaining their autonomy. They have thus generally acted as a stronger source of opposition to secular policies than their Sunni counterparts.

Incremental secularization and democratization

Middle Eastern societies came into direct contact and conflict with the secular West as early as the military defeats they experienced. The landing of Napoleon in Egypt in 1798 was the most dramatic of these events. Although the French were expelled in 1802 by the combined forces of British and Ottoman troops, the shock of contact started a secularization process that continues to this day. For the Ottoman Empire, the loss of Greece and Egypt in the early nineteenth century brought military defeat home. For Qajar Iran, defeat took place in the early nineteenth century as a result of two successive wars with Russia in which the country lost its control over the Caucasus and Central Asia. The resulting shock awakened the governments in Ottoman Turkey, Iran, and Egypt to the need for reform.

Reform began first with military institutions. Reorganization of armies along Western models of conscription, armament, and warfare was the first item on the agenda. In Ottoman Turkey, the Tanzimat Reforms of 1836–76 took the lead. A proclamation in 1839 upheld the principles of individual liberty, freedom from oppression, and equality before the law, and a section of the 1856 edict concerned itself with the rights of Christians. However, such declarations by the Ottoman Sultans were primarily window dressing aimed at pleasing Western powers. The real reforms were in the army, including the major reorganizations of 1842 and 1869 following the pattern of the successful Prussian conscript system.

In Iran, military reform was conducted under the leadership of Crown Prince Abbas Mirza. A French military mission sent to Iran by Napoleon assisted him in the task. However, as soon as France reached an agreement with Russia against Britain, the mission was withdrawn and Iran suffered defeat at the hands of the Russians.[9]

In Egypt, an ambitious Albanian military officer named Muhammad Ali led the modernization and secularization drives. As a society ruled by the control of a single superhighway, the Nile, Egypt presented the greatest opportunity in the Ottoman Empire for a total restructuring of society. The three-year French occupation (1798–1801) had undermined the country's traditional system. Muhammad Ali completed the task by putting an end to Egypt's traditional society. He organized a modern army, eliminated the former ruling oligarchy, expropriated the old landholding classes, turned the religious class into government pensioners, restricted the activities of the native merchants and artisans, neutralized the Bedouins, and crushed all movements of rebellion among the peasants. The task of rebuilding Egypt along modern lines now lay before him. Although he largely failed in this task by refusing to democratize the political system, his secular policies in administration, education, and law laid the foundation. Disbanding his mercenary army, he created a fleet and an army of Egyptians conscripted from the peasant class. To supply services for his armed forces, he created Western-style schools to train doctors, engineers, veterinarians, and other specialists. He also began sending students to European countries for training in modern techniques.

After military reform, educational secularization made the greatest progress. Education in Islamic societies had been the responsibility of the various *millets* (religious communities) recognized by the state as the Peoples of the Book, including Zoroastrian, Jewish, Christian, and Islamic communities. Education for Muslims was controlled by the ulama and directed toward religious learning. The first inroads into the Ottoman educational system had been made with the creation of naval engineering (1773), military engineering (1793), medical (1827), and military science (1834) colleges. Similar institutions for diplomats and administrators were founded, including the translation bureau (1833) and the civil service school (1859). The latter was reorganized in 1877 and eventually became the political science department of the University of Ankara and the major training center for higher civil servants.

In 1846, the first comprehensive plan for state education was put forward. It provided for a complete system of primary and secondary schools leading to the university level, all under the Ministry of Education. A still more ambitious educational plan, inaugurated in 1869, provided for free and compulsory primary education. Both schemes progressed slowly because of a lack of money, but they provided a framework within which development toward a systematic, secular educational program could take place. By 1914 there were more than 36,000 Ottoman schools, although the great majority were small, traditional primary schools. The development of the state system was aided by the example of progress among the non-Muslim *millet* schools, in which the education provided was more modern than that in the Ottoman schools. These included more than 1,800 Greek schools with about 185,000 pupils, and some 800 Armenian schools with more than 81,000 pupils. Non-Muslims also used schools provided by foreign missionary groups in the empire; there were 675 US, 500 French Catholic, and 178 British missionary schools, with more than 100,000 pupils between them. These foreign schools included such famous institutions as Robert College (founded 1863), the Syrian Protestant College (1866; later the American University of Beirut), and the Université Saint-Joseph (1874). In Iran and Egypt, secularization by state expansion of military, civilian, and educational bureaucracies followed similar patterns to those in the Ottoman Empire, but with significant lags.

Middle Eastern efforts toward state-building, centralization, and secularization resembled the European models of benevolent despots such as Louis XIV in France (1638–1715), Frederick the Great in Prussia (1712–86), and Peter the Great in Russia (1672–1725). However, the results were radically different. From the nineteenth century onwards, European powers and cultural influences were increasingly penetrating Middle Eastern polities and societies. That in turn led to strongly ambivalent feelings about modernization and secularization *cum* Westernization. Modernization was thus viewed by some as Western imperialism and to be resisted. To the ulama, the process seemed to be not only undermining their authority but also destroying the very fabric of Islamic culture and civilization.

The seeds of dualistic cultural and educational development in the Middle East were thus sown during the nineteenth century. Although Turkey and Iran were not formally colonized, they too developed dualistic systems of religious and secular schools alongside the countries that were colonized (Egypt, Syria, Lebanon, Palestine, Iraq, and Jordan).

Iran followed Turkey and Egypt by establishing in 1852 its first modern university, *dar al-funun*, with the explicit objective of teaching modern sciences and technology. Missions of Middle Eastern students were also sent to Europe to learn Western science, technology, and culture. The returning students inaugurated the translation of European works into Arabic, Persian, and Turkish. Schools, especially in the Levant, soon established printing presses in Ottoman Turkey (1727), Iran (1812), Egypt (1815), and Iraq (around 1870). Introduced earlier by Protestant and Roman Catholic missionaries, printing presses stimulated the growth of Beirut's publishing industry, mainly in Arabic but also in French and English. By 1900 Beirut was in the vanguard of Arabic journalism. A group of intellectuals sought to revive the Arabic cultural heritage and eventually became the first spokespeople of a new Arab nationalism.[10]

The modern educational institutions involved only a small percentage of the people, whereas the masses continued to receive traditional education in the Islamic schools. An unintended consequence of all this was the rise of an anti-imperialist and reformist pan-Islamic movement. A charismatic and forceful cleric, Seyyed Jamal ed-Din al-Afghani (1838–97), led the way. In the career of this single leader, we can see how the religious and secular forces were going to confront each other in the next century or so of Middle Eastern history.[11] Born in Asadabad, Afghani followed an extraordinary career of religious and political agitation that took him from Iran to Afghanistan, India, Egypt, France, Britain, Russia, and finally the Ottoman court in Istanbul. Wherever he went, he counseled the leaders, led religious and political agitation against Western colonialists and their native allies, and called for external unity and internal reform of the Islamic world. He was followed by Islamic reformists such as Muhammad 'Abduh and Rashid Reda in Egypt, and constitutional revolutions such as those in Iran, Egypt, and Turkey. He was clearly the precursor to the late twentieth-century resurgence of Islamic movements in many parts of the Middle East.[12] He may be considered as the godfather of the Muslim Brotherhood (Ikhwan al-Muslimun) in the Arab world and the Islamic republican movement in Iran.

Afghani's legacy was fourfold: anti-imperialism, anti-absolutism, Islamic militancy, and Islamic reform. The four legacies converged in the constitutionalist movements in Ottoman Turkey, Egypt, and Iran. Revolutionary sentiments were also encouraged by the Japanese defeat of Russia in 1905 and the Russian Revolution of 1905. Although the Ottoman constitution of 1876–8 was short-lived, followed by Sultan Abdul-Hamid's autocratic rule, the Young Turks Revolution of 1908 reinstated it.[13] In Iran, the Tobacco Revolt of 1891, the assassination of Nasser ed-Din Shah in 1898, and the Constitutional Revolution of 1905–9 can be all traced back to Afghani's influence. However, the Shi'a ulama in Iran were somewhat divided on constitutionalism. A dominant faction led by two ayatollahs, Behbahani and Tabatabai, supported the constitutional movement. Another faction, led by a more learned and respected Ayatollah Nuri, opposed constitutionalism on the ground that secular, parliamentary legislation violated the Shari'a codes. Following the success of the revolutionaries, Nuri was hanged on charges of murder; 70 years later, in the Islamic Republican Revolution of 1979, Nuri was resurrected as the hero of the Islamic revolutionaries.[14]

The nascent nationalist and democratic movements were facing strong foreign enemies. In Iran, the secret Anglo-Russian Treaty of 1907 divided the country into three spheres of influence, with Russia controlling the northern provinces and Britain controlling the southern provinces. The central provinces were left to the Iranian government to operate as a buffer zone.[15] In Egypt, the revolt of Egyptian military officers in 1881 under Colonel Ahmed Arabi was inspired by Afghani. This was the first open expression of a nationalist movement directed against foreign and Turkish domination that also called for constitutional government. After a period of turmoil, in 1888 the British in effect turned Egypt and the Suez Canal into their own protectorate. Under Lord Cromer and Lord Kitchener, Egypt as well as Sudan became virtual British colonies.

Incremental secularization and democratization during the nineteenth century thus had a patchy and lop-sided achievement. The new constitutions of Iran, Turkey, and later Egypt (1922) were copies of the constitutions of Western parliamentary monarchies, introducing democratic and secular legislation. Although Western powers paid lip-service to the democratic ideals, their policies were dictated more by their inter-imperialist rivalries or cooperation than by a genuine desire to see the

Middle East move toward secular and democratic societies. As a result of increasing Western penetration of the Middle East, dualistic cultural and political development became the main historic trend in the twentieth century. In the Iranian constitution, for instance, an article called for a committee of five *mujtahids* to pass judgment on the laws passed by the Majlis (National Assembly) to make sure that they conform to the Shari'a. But this article was never enacted. Narrowly based ruling elites often sided with Western powers in policies of secularization without democratization. In the meantime, the masses were kept relatively un-educated and steeped in their religious beliefs and practices.

Radical secularization without democratization

The next chapter in Middle Eastern secularization begins with the inter-war period (1918–40). The defeat of the Ottomans and the occupation and fragmentation of Iran brought into play two strongmen on horse-back. In the name of national salvation, Kemal Ataturk in Turkey and Reza Shah in Iran led vigorous national unification, modernization, and secularization campaigns that excluded democratization from their agen-das. In this respect, Turkey was generally ahead of Iran. Reza Shah thus followed Ataturk's lead. However, given the exceptional power of the Shi'a ulama in Iran, Reza Shah's achievement was perhaps the more re-markable. As prime minister, Reza Khan (later Reza Shah Pahlavi) toyed with the idea of replacing the Qajar monarchy with a republic. But the ulama's opposition dissuaded him. The ulama clearly saw Ataturk's example as a threat to their own power. Instead, under Reza Khan's direction, the Majlis passed a resolution in 1925 to replace the Qajar Dynasty with the Pahlavi Dynasty, a name that invoked pre-Islamic na-tionalist memories.

In the rest of the Middle East (Egypt, Syria, Lebanon, Iraq, Palestine, Transjordan, and the Persian Gulf emirates), the British and French co-lonial powers were directly in charge. Although they followed less rigor-ous secularization policies than did Ataturk or Reza Shah, their agents were eager to reduce the power of the ulama. In contrast to Iran and Turkey, where authoritarian secular nationalism dominated the scene, liberal nationalism in the Arab world proved a more potent weapon against the colonial powers. Only in Saudi Arabia, where a new dynasty had come to power in the name of Wahhabi puritanism, was the Shari'a the exclusive law.

The winds of nationalism in the Middle East at the turn of the twen-tieth century were so strong that they often swept the ulama along. Na-tionalism, however, converged with a number of other ideological trends, including pan-Islamism, pan-Arabism, pan-Turkism, pan-Iranism, as well as liberalism and Marxism. What unified these disparate ideologies was anti-imperialism. The sentiments were directed against Western domination, although the primary attitude toward Western science, technology, and culture was positive. This was particularly true of Westernized intellectuals. Even among the ulama, many wished to adopt Western constitutional limits on the power of the ruling despots.

The authoritarian nationalism of Ataturk and Reza Shah was heavily focused on state- and nation-building rather than institutions of political participation. Ataturk's instrument of modernization was the Republican People's Party, formed on 9 August 1923, replacing all other political organizations. Its program consisted of "Six Arrows: Republicanism, Nationalism, Populism, Statism, Secularism, and Revolution." The arrow of Secularism hit its targets most expeditiously one after another:

- abolition of the Caliphate on 3 March 1924 (since the early sixteenth century, the Ottoman sultans had laid claim to the title of Caliph of the Muslims);
- abolition of religious schools and courts;
- adoption of Western-style clothing;
- abolition of Sufi brotherhoods;
- emancipation of women, including the rights to vote and stand for election, abolition of polygamy, turning marriage into a civil contract and divorce into a civil action;
- adoption of the Swiss civil code, the Italian penal code, and the German commercial code in place of the Shari'a;
- adoption of the Latin alphabet to replace the Arabic script in which Ottoman Turkish had been written; this had the effect of cutting the younger generation off from Islamic historical memories and literature, but it also led to an increase in literacy;
- adoption of Western-style surnames in place of old Islamic names and titles.

With some delay, Reza Shah in Iran followed essentially the same secularization policies. He did not, however, have the instrument of a political party and faced the opposition of a retrenched ulama. He took away the schools and the courts from the control of the ulama, but left personal affairs (marriage, divorce, and inheritance) largely under the control of the Shari'a. Although he succeeded in some of his social secularization policies (unveiling of women, institution of Western-style clothing, adoption of surnames, and compulsory military conscription), he could not go so far as to grant suffrage to women or to abolish polygamy. Even so, his social reforms were strongly resisted in some provinces.[16]

There was initially a high degree of consensus on secularization among the ruling elite in Turkey and Iran. As many of its goals were achieved, many Turkish and Iranian nationalists wished to see more democratic regimes. In fact, Ataturk experimented in 1930 with the creation of an opposition party led by his longtime associate Ali Fethi, but its immediate and overwhelming success caused Ataturk to suppress it. In their later years, both Ataturk and Reza Shah grew more remote from their people – Ataturk by reason of excessive drinking and ill health; Reza Shah by reason of excessive autocracy and greed. Ataturk left a secular republican legacy behind in Kemalism that continues to this day as the dominant ideology of the Turkish ruling elite. By contrast, Reza Shah's legacy was challenged from the secular left as well as the religious right as soon as he was forced into exile by the Allied powers in 1941.

In contrast to Iran and Turkey, the Egyptian monarchy (1922–52) was torn between the king, the Wafd Party, and the British. The constitution (promulgated in 1923) was, like the Iranian constitution, based on that of Belgium. But Egyptian constitutionalism was as illusory as Egyptian independence. King Fu'ad was never popular and was prepared to intrigue with the nationalists or with the British to secure his power. The Wafd, with its mass following, elaborate organization, and charismatic leadership of Sa'ad Zaghlul, was the only truly national party in Egypt. Ideologically, it stood for national independence against the British and for constitutional government against royal autocracy. In practice – and increasingly after the death of Zaghlul in 1927 – its leaders were prepared to make deals with the British or the king to obtain or retain power. Personal and political rivalries led to the formation of splinter parties, the first of which, the Liberal Constitutionalist Party, broke off as early as 1922. The primary aim of the British government was to secure its imperial interests, especially control of the Suez Canal. Egyptian political conditions thus bred competition and maneuvering among the parties representing different factions of the ruling elite.

Nevertheless, the dominant ideological trend in Turkey, Iran, and Egypt during the inter-war period was the same – secular nationalism. A return to pre-Islamic mythologies and memories was a distinctive feature of this nationalism. Secular intellectual and political leaders considered religion to be a barrier to modernization and turned to pre-Islamic lore for salvation. In Turkey, Kemalism looked to the Turkik past in Central Asia and Anatolia to transform Ottomanism into a Turkish identity not dependent on Islam. "Islamic" dress was discouraged. Turkish was purged of its Arabic and Persian vocabularies and Turkik equivalents were found or coined to replace them. History was rewritten to glorify Turkish origins and achievements. Zia Gökalp (1876–1924), a leading Turkish intellectual, had already laid the ideological foundations for pan-Turkism and later secular Turkish nationalism confined to the Ottoman Turks. Although he did not live long enough to see his dreams realized, he was elected to the parliament of the new republic shortly before he died. His influence on the development of Turkish secular nationalism was next to that of Ataturk himself.[17]

In Iran, the secularists argued that the Arabs had imposed Islam on the Iranians and that the Islamic period represented a decline in Iranian civilization. A return to ancient Iranian architecture, names, celebrations, and customs was encouraged. Zoroastrianism as the religion of pre-Islamic Iran was celebrated. An Academy of Iranian Languages was established to purge Persian of its Arabic vocabulary and to replace it with revived or newly coined words. The leading Iranian intellectuals in the development of a secular nationalist ideology were Mirza Malkam Khan, Mirza Fath Ali Akhundzadeh, Mirza Agha Khan Kermani, Hassan Taqizadeh, Seyyed Jamal ed-Din Esfahani and his son Seyed Muhammad Ali Jamalzadeh, Sadeq Hedayat, and Ahmad Kasravi.[18] Some of these intellectuals, novelists, preachers, and politicians came from clerical backgrounds, adopting a secular, freethinking ideology. Among them, Ahmad Kasravi (1880–1946) went furthest in his anti-clerical views by establishing a religion of *pakdini* (pure religion) that tried to purge all metaphysics and superstition. He paid for his beliefs when, in 1946, a Fadaii Islam zealot assassinated him.[19]

In Egypt, an influential intellectual, Taha Hussein (1889–1973), connected his country's national identity with Pharaonic times and with Mediterranean–European culture. Having been educated at al-Ahzar (the oldest Islamic university), the newly established secular Cairo University, and the Sorbonne, he was uniquely qualified to challenge religious beliefs and establishments. He was eventually declared an apostate by the ulama. But this did not prevent him from serving as Minister of Education (1950–2) in the last Wafd government before the overthrow of the monarchy. During his tenure, he vastly extended state education and abolished school fees. Secularists such as Taha Hussein considered Egypt capable of easily sharing in modern Western civilization. Religious differences were considered of no consequence; Muslims, Copts, and Jews were seen as equally Egyptian. The development of a standard literary Arabic, *fusha*, emphasized the unity of all Arabs, regardless of confession.

In all three countries (Turkey, Iran, and Egypt), these approaches allowed, indeed required, all religious communities to partake in a single legal and societal system, at the price of denying the Muslim loyalty of the majority of the population. In Saudi Arabia and Pakistan, by contrast, Islam played a primary role in the formation of a national identity. In Pakistan, it provided an alternative for Muslims who would otherwise have had to share in an identity defined by a Hindu majority in independent India. In spite of the fact that Muhammad Ali Jinah (1876–1948) was himself a thoroughly secular, British-educated barrister, he led the Muslims into partition from India. In Saudi Arabia, the state was forged in the image of the Wahhabi fundamentalist faith. Elsewhere in the Arab world, especially in the Maghrib, secular nationalism's downgrading of Islam was muted by a qualified acceptance of Islam as one important source of loyalty, but not the only one.

Secular education

The main instrument of secular nationalism, in turn, was secular education. This was as true for the three large states as for the smaller ones in the region. Not only could secular education provide skilled workers for modernization; it also could inculcate the civic virtues necessary for modern citizenship. Educational expansion, however, was more rapid in independent countries (Turkey and Iran) than in the colonies. In Lebanon, Syria, Tunisia, Morocco, and Algeria, educational policy mirrored French interests. In Egypt, Jordan, Palestine, and Iraq, British policy was dominant. Both colonial powers followed similar policies: to preserve the status quo, train a limited number of native administrators, arrest nationalism, and, in the case of France, promote its own culture and language. Accordingly, they limited educational growth. The colonial powers favored private, foreign, and missionary schools for the upper classes. The public systems were centrally administered. Their curricula were often copied from the British or the French and therefore were of limited relevance to local needs. The quantity and quality of teachers were inadequate, and dropout rates were high. Few modern schools were to be found in the Arabian Peninsula. Only in Lebanon and in the Jewish community in Palestine were large numbers of students enrolled in modern schools. Elsewhere, only a small percentage of the populace (including a few women) received a modern education.

Following independence, each country nationalized some of its private schools, which were regarded as promoting alien religions and cultures. Each country also greatly expanded educational opportunities, especially at the upper levels. In 1925, Egypt nationalized a private institution founded in Cairo in 1908 and made it into a national university, and subsequently opened state universities in Alexandria (1942) and 'Ain Shams (1950). The newly independent countries also sought to equalize educational opportunities. Iraq provided free tuition and scholarships to low-income students. In 1946, Syria made primary education free and compulsory. Jordan enacted a series of laws calling for free and compulsory education and placed strict controls on foreign schools, especially missionary schools.

Despite progress, secular education could not overcome the existing cultural and social obstacles to universal education. The modern educational systems were divided into schools for the masses and for the elite. Both types coexisted uneasily with the traditional Islamic schools, which ran the gamut from traditional *maktabs* (primary schools) to the venerable al-Azhar University. Educational participation rates in the secular schools stood at relatively low levels.

In both Turkey and Iran, progress toward secular education was more strident. Ataturk and, to a lesser degree, Reza Shah were determined secularizers. Ataturk closed the religious schools, promoted coeducation, prepared new curricula, emphasized vocational and technical education, launched a compulsory adult education project, and established the innovative Village Institutes program to train rural teachers. In 1933, he reorganized Istanbul University into a modern institution and later established Ankara University. In Iran, Reza Shah followed similar policies. He integrated and centralized the educational system, expanded the schools, especially at the higher levels, founded the University of Tehran (1934), sent students abroad for training, moved against the Islamic schools, promoted the education of women, and inaugurated an adult education program. Nevertheless, the Iranian educational system remained small and elitist.[20]

Following World War II, secular socialist "revolutions" led by the military regimes called for universal primary education, an emphasis upon vocational training, expansion of the higher levels, and the promotion of women's education. Gamal Abdul-Nasser in Egypt and the Ba'athist regimes in Syria and Iraq promoted their secular pan-Arab ideologies by means of the mass media (notably newspapers and radio broadcasting). Their aim was to transform society and culture. They integrated and unified the educational system by bringing the religious schools under secular control. All public education was made free, and strong efforts were made to universalize primary education, to upgrade technical and vocational education, and to improve the quality of education generally.

In North Africa, the substitution of Arabic for French as the language of instruction presented yet other difficulties. When Tunisia, Algeria, and Morocco gained independence from France, most teachers taught only in French. Appropriate texts in Arabic were not available. By the 1980s the Arabization process remained incomplete; in all three countries, some instruction was still being given in French.

Generally speaking, the educational reforms did not always produce the anticipated results. Egypt failed to devise a coherent fit between educational expansion and developments in other sectors. Tunisia, too, despite large investments, was unable to coordinate educational expansion with the needs of the economy. Above all, secular education was no match for the powerful religious beliefs of incoming students from the more traditional lower strata of society, who had Islamic rather than secular orientations.

Islamization with or without democratization

Recent decades have witnessed mounting social and political mobilization in the Middle East. An Islamic resurgence against the secular policies of the twentieth century has been an integral part of this mobilization. Rapid urbanization, increasing literacy, deepening media exposure, and a demographic revolution that has tilted the population composition toward the young have catapulted the more religious, lower strata of society onto the political scene. Yet the formation of democratic institutions of political participation (trade unions, voluntary associations, political parties, and free elections) has not kept pace with increasing mobilization. If we consider political development and democracy to be a function of the institutionalization of political participation, the outcome of this lag has been political decay rather than development, i.e. the rise of underground political activism, violence, and terrorism.[21]

Much of this activism has expressed itself in Islamic terms. As the lower strata of society have gained increasing access to cities, literacy, and the media, their Islamic leaders and movements have best articulated their political aspirations. The secular elites, in contrast, through their close association with Western powers and interests, have largely lost the competition for the political imagination and loyalties of this mobilized, semi-urbanized, youthful, and often unemployed or underemployed population.

The historical roots of Islamic resurgence are embedded in the social structure of Middle Eastern societies. As a crossroads of major population movements in history, the Middle East has been an ethnic melting pot for centuries. Iranians, Arabs, Turks, Kurds, Armenians, Jews, Copts, Maronites, Druzes, and Assyrians have lived, intermarried, and interacted with each other for a very long time indeed. The Medina Constitution of Prophet Muhammad (622–32) had found an ingenious solution to the problem of ethnic and religious diversity. It gave religious and political autonomy to the Peoples of the Book (*ahl al-kitab*), requiring them to pay special taxes (*jizyah*) in return for protection. Successive Islamic empires adopted this constitutional regime under what came to be known as the *millet* system. The system produced a high level of tolerance for the minorities.

Modeled after the European Westphalian order of territorial nation-states, secular nationalism inevitably exacerbated ethnic and religious tensions. As Iranian, Arab, and Turkish secular nationalist regimes reconstructed the Middle Eastern states in the image of newly defined, purist models of "nations," their traditional Muslim populations as well as their ethnic minorities were increasingly put into a defensive position. Long before the 1979 Islamic Revolution in Iran, which dramatized the vulnerability of the secular nationalist regimes, a number of Islamic thinkers had opposed nationalism altogether. In India, Mawlana Abu'-'Cia' Mawdudi, who was the founder of the Jama'at-i Islami, opposed both secular and religious nationalism and argued for the Islamization of society as an alternative to nationalism. Mawdudi later became the most influential Islamic ideologue in the formation of Pakistan. In Egypt, Sayyid Qutb and Hasan al-Banna', who were the mentors of the Muslim Brotherhood, fought for the educational, moral, and social reform of Egyptian society and indeed of all Islamdom. In Iran, Ayatollah Shaikh Fazlullah Nuri (died in 1909), Ayatollah Ruhollah Musavi Khomeini (1902–89), and a French-educated sociologist Ali Shariati led the charge against secular nationalism. Among the Islamic ideologues, Khomeini was perhaps the most daring to call for the overthrow of all secular regimes and their replacement with Islamic republics led by Islamic jurists (*fuqaha*, or vicars of God on earth).[22]

Given their significantly different conditions, Middle Eastern societies have experienced the Islamic resurgence in different ways. At the risk of oversimplifying a very complex and evolving situation, Middle Eastern countries can be divided into five groups with respect to relations between mosque and state:

1. convergence of mosque and state: Saudi Arabia, Iran, Sudan, Afghanistan;
2. suppression of mosque by state: Turkey, Algeria, Iraq, Syria;
3. confessional: Lebanon;
4. uneasy coexistence: Egypt, Israel;
5. evolving coexistence: Jordan, Kuwait.

For reasons that have already been reviewed in this chapter, the Shi'a ulama in Iran were possessed of sufficient financial and administrative autonomy to be able to fill the political vacuum left by a monarchical regime. The story of the Iranian Revolution has been extensively researched and published and need not detain us here.[23] Two men who are not normally credited for it paved the way for the Islamic revolution. During his long tenure as the chief Shi'a *mujtahid* (*marja' taqlid*), Ayatollah Boroujerdi (died in 1961) created a virtual state within the state by developing the most extensive financial and administrative system that the Shi'a ulama had achieved up to that time. By pursuing a policy of modernization without democratization, Muhammad Reza Shah also had created a political vacuum. By destroying all secular communist and liberal sources of opposition, the Shah's regime had paved the way for the Shi'a clerical hegemony. Given the fact that the Shi'a ulama are rather decentralized in organization and financing, following the death of Ayatollah Khomeini in 1989 significant differences among them have gradually emerged. Three groups may be identified: the conservatives, led by

Ayatollah Seyyed Ali Khamanei (Supreme Leader); the liberals, led by Seyyed Muhammad Khatami (president since 1997); and the pragmatists, led by Hojjaul-Islam Ali Akbar Hashemi Rafsanjani (president during 1989–97). All three groups are united in their goal of upholding the Islamic regime, but they differ on how to respond to the democratic pressures from below.

By comparison with the revolutionary regime in Iran, the theocratic regimes in Saudi Arabia, Afghanistan, and Sudan are politically repressive and socially conservative. The Saudi regime has been intolerant toward the rights of women and minorities. The Taliban in Afghanistan were brought to power by United States arms, Saudi money, and Pakistan military leadership. They suppressed women and minorities. The Sudanese regime has been engaged in a bloody civil war against its own Christian population in the south. In December 1999, however, President Omar el-Bashir deposed the clerical parliamentary speaker and political strongman Hassan Tourabi. The president's increasing power suggests that he can normalize relations with Sudan's neighbors and perhaps bring some stability to this corner of the African continent.

The second group of regimes, including those in Turkey, Algeria, Iraq, and Syria, are secularist with little tolerance toward their Islamic oppositions and critics. As Hakan Yavuz argues,

The social fault lines that have emerged in Turkey because of the crisis of Kemalism and growing economic inequalities involve four major actors: the military, which uses Kemalism to legitimize its dominant institutional position; the TUSIAD [Association of Turkish Industrialists and Businessmen], which also controls the major media outlets; Sunni Islamic groups, which are divided into four major factions; and Turkish ethnic and sectarian minorities, mainly the Kurds and Alevis. The fault lines these actors straddle do not represent "ancient hatreds" between competing groups. They are instead a product of a closed political system whose military–bureaucratic guardians have played an active role in aggravating societal divisions.[24]

Although the situation in each country is unique and requires its own analysis (see the relevant chapters in this volume), many of the same problems apply to Algeria, Iraq, and Syria, where military–bureaucratic regimes preside over restive civil societies. By contrast to Turkey, where the Islamic resurgence has been relatively non-violent, Algeria, Iraq, and Syria have experienced militant and violent Islamist movements. In Iraq and Syria, the iron hand of the state has so far squashed the movements. In Algeria, following the cancellation of the 1992 elections in which the Front Islamique du Salut (FIS, or Islamic Salvation Front) won a majority of the National Assembly seats, a merciless civil war started pitting the military regime against the militant Muslims. However, by the election of Abdelaziz Bouteflika to the presidency in 1999, Algeria has inaugurated a new phase of reconciliation between the secular and religious elements. According to Robert Mortimer, "despite his lack of electoral legitimacy, Bouteflika has the skills to lead Algeria out of the nightmare of the 1990s."[25] That may or may not prove to be the case.

Because of its high literacy and civil society strength, Lebanon has always enjoyed a greater level of democratic freedoms than most other Middle Eastern societies.[26] Through a national compact, the Lebanese political system has attempted to maintain a delicate balance between its main religious–ethnic communities. The resulting confessional system has reserved the presidency for a Maronite, the premiership for a Sunni, and the speakership of the parliament for a Shi'a. The civil war of the 1980s disturbed this delicate balance, which had to be reconstructed through difficult negotiations by giving more power to the underrepresented Shi'a population. The presence of Syrian forces in Lebanon currently guarantees short-term stability but undermines long-term stability. Nevertheless, Lebanon is now trying to restore its democratic tradition.

Having had the longest experience with Islamic movements, the Egyptian military–bureaucratic regime has had an uneasy coexistence with its militant Muslims. President Gamal Abdul-Nasser (1954–70) attempted to co-opt the Ikhwan members by advancing reforms at home and militancy abroad while waging battle against Israel. For a while in the 1960s, Nasser's banner of pan-Arabism could not be easily challenged. President Anwar Sadat (1970–81) reversed Nasser's policies by entering into a peace accord with Israel, befriending the West, and inaugurating economic liberalization. He also confronted the Muslim militants by repressive measures that led to his assassination.

Democratization from above is thus the norm in the Middle East wherever pressures from below build up sufficiently to threaten the regimes. In the aftermath of the Iranian Revolution, decline of oil revenues in the 1980s and 1990s, and the Persian Gulf War of 1991, several Middle Eastern regimes had to liberalize to survive. The logic of rentier states, which generally deny participation in recompense for no taxation, has been greatly undermined. In Jordan, for example, high levels of debt and inflation and the expulsion of Palestinians from Kuwait into Jordan strained the financial capabilities of the state.[27] The 1989 riots in southern towns populated by Jordanian tribes loyal to the Hashemite throne awakened King Hussein to the need for democratization. The parliamentary elections that were subsequently held allowed multiparty competition, including some Islamic militants who made it to the parliament; following the ascension of King Abdullah to the throne in February 1999, however, severe limits on political activity have been reintroduced. Similarly in Kuwait after the Gulf War, the regime could no longer resist demands for the revival of the parliament. In 1999, however, the parliament rejected the Amir's proposal for the extension of suffrage to women. As demonstrated also in the Iranian and Algerian revolutions, political participation by patriarchal Middle Eastern men often denies political democracy to women.

Conclusion

This chapter has limited its analysis of secularization and democratization in the Middle East to primarily internal rather than external factors. In a region that has been dominated by foreign powers for the past two centuries, this analysis may be considered incomplete. Nevertheless, it has been argued here that foreign domination has played a critical role in creating serious obstacles to secularization and democratization. Although Western powers have generally supported secularization, they have often stood in the way of democratization by supporting client dictatorial regimes. In contrast to the Western historical experience in which secular nationalism and liberal democracy undermined the authority of the church, Middle Eastern anti-imperialism has brought the ulama, nationalists, and democrats into an uneasy alliance. In recent decades, however, that alliance has been fractured by the increasing militancy of Islamism, as evidenced notably in Iran, Sudan, Afghanistan, and Algeria.

The chapter also has identified the varieties of state–mosque relations with respect to secularization and democratization trends. These varieties include convergence of state and mosque, suppression of the mosque by the state, confessionalism, and uneasy and evolving coexistence. The interactions of secularization and democratization have thus been too complex to lend themselves to any facile generalization. Radical secularization as typified by Kemalist Turkey and Iran under the Pahlavis followed an authoritarian path. A more liberal secularization regime, as typified by Egypt, has led to an evolving coexistence between state and the mosque. The Middle East's multi-ethnic and multi-religious societies, however, best lend themselves to constitutional regimes that allow freedom and autonomy for the varieties of religious communities. The Lebanese confessional system best typifies such a regime.

If we consider democracy as a process of broadening and deepening of political participation, its minimal requirements are popular sovereignty, electoral representation, and civil liberties, which together may be identified as political democracy. Social democracy goes beyond this minimum requirement by providing equality of opportunity and social security for all citizens. Cultural democracy goes even further by providing freedom of identity negotiations with respect to language, religion, ethnicity, gender, and lifestyles. Although some Middle Eastern societies have made halting progress toward political democracy, most of them have failed to make any significant strides toward social or cultural democracy. In rentier states where falling windfall revenues (from oil or immigrants' remittances) are forcing the states to concede democratic freedoms to their civil societies (notably Iran, Jordan, and Algeria), prospects for democracy currently seem more encouraging.

Notes

1. http://www.members.eb.com/bol/topic?eu=115569&sctn=11; accessed 7 January 2000.
2. Nur Yalman, "Some Observations on Secularism in Islam: The Cultural Revolution in Turkey," *Daedalus*, vol. 102, no. 1, Winter 1973; Nur Yalman, "On Secularism and Its Critics: Notes on Turkey, India and Iran," *Contributions to Indian Sociology*, vol. 25, no. 2, 1991, New Delhi: Sage Publications.
3. Bible, Mark 12: 17.
4. Edward Mortimer, *Faith and Power: The Politics of Islam*, New York: Random House, 1982, pp. 76–9.
5. Ibid., pp. 74–6.
6. Emmanuel Sivan, *Radical Islam: Medieval Theology and Modern Politics*, New Haven, CT: Yale University Press, 1985, pp. 86–90.
7. Fred Warren Riggs, *Administration in Developing Countries: The Theory of Prismatic Society*, Boston: Houghton Mifflin, 1964.
8. Dale Eickelman and Jon W. Anderson, eds., *New Media in the Muslim World: The Emerging Public Sphere*, Bloomington, IN: Indiana University Press, 1999; Bruce B. Lawrence, Angelique Ward, and Nick Goetz, eds., *The Complete Idiot's Guide to Online Religion*, Indianapolis, IN: Macmillan Computer Publishing, 1999.
9. Iradj Amini, *Napoleon and Persia: Franco–Persian Relations under the First Empire*, Washington, DC: Mage Publishers, 1999.
10. Albert Habib Hourani, *Arabic Thought in the Liberal Age, 1798–1939*, Cambridge: Cambridge University Press, 1983.
11. Nikki R. Keddie, *Religion and Rebellion in Iran: The Iranian Tobacco Protest of 1891–1892*, London: Frank Cass, 1966; Nikki Keddie, *An Islamic Response to Imperialism: Political and Religious Writings of Sayyid Jamal al-Din "Al Afghani"*, Berkeley and Los Angeles: University of California Press, 1968; Nikki Keddie, *Sayyid Jama al-Din "al-Afghani": A Political Biography*, Berkeley: University of California Press, 1972; Nikki Keddie, *Roots of Revolution: An Interpretive History of Modern Iran*, New Haven, CT: Yale University Press, 1981; Nikki Keddie, ed., *Religion and Politics in Iran: Shi'ism from Quietism to Revolution*, New Haven, CT: Yale University Press, 1983; Nikki Keddie and Eric Hoogland, eds., *The Iranian Revolution and the Islamic Republic*, New York: Syracuse University Press, 1986.
12. Eli Kedourie, "Jamal ad-Din al-Afghani," *Encyclopedia Britannica Online*, http://www.members.eb.com/bol/topic?eu=44263&sctn=1; accessed 6 January 2000.
13. Hasan Kayali, "Elections and the Electoral Process in the Ottoman Empire, 1876–1919," *International Journal of Middle East Studies*, vol. 27, no. 3, August 1995.
14. Nikki R. Keddie, *Qajar Iran and the Rise of Reza Khan, 1796–1925*, Costa Mesa, CA: Mazda Publishers, 1999, p. 61.
15. W. Morgan Shuster, *The Strangling of Persia: Story of the European Diplomacy and*

Oriental Intrigue That Resulted in the Denationalization of Twelve Million Mohamme-dans, A Personal Narrative, Washington, DC: Mage Publishers, 1987.

16. Jalil Bahar and Majid Tafreshi, *Shenasnameh: zendegani va aasar-I-sheikh ahmad bahar* [Identity: Life and Works of Sheikh Ahmad Bahar], Tehran: Neda, n.d.

17. Encyclopedia Britannica Online, "Gökalp, Ziya," http://www.members.eb.com/bol/topic?eu=37950&sctn=1; accessed 16 January 2000.

18. Ahmad Kasravi, *T⁻ar⁻ikh-i mashr⁻utah-i ⁻Ir⁻an* [History of the Constitutional Revolution of Iran], Tehran: Amir Kabir Publishers [1940/41–43/44].

19. Keddie, *Roots of Revolution*, chapter 8; Ahmad Kasravi, *On Islam and Shi'ism*, translated from Persian by M. R. Ghanoonparvar, Costa Mesa, CA: Mazda Publishers, 1990.

20. David Menashri, *Education and the Making of Modern Iran*, Ithaca, NY: Cornell University Press, 1992.

21. Samuel P. Huntington, *Political Order in Changing Societies*, New Haven, CT: Yale University Press, 1968.

22. Ruh Allah Khomeini, *Islam and Revolution*, translated and annotated by Hamid Algar, Berkeley, CA: Mizan Press, 1981; Keddie, *Roots of Revolution*, pp. 205–13; Majid Tehranian, "Fundamentalist Impact on Education and the Media: An Overview," in Martin E. Marty and R. Scott Appleby, eds., *Fundamentalism and Society*, Chicago: University of Chicago Press, 1993; Majid Tehranian, "Islamic Fundamentalism in Iran and the Discourse of Development," in Martin Marty and Scott Appleby, eds., *Fundamentalism and Society*, vol. 2, Chicago: University of Chicago Press, 1993.

23. Keddie, *Roots of Revolution*; Amin Saikal, *The Rise and Fall of the Shah*, Princeton, NJ: Princeton University Press, 1980; Tehranian, "Fundamentalist Impact on Education and the Media," and "Islamic Fundamentalism in Iran."

24. H. Hakan Yavuz, "Turkey's Fault Lines and the Crisis of Kemalism," *Current History*, vol. 99, no. 633, January 2000, p. 34.

25. Robert Mortimer, "Bouteflika and Algeria's Path from Revolt to Reconciliation," *Current History*, vol. 99, no. 633, January 2000, p. 13.

26. Saad Eddin Ibrahim, "Constitutional Monarchies in the Arab World?!" *Civil Society*, vol. 8, no. 93, December 1999.

27. Quintan Wiktorowicz, "The Limits of Democracy in the Middle East: The Case of Jordan," *Middle East Journal*, vol. 53, no. 4, Autumn 1999.

6

The influence of Islam on attitudes toward democracy in Morocco and Algeria

Mark Tessler

Both academic and policy discussions about democracy in the Arab world, as well as inquiries about the relationship between democracy and peace, usually include attention to the political orientations of ordinary men and women. In particular, questions are raised about whether popular attitudes and beliefs constitute an obstacle to democratization, possibly because the religious or cultural traditions that predominate in most Arab countries inhibit the emergence of a democratic political culture.

Although questions are frequently raised about the views of ordinary citizens, about what is sometimes described as "the Arab street," answers are most often based on impressionistic and anecdotal information. Indeed, some analyses appear to be influenced by Western stereotypes about Arabs and Muslims. By contrast, systematic empirical inquiries into the nature, distribution, and determinants of political attitudes in the Arab world are rare.

Similarly, there is a growing body of scholarly (and popular) literature devoted to the relationship between Islam and democracy. Again, however, there has been almost no systematic research at the individual level of analysis, and so there is little evidence with which to answer questions about whether, and if so how, religious attachments influence the political orientations of ordinary citizens.

Against this background, this chapter examines the influence of Islam on attitudes toward governance in general and democracy in particular through the analysis of public opinion data collected in Morocco and Algeria. Based on interviews with representative samples of adults in Rabat and Oran, these data were collected through survey research designed and carried out in collaboration with Moroccan and Algerian scholars. The interview schedule includes questions about governance and democracy and also about conceptions and practices relating to Islam. Although more research will be needed before generalizable conclusions can be advanced with confidence, these data provide a solid empirical foundation for considering questions that are usually discussed with little or no systematic evidence.

To place this research within the context of the overall volume's concerns, and thereby to establish its relevance and potential utility, the discussion begins by briefly reviewing: the importance of democracy in the Arab world; the elements of democratic transitions in other world regions, with particular reference to citizen orientations; the possible salience of Islam in assessments of Arab democratization; and findings from research in the West about the influence of religion on political attitudes. The data are then presented in order to shed light on the degree to which Islamic attachments have an impact on attitudes toward democracy and governance in Morocco and Algeria.

The importance of democracy in the Arab states

With a few exceptions, the Arab world has made relatively little progress toward political liberalization in recent years. On the contrary, many of the experiments in democratization that were launched a decade or so ago have been cut back substantially or even abandoned. Lisa Anderson describes the situation as "exceptionally bleak ... from the spectacular crash and burn of Algeria's liberalization to Tunisia's more subtle but no less profound transformation into a police state, from Egypt's backsliding into electoral manipulation [and repression of Islamic political movements] to the obvious reluctance of Palestinian authorities to embrace human rights."[1]

Yet the importance of democracy has been repeatedly emphasized by Arab as well as Western scholars. A concern for political liberalization, and ultimately for democracy, does not reflect an uncritical infatuation with globalization or a belief that Western political forms are inherently superior. It rather reflects a deep desire for accountability and morality on the part of political leaders and a rejection of political and economic relationships through which, as described by a Jordanian journalist, "autocratic rulers and non-accountable power elites pursue whimsical, wasteful and regressive policies."[2]

Indeed, discontent with the political and economic situation has led to outbursts of citizen anger, including rioting, in a number of Arab countries.[3] Thus, as expressed by an American scholar of Egyptian origin, "a severe, multi-dimensional, and protracted crisis is faced by many regimes in the Muslim [and Arab] world. This is evidenced by a decline of state legitimacy and has resulted in 'state exhaustion'."[4] The result, according to a Lebanese political scientist, is that unchecked authoritarianism in many Arab countries is "paving the way to a deep crisis in the fabric of society."[5] Similarly, an Egyptian sociologist argues that "political reform must be initiated, or else there is a real danger of political chaos," and a second Egyptian scholar states that "I dreamed of democracy in my youth and now I see that our country is regressing politically."[6]

Additionally, there is at least some evidence that democratization in the Arab world would contribute to the peaceful resolution of regional conflicts[7] and also to regional economic integration.[8] These assessments are consistent with the thesis, well established in the scholarly literature (and discussed in Solingen's chapter in this volume), that a state's international behavior is strongly influenced by the pattern of its domestic governance.[9]

Alternatively, the absence of democracy may produce support for adventurism and militarism in international affairs, as Arab and other scholars have observed when seeking to explain the support for Saddam Hussein among ordinary citizens in many Arab countries.[10] According to a Moroccan analyst, many judged the anti-Iraq coalition in the Gulf War to be "enemies of the people ... The sole motivation of the sultans of the Gulf, of Mubarak, and even of Assad, all of whom joined in the war against Saddam, was to remain in power and protect their personal interests ... to defend themselves against their own people."[11] Had these governments been more democratic and hence legitimate, their campaign against Iraq's adventurism would presumably have had much more popular support among their citizens.

It should be repeated that the motivation for democratic governance is not based on a desire to imitate the West. Nor does it necessarily reflect a belief that democracy will contribute to regional peace and integration, even though these may be desirable by-products. There is rather an awareness that mechanisms by which ordinary men and women can hold their governments accountable are necessary to limit mismanagement and corruption and to push for policies that address the needs of all citizens, rather than simply deliver resources to the ruling elite. These themes continue to be emphasized in a wide range of settings, as, for example, at a December 1999 conference in Amman attended by intellectuals from 13 Arab countries. The meeting, which focused on the challenges of globalization, issued a call for "greater political freedoms and intellectual pluralism," as well as the preservation of Arab specificity.[12]

In view of the importance of democratic governance, and despite the pessimism of most present-day assessments, there is at least some hope for renewed political liberalization in the years ahead. On the one hand, there are new rulers and/or regimes in a number of important countries, including Jordan, Morocco, and Algeria. On the other, various domestic and international forces will keep issues of governance on the agenda and, in all probability, exert pressure for at least gradual democratization. Relevant considerations include popular demands for more responsive and accountable government;[13] pressures for economic liberalization, which may lead to greater pluralism in the shaping of public policy;[14] and a growing number of civil society organizations.[15]

The role of citizen attitudes

Studies of democratic transitions and democratic consolidation usually identify two analytically distinct dimensions to which attention must be devoted.[16] One involves political institutions and processes. The other involves citizen attitudes and values, often described as political culture. Institutional and process considerations call attention to the need for mechanisms that make political leaders accountable to those they govern, including free, competitive, and regular elections. Political culture calls attention to the orientations of ordinary men and women and, so far as democracy is concerned, to the need to develop civic and participatory norms at the individual level of analysis.

With respect to political culture more particularly, the constellation of citizen attitudes necessary for a mature democracy is variously described as "participant citizenship," a "civic culture," and a "democratic culture." This is defined in the following terms by a prominent student of democratization in Russia and Eastern Europe: a democratic citizen "believes in individual liberty and is politically tolerant, has a certain distrust of political authority but at the same time is trusting of fellow citizens, is obedient but nonetheless willing to assert rights against the state, and views the state as constrained by legality."[17]

Important questions are raised about the relationship between the institutional and political culture dimensions of democratization. Specifically, there is discussion and disagreement about whether reasonably high levels of participant citizenship are a prerequisite for successful democratization, or whether citizens can acquire democratic orientations at a somewhat later stage, as a result of exposure to a political environment in which political life is characterized by pluralism and competition. As noted by Rose, a student of democratization in post-communist countries, "some theorists argue that a democratic culture is a consequence that follows the establishment of democratic institutions, while others consider it a prerequisite for achieving stable democracy."[18]

Huntington summarizes the precondition thesis, noting that "a profoundly antidemocratic culture would impede the spread of democratic norms in the society and deny legitimacy to democratic institutions."[19] Yet, as noted by Rose, "if this is the case, it could take generations before democracy is secure in a given country." In fact, however, Rose asserts that most scholars take a "realist" position and tend to see the emergence of democratic attitudes among ordinary citizens as a consequence of democratization at the institutional level. Progress toward democracy, he suggests, begins with "teams of elites competing for votes to win office. This does not require every voter to believe in democracy or that every politician believe in anything – the latter are simply advocating policies they think the public wants."[20]

Debates about sequencing notwithstanding, there is general agreement that ordinary men and women must eventually possess the kinds of orientations associated with a civic or democratic political culture if democratic transitions are to succeed and be consolidated. As a consequence, it is necessary to identify the experiences and conditions that either encourage or hinder the emergence of such orientations, and studies devoted to this question are increasingly common in some postauthoritarian polities. This includes research in Eastern Europe,[21] Latin America,[22] and, to a lesser extent, East Asia[23] and Africa.[24]

Despite numerous calls for the investigation of political attitudes, some going back almost two decades, individual-level research focusing on political culture has lagged in the Arab world.[25] The primary reason, according to both Arab and non-Arab observers, is the authoritarian political climate that prevails in most Arab states.[26] There have been a few exceptions in recent years, primarily, though not exclusively, involving work in Palestine.[27] Moreover, one recent review asserts that "the limited survey research done in the Arab world has had disproportionately high payoffs."[28] Still, opinion studies focusing on democracy and governance in Arab countries remain few in number and also, for the most part, limited in analytical scope. Consequently, relatively little is known about the nature, distribution, and determinants of the political attitudes held by ordinary Arab men and women.

Islam and democracy

Against this background, there is discussion, and often disagreement, about the relationship between democracy and Islam. Although stereotypes are sometimes advanced, questions about the influence of Islam are not inappropriate. There is a strong historic connection between religion and politics in the Muslim world, reflecting Islam's character as a religion of laws pertaining to societal organization as well as individual morality.

In addition, Islam has become increasingly influential in Arab political and cultural life during the past quarter-century. New Muslim cultural associations, study groups, welfare organizations, and financial institutions have emerged, accompanied by a sharp increase in such expressions of personal piety as mosque attendance and public prayer.

Islam has also become an important point of reference in debates about how the Arab world should be governed.[29] Emphasizing political and economic problems and campaigning under the banner "Islam is the solution," Muslim political organizations have had notable success in attracting new followers. Adherents include younger individuals, women as well as men, and many well-educated persons.[30] These "Islamist" groups, as they are called, have also shown significant electoral strength when citizens have had an opportunity to express their preferences at the polls.[31]

Morocco and Algeria, the focus of this study, are prominent among the Arab countries to which these generalizations about Islam apply. In Morocco, both the monarchy and one of the country's oldest political parties, the Istiqlal, have a historically established and continuing identification with Islam. More recently, Islamist opposition movements have come to prominence on university campuses and elsewhere, and several representatives of these movements won seats in parliament in the 1999 elections. In Algeria, Islamists won the elections of 1990 and 1991, demonstrating at the time both their organizational ability and the strength of their appeal.

So far as democracy is concerned, some observers, particularly some Western observers, assert that democracy and Islam are incompatible. Whereas democracy requires openness, competition, pluralism, and tolerance of diversity, Islam, they argue, encourages intellectual conformity and an uncritical acceptance of authority. In the words of one authority, "the idea of democracy is quite alien to the mind-set of Islam."[32] Equally important, Islam is said to be anti-democratic because it vests sovereignty in God, who is the sole source of political authority and from whose divine law must come all regulations governing the community of believers. In the view of some, this means that Islam "has to be ultimately embodied in a totalitarian state."[33]

But many others reject the suggestion that Islam is an enemy in the struggle to establish accountable government. They point out that Islam has many facets and tendencies, making unidimensional characterizations of the religion highly suspect.[34] They also report that there is considerable variation in the interpretations of religious law advanced by Muslim scholars and theologians, and that among these are expressions of support for democracy, including some by leading Islamist theorists.[35] Finally, they insist that openness, tolerance, and progressive innovation are well represented among traditions associated with the religion, and are thus entirely compatible with Islam.[36]

As the preceding suggests, within Islamic doctrine and Muslim traditions one can find both elements that are and elements that are not congenial to democracy; and this in turn means that the influence of the religion depends to a very considerable extent on how and by whom it is interpreted. There is no single or accepted interpretation on many issues, and sometimes not even a consensus on who speaks for Islam. As one study demonstrated with respect to Islamic strictures about family planning and contraception, different religious authorities give different advice about what is permissible in Islam.[37] In addition, serious doubts have been expressed about the motivation of some religious authorities. As one Arab scholar asks, focusing in particular on the relationship between Islam and democracy:

Can democracy occur if the *ulama* or jurists have sole charge of legal interpretation? May not the *ulama*'s ability to declare laws compatible or incompatible with the teaching of the *shariah* lead to abuse? There are numerous examples of *ulama* manipulating Islamic teachings to the advantage of political leaders. Indeed, the religion has been dominated by the state since its inception and the *ulama* have often played a role that sometimes also has been played by Christian clergy: motivated by political rather than religious considerations, they have offered doctrinal interpretations that are deliberately designed to justify the behavior of political leaders.[38]

Research in the West on religion and politics

This study seeks to provide information about the influence of religious orientations on attitudes toward governance in North Africa. It does not aspire to resolve debates about the relationship between Islam and democracy. It is limited to the individual level of analysis, and even here it is only one among the many studies needed to lay an empirical foundation for serious consideration of this issue. At the same time, it does draw upon an unusually solid base of original public opinion data collected in Morocco and Algeria, and it may accordingly make a contribution that moves beyond broad generalizations and stereotypes.

Further, the study can contribute to a more objective assessment of whether and how Islam influences political orientations in Muslim societies. It can also help to incorporate insights drawn from these societies into comparative research concerned with the locus of applicability of particular connections between religion and politics. Such research, like that in the Arab world, is still at an early stage. But there have been a number of studies in Western countries concerned with the relationship between religious orientations and political attitudes among ordinary citizens, and these may be briefly summarized in order to place the present investigation in comparative perspective.

This comparative perspective also serves as a reminder that questions about the influence of religion are not unique to the Arab world or to Islam. Social scientists in the West have also called for, and carried out, studies of the relationships between religion and politics. These include individual-level research that assesses the utility of religious orientations in accounting for variance in political attitudes. The existence of such studies should discourage stereotypes that emphasize Islamic exceptionalism.

Findings from a number of empirical studies in Western countries, although not entirely consistent, suggest a nuanced and conditional relationship between religion and politics, one in which religious orientations are neither consistently useful nor consistently irrelevant in accounting for variance in political attitudes and behavior. Several opinion surveys report, for example, that personal religiosity is strongly and positively related to the degree of importance that individuals attach to issues of public policy pertaining to personal conduct, especially when, as in the case of abortion, homosexuality, and gender roles, this conduct is deemed to involve an ethical or moral dimension.[39] Another study, using data from the United States, looked at religiosity defined in terms of a tendency to seek religious guidance and biblical literalism and found a positive correlation with anti-communism and higher levels of support for military and defense-related spending.[40]

Although these findings suggest that religiosity frequently pushes toward conservative and nationalistic political views, a study using European data found that greater religiosity was positively correlated with higher levels of internationalism, and specifically with more support for European integration and for aid to developing countries.[41] In this case, religiosity was measured by the degree to which respondents reported that religion was important in shaping their political outlook.

The findings of yet another scholar are similarly diverse.[42] Using data from the United States, Jelen found that respondents with evangelical beliefs associated with Protestantism were more likely to display hawkish foreign policy attitudes related to defense spending, the use of military power to achieve foreign policy goals, and the bombing of civilian targets in war-time situations. Roman Catholics, by contrast, took more dovish positions on a number of foreign policy questions. A less consistent pattern emerged from his analysis of cross-national European data, however. Specifically, there was a direct positive correlation between religiosity and support for military security in three countries, a direct but negative correlation between these variables in two countries, and a positive but indirect correlation in seven countries.[43]

Several other studies have constructed attitudinal scales measuring different normative dimensions associated with religion and then examined the correlation between each scale and a series of political attitudes. This research found that more individualistic orientations, such as an emphasis on a personal relationship with God rather than religion's contribution to solving societal problems, were correlated with greater conservatism in ideology, partisanship, and policy preferences.[44] These findings suggest that the type of religious orientation, as well as the degree of religiosity, may be useful in accounting for variance in individual political attitudes.

Taken as a whole, this research suggests that religion in the West often pushes toward political conservatism and nationalism, but also that these tendencies are both inconsistent and in all probability conditional. A more coherent picture may emerge as additional research is undertaken.

Data from opinion research in North Africa

This study's empirical contribution draws upon a cross-national opinion survey carried out in North Africa in late 1995 and early 1996 under the auspices of the American Institute for Maghrib Studies, with supplementary financial support provided by the Ford Foundation and United States Information Agency. The survey was conducted in Rabat, Morocco, and Oran, Algeria. Tunisian government permission to conduct the survey in Tunis was initially denied but has since been obtained, and so the Tunisian component of the project is presently being carried out.

Although limited to a single city in each country, the surveys are based on carefully drawn random samples of 1,000 households in each city, and they are thus representative of large and very heterogeneous populations. Further, extensive care was taken in the training of interviewers, and a lengthy "interviewer manual" was prepared for use in each country. In addition, not only was the survey instrument carefully prepared and pre-tested, it included a very broad array of items, thus making the data of interest to students and scholars in many different disciplines. Finally, an innovative, multi-stage procedure was developed for selecting respondents. One battery of questions was administered to household heads; another, composed of questions dealing with political, social, and economic attitudes, was given to a second, randomly selected member of each household; and, when this second respondent was a woman of child-bearing years, an additional set of questions pertaining to fertility and family planning was asked.

Perhaps the most notable feature of the project was the composition of the research team. This was a truly international effort, involving 15 social scientists from Tunisia, Algeria, Morocco, and the United States. Each country was represented in approximately equal measure and all national "delegations" included scholars from at least three different academic disciplines. The group met regularly over a three-year period, first to develop and then to refine both conceptual and methodological aspects of the project and later to exchange findings from preliminary analyses. I have written or co-authored several papers that report selected findings and give additional information about the study.[45]

For this chapter, a multidimensional scaling technique known as factor analysis has been used to select items from the interview schedule to measure attitudes toward Islam and toward governance. Used in this way, factor analysis has a number of important advantages.[46] First, it provides an objective basis for selecting the items. Although selection is of course limited by the composition of the interview schedule, factor analysis identifies those items that are most closely associated with whatever conceptual property or properties characterize the collection of items that ask about Islam and about governance. Secondly, factor analysis offers evidence of reliability and validity. High loadings on a common factor indicate reproducibility, and hence reliability. They also indicate unidimensionality, meaning that the items measure a common conceptual property, which is a basis for inferring validity. Thirdly, factor analysis permits the construction of multi-item scales, or indices, which add precision when measuring the views of respondents. This is accomplished either by computing factor "scores" or by summing the items associated with a given dimension, those that factor analysis indicates "belong together."

A factor analysis of items from the Moroccan and Algerian survey instruments has identified a number of dimensions, or factors, four of which are of interest to our present analysis. These include two dimensions pertaining to Islam: personal piety and attitudes toward Islamic guidance in public affairs. The other two dimensions involve political orientations: attitudes toward democracy and civic participation.

The Moroccan and Algerian data yield nearly identical results with respect to both the nature of the dimensions and the individual survey items associated with each, thereby inspiring additional confidence in the validity and reliability of these measures. Further, confidence that respondents understood the survey items properly and gave coherent responses is indicated by the comparability of the observed patterns to findings from other empirical studies. Reports based on data from Egypt, Palestine, Kuwait, Lebanon, and Jordan, as well as from Morocco and Algeria, consistently show the same two dimensions of Islamic orientation.[47] Similarly, research on political culture in the context of democratization confirms the salience of the civic attitudes identified in the present study.[48] Against this background, the items associated with each of the dimensions identified by factor analysis are shown below.

Personal piety:
1. prays regularly
2. consults *imam* or *f'kih* if has a personal problem
3. often reads works on religion (only for Morocco)

Islamic guidance:
1. believes that religion should guide political and administrative affairs
2. believes that religion should guide economic and commercial affairs

Attitudes toward democracy:
1. believes openness to diverse ideas is an important criterion for political leadership
2. believes the development of democratic institutions is a high priority for government

Civic participation:
1. belongs to one or more civic associations
2. participates in public service projects

Findings

Prior to examining the connections between religious orientations and political attitudes, it may be instructive to present descriptive information about the nature and distribution of responses to selected items from the survey instrument. Accordingly, two tables are included in an appendix. Table 6A.1 gives the aggregate percentage of respondents in each country reporting various attitudes and behavior patterns. Table 6A.2, which presents responses to one item from each dimension, shows the distributions of attitudes and behavior patterns across demographic categories based on gender, education, and age. Although these tables do not shed light on the relationship *between* Islam and democracy, they do provide valuable information about some of the normative and behavioral characteristics of the populations under study with respect to Islam and politics.

Correlation and regression analysis have been used to examine the relationships between religious dimensions and political dimensions. The latter method, which treats political orientations as dependent variables and religious orientations as independent variables, is the more powerful of these techniques. It assesses the explanatory power of each independent variable with all others held constant, thus addressing the problem of multicolinearity.

Morocco

Turning first to Morocco and beginning with attitudes toward democracy, there are statistically significant correlations involving both personal piety and attitudes toward Islamic guidance. Specifically, in both cases, individuals with *stronger* religious orientations are significantly *less* likely to attach high priority to democratic institutions and values. Regression analysis shows that the relationship between personal piety and attitudes toward democracy is spurious, however. Personal piety and support for Islamic guidance are themselves strongly intercorrelated and, when the latter variable is held constant, personal piety's relationship to support for democracy loses much of its statistical significance. Further, it loses *all* of its statistical significance with the introduction of two additional control variables: age and education. By contrast, the inverse relationship between support for Islamic guidance and priority attached to democracy remains statistically significant when piety, age, and education are held constant.

These patterns are shown in table 6.1, which reports correlation coefficients for the correlations and *t*-values for the regressions, both of which show the direction as well as the strength of relationships. Probability values are given in parentheses. The lower the probability value (p), the greater the likelihood that the variables are actually related in the population from which the sample has been drawn. The generally accepted cut-off point for statistical significance is $p < .05$; when significance at or beyond the .05 level is attained, the values are in bold in the table. Note also that the larger the number of variables held constant, the greater the likelihood that the relationship is causal, meaning that the independent variable is a determinant of variance on the dependent variable.

Additional insight is provided by two further analyses. The first replaces the scale measuring attitudes toward Islamic guidance by its two constituent items. The regression in this case shows that the item pertaining to guidance in economic and commercial affairs provides the scale's explanatory power; it remains statistically significant in the new regression model, whereas the item pertaining to guidance in political and administrative affairs loses its statistical significance. The second involves disaggregating, with separate analyses undertaken for men and women. When this is done, the previously reported pattern holds for women but not for men. These patterns, too, are shown in table 6.1.

Table 6.1 Religious orientations and attitudes toward democracy in Morocco

		Regressions				
	Corre-lation	Full sample	Full sample	Full sample	Men only	Women only
Personal piety	**−.101**	−1.74	−0.48	0.08	−0.24	−0.09
	(.009)	(.083)	(.706)	(.937)	(.810)	(.926)
Islamic guidance in	**−.153**	**3.16**	**−2.50**			
public affairs	**(.000)**	**(.002)**	**(.013)**			
1. in politics and				−1.23	−1.67	−0.15
administration				(.218)	(.097)	(.882)
2. in economics				**−2.43**	−1.20	**−2.17**
and commerce				**(.015)**	(.232)	**(.031)**
Age				−1.37	−1.48	−0.58
				(.171)	(.140)	(.565)
Education			**10.70**	9.75	7.54	**−5.36**
			(.000)	**(.000)**	**(.000)**	**(.000)**

Notes: Reported for correlations are correlation coefficients, and reported for regressions are *t*-statistics; both show the direction as well as the strength of relationships. Figures in parentheses are probabilities; $p < .05$ is the generally accepted minimum level of statistical significance, indicated in bold when attained.

One conclusion to be drawn from this analysis is that personal piety has no independent explanatory power. With other variables held constant, there are no significant differences in the attitudes toward democracy held by individuals who are more pious and observant and those who are less pious and observant. Conversely, attitudes about Islamic guidance in public affairs *do* have an influence on attitudes toward democracy. However, although an inverse relationship persists when controls are included in the analysis, the relationship is nonetheless limited and conditional. It is limited to attitudes involving guidance in economic and commercial affairs, and it is significant only in the case of women.

The pattern is much less elaborate with respect to civic participation. In neither the regression analysis nor even the correlation analysis is participation related to a statistically significant degree to either personal piety or attitudes toward Islamic guidance. In other words, in both bivariate and multivariate analyses, individuals with stronger religious orientations are neither more likely nor less likely to participate in civic associations and public service projects than are individuals with weaker religious orientations. Islamic attachments thus have no influence on civic participation.

Algeria

Findings from Algeria are similar to those from Morocco with one important exception. As in Morocco, there is an inverse and statistically significant relationship between support for democracy and both personal piety and support for Islamic guidance in public affairs. In contrast to Morocco, however, the statistical significance of personal piety does not disappear in the regression analysis. This is the case even when age and education are introduced as control variables. These findings are presented in table 6.2.

Additional regression models are also presented in table 6.2. First, as in Morocco, the scale measuring attitudes toward Islamic guidance has been replaced by its constituent items. Further, precisely as observed in Morocco, it is views about Islamic guidance in economic and commercial affairs that provide the scale's explanatory power. Views about Islamic

Table 6.2 Religious orientations and attitudes toward democracy in Algeria

		Regressions				
	Corre-lation	Full sample	Full sample	Full sample	Men only	Women only
Personal piety	−.114 (.001)	−2.57 (.010)	−2.50 (.013)			
1. prays regularly				−2.05 (.041)	−0.23 (.819)	−2.58 (.010)
2. consults *imam* or *f'kih*				−1.61 (.108)	−0.69 (.490)	−1.74 (.082)
Islamic guidance in public affairs	−.140 (.009)	−2.93 (.004)	−2.63 (.009)			
1. in politics and administration				0.88 (.382)	0.80 (.422)	0.44 (.659)
2. in economics and commerce				−3.38 (.001)	−1.47 (.142)	−3.29 (.001)
Age				−0.59 (.558)	−0.85 (.395)	−0.17 (.869)	−1.06 (.289)
Education			2.87 (.000)	3.09 (.002)	2.06 (.040)	−2.32 (.021)

Notes: Reported for correlations are correlation coefficients, and reported for regressions are *t*-statistics; both show the direction as well as the strength of relationships. Figures in parentheses are probabilities; $p < .05$ is the generally accepted minimum level of statistical significance, indicated in bold when attained.

guidance in political and administrative affairs are not independently related to attitudes toward democracy.

Second, constituent items have also been substituted for the personal piety scale, since in Algeria this scale is also related to attitudes toward democracy to a statistically significant degree. In this case, it is regular prayer that carries the scale's explanatory power. Consulting an *imam* or *f'kih* is not independently related to attitudes toward democracy.

Third, separate regressions have again been undertaken for men and women, and as in Morocco the statistically significant relationships hold in the case of women but not men. Thus, to summarize, women who pray more regularly are less likely to attach importance to democratic institutions and values, as are women who are more favorably disposed toward Islamic guidance in economic and commercial affairs. This pattern is observed with age, education, and the other constituent items of the two Islamic orientation scales held constant. Among Algerian men, by contrast, as among men in Morocco, none of the Islamic orientations examined is related to attitudes toward democracy to a statistically significant degree.

Turning finally to civic participation, findings again parallel those observed in Morocco. No statistically significant relationships have been observed. In both the bivariate and multivariate analyses, individuals with stronger religious orientations are neither more likely nor less likely than those with weaker religious orientations to participate in civic associations or public service projects. Islamic orientations thus do not account for variance in levels of civic participation.

Conclusion

Survey data from the Maghrib suggest that, although religious orientations do have some influence on attitudes toward democracy and governance, this influence is limited and conditional. In Morocco, personal piety does not predispose individuals either favorably or unfavorably toward democracy or, similarly, toward civic participation. In Algeria, regular prayer is the only aspect of religious piety that influences political orientations, more frequent prayer being associated with less support for democracy. But this relationship holds only among women, and frequency of prayer is unrelated to civic participation. In both Morocco and Algeria, one but only one aspect of support for religious guidance in public affairs is associated with political orientations. This is support for guidance in economic and commercial affairs, which is inversely related to support for democracy. Again, however, this relationship holds only among women. Support for Islamic guidance in economics and commerce is unrelated to civic participation among either women or men, and among both men and women support for guidance in political and administrative affairs is unrelated either to attitudes toward democracy or to civic participation. All of the latter findings obtain in both Morocco and Algeria.

Three sets of conclusions may be tentatively advanced on the basis of these findings. All raise questions that deserve additional research. First, despite some statistically significant relationships, Islam appears to have less influence on political attitudes and behavior than is frequently suggested by students of Arab and Islamic society. The present study is of course limited in both space and time, and it is also restricted to the individual level of analysis. Nevertheless, it strongly suggests that Islam should not be reified when attempting to explain Arab political orientations, and, more specifically, it offers evidence that support for democracy and participation in civic affairs are not in most cases lower among individuals with the strongest Islamic attachments.

Secondly, the locus of those relationships that *are* statistically significant is noteworthy. In both of the countries for which data are available, support for Islamic guidance has explanatory power only among women, and only with respect to guidance in economic and commercial affairs. This suggests that it may be economic concerns that discourage support for democracy, rather than a desire for the broad application of Islamic codes to public affairs. And it is also possible, although additional research is needed to test this hypothesis, that this is because democracy is perceived to include an economic opening that will increase inequality and is therefore less attractive to those for whom economic concerns are more pronounced. Further, it may be that such concerns are greater among women than men, a hypothesis that is supported by a recent study exploring the consequences for Maghribi and other Arab women of political and economic liberalization.[49]

Thirdly, studies in the United States and Europe report that religious orientations have more explanatory power than has been observed in the present investigation. The difference should not be overstated, since findings from Western countries are not entirely consistent and since the present study indicates that religion has at least a limited and conditional impact on political orientations in North Africa. Further, research in the United States and Europe has not examined the same political orientations. Nevertheless, perhaps surprisingly, the present study suggests that religion influences political orientations more frequently and consistently in the West than in the Arab world. This may be because levels of personal piety are higher in the Arab world and also because of a strong and historically legitimated connection between Islam and politics, thereby making religious orientations less useful in distinguishing among individuals with dissimilar political inclinations.

If correct, this suggests that aggregate religiosity at the system level constitutes a conditionality affecting the relationship between religion and politics at the individual level of analysis. Specifically, whereas religiosity tends to push toward political conservatism in more secular societies, it frequently does not push toward any particular political tendency in more religious societies. It remains to be seen whether future research supports this hypothesis. For the present, however, findings from North Africa do indicate a need for comparative analyses aimed at identifying system-level characteristics that specify the locus of religion's influence on the political orientations of ordinary citizens.

More opinion studies, as well as research at other levels of analysis, are necessary in order to arrive at a fuller understanding of whether and how Islam influences the prospects for successful democratic transitions in the Arab world. This study aspires to encourage and advance this effort, while at the same time making a contribution to scientific cumulativeness that is significant despite its limitations. And the evidence presently available from Morocco and Algeria suggests that Islam is not the obstacle to democratization that some Western scholars allege it to be. A democratic, civic, and participant political culture may indeed be necessary for mature democracy, but there is nothing in the present study's findings to suggest that the emergence of such a political culture is discouraged by the Islamic attachments of Arab men and women.

Appendix

Table 6A.1 Aggregate attitudes toward Islam and governance (percent)

	Morocco	Algeria
Personal piety		
Prays regularly	73	78
Consults *imam* or *f'kih* if personal problems	29	12
Islamic guidance		
Religion should guide economic and social affairs	62	50
Religion should guide political and administrative affairs	50	31
Attitudes toward democracy		
Development of democratic institutions is a high priority	20	17
Openness to diverse ideas an important leadership criterion	16	26
Political participation		
Belongs to one or more civic associations	11	5
Participates in public service projects	14	13

Table 6A.2 Distributions of attitudes and behavior patterns across demographic categories (percent)

	Male				Female			
	Young Lo Ed. (MYL)	Old Lo Ed. (MOL)	Young Hi Ed. (MYH)	Old Hi Ed. (MOH)	Young Lo Ed. (FYL)	Old Lo Ed. (FOL)	Young Hi Ed. (FYH)	Old Hi Ed. (FOH)
Respondents who pray regularly								
Algeria	50	92	60	87	47	96	74	86
Morocco	42	89	56	81	31	90	61	80
Respondents who believe religion should guide political and administrative affairs								
Algeria	47	34	28	15	43	40	33	18
Morocco	33	56	46	44	42	50	53	37
Respondents who consider openness to diverse ideas an important leadership criterion								
Algeria	13	25	32	18	22	19	35	27
Morocco	25	11	31	25	11	6	30	15
Respondents who participate in public service projects								
Algeria	21	17	16	41	5	7	7	14
Morocco	11	10	23	29	0	5	17	21

Notes

1. Lisa Anderson, "Politics in the Middle East: Opportunities and Limits in the Quest for Theory," in Mark Tessler, with Jodi Nachtwey and Anne Banda, eds., *Area Studies and Social Science: Strategies for Understanding Middle East Politics*, Bloomington, IN: Indiana University Press, 1999, p. 6.
2. Rami G. Khouri, "A Lesson in Middle East History and Humanity," *Jordan Times*, 28 May 1991.
3. Mark Tessler, "The Origins of Popular Support for Islamist Movements: A Political Economy Analysis," in John Entelis, ed., *Islam, Democracy, and the State in North Africa*, Bloomington, IN: Indiana University Press, 1997, pp. 97–9.
4. Ibrahim A. Karawan, " 'ReIslamization Movements' According to Kepel: On Striking Back and Striking Out," *Contention*, vol. 2, Fall 1992, p. 162.
5. Hilal Khashan, "History's Legacy," *Middle East Quarterly*, vol. 5, March 1998.
6. As quoted in Miral Fahmy, "Mubarak to Put Economy before Politics," *Reuters Global Newsbank*, 27 September 1999.
7. Mark Tessler and Marilyn Grobschmidt, "Democracy in the Arab World and the Arab–Israeli Conflict," in David Garnham and Mark Tessler, eds., *Democracy, War and Peace in the Middle East*, Bloomington, IN: Indiana University Press, 1995; James Ray, "The Future of International War," in Garnham and Tessler, eds., *Democray, War and Peace in the Middle East*.
8. Etel Solingen, chapter 3 in this volume and "Democratization in the Middle East: Quandaries of the Peace Process," *Journal of Democracy*, vol. 7, July 1996; Kirk Van-

dewalle, "The Middle East Peace Process and Regional Integration," *Survival*, vol. 36, Winter 1995.

9. Zeev Maoz and Bruce Russett, "Normative and Structural Causes of Democratic Peace: 1946–1986," *American Political Science Review*, vol. 87, September 1993; Michael Ward and Kristian Gleditsch, "Democratizing for Peace," *American Political Science Review*, vol. 92, March 1998; Dan Reiter and Allan Stam, "Democracy, War Initiation, and Victory," *American Political Science Review*, vol. 92, June 1998.

10. *La Guerre du Golfe et l'Avenir des Arabes: débats et réflexions*, Tunis: Cérès Productions, 1991; David Pollock, *The "Arab Street"? Public Opinion in the Arab World*, Washington DC: Washington Institute for Near East Policy, Policy Paper no. 32, 1992.

11. Mounia Bennani-Chraibi, *Les Représentations du Monde des Jeunes Marocains*, Paris: Thèse de doctorat de l'Institut d'Etudes Politiques, 1993, pp. 417–18.

12. Oula Al-Farawati, "Arab Intellectuals Review Challenges of Globalization," *Jordan Times*, 9–10 December 1999.

13. William Quandt, "The Urge for Democracy," *Foreign Affairs*, vol. 73, July–August 1994; I. William Zartman, "A Search for Security and Governance Regimes," in Garnham and Tessler, eds., *Democracy, War and Peace in the Middle East*; Augustus Richard Norton and Robin Wright, "The Post-Peace Crisis in the Middle East," *Survival*, vol. 36, Winter 1995.

14. Solingen, "Democratization in the Middle East," p. 151; Clement Henry, *The Mediterranean Debt Crescent: Money and Power in Algeria, Egypt, Morocco, Tunisia, and Turkey*, Gainesville, FL: University Press of Florida, 1996.

15. Augustus Richard Norton, *Civil Society in the Middle East*, Leiden: E. J. Brill, 1996.

16. Samuel Huntington, "Democracy's Third Wave," in Larry Diamond and Marc Plattner, eds., *The Global Resurgence of Democracy*, Baltimore, MD: Johns Hopkins University Press, 1993, pp. 13–15.

17. James Gibson, "The Resilience of Mass Support for Democratic Institutions and Processes in the Nascent Russian and Ukrainian Democracies," in V. Tismaneanu, ed., *Political Culture and Civil Society in Russia and the New States of Eurasia*, New York: M. E. Sharpe, 1995, p. 55.

18. Richard Rose, "Where Are Postcommunist Countries Going?" *Journal of Democracy*, vol. 8, July 1997, p. 97.

19. Huntington, "Democracy's Third Wave," p. 13.

20. Rose, "Where Are Postcommunist Countries Going?", p. 98.

21. Richard Rose, William Mishler, and Christian Haerpfer, *Democracy and Its Alternatives: Understanding Post-Communist Societies*, Baltimore, MD: Johns Hopkins University Press, 1998; Rose, "Where Are Postcommunist Countries Going?"; Gibson, "The Resilience of Mass Support for Democratic Institutions and Processes in the Nascent Russian and Ukrainian Democracies."

22. Marta Lagos, "Latin America's Smiling Mask," *Journal of Democracy*, vol. 8, July 1997.

23. Doh Chull Shin and Huoyan Shyu, "Political Ambivalence in South Korea and Taiwan," *Journal of Democracy*, vol. 8, July 1997.

24. Dan Ottemoeller, "Popular Perceptions of Democracy: Elections and Attitudes in Uganda," *Comparative Political Studies*, vol. 31, February 1998; Robert Mattes and Hermann Thiel, "Consolidation and Public Opinion in South Africa," *Journal of Democracy*, vol. 9, January 1998.

25. Malcolm Kerr, "Foreword," in Tawfic Farah, ed., *Political Behavior in the Arab States*, Boulder, CO: Westview Press, 1983; Michael Hudson, "The Political Culture Approach to Arab Democratization: The Case for Bringing It Back in, Carefully," in Rex Brynen, Bahgat Korany, and Paul Noble, eds., *Political Liberalization and Democratization in*

the Arab World, Boulder, CO: Lynne Rienner Publishers, 1995; Anderson, "Politics in the Middle East."

26. Mark Tessler, "Arab Politics and Public Opinion," paper presented at a U.S. Government inter-agency conference on "Next Generation Politics in the Muslim World," Washington, DC, 1999; Iliya Harik, "Some Political and Cultural Considerations Bearing on Survey Research in the Arab World," in Mark Tessler, Monte Palmer, Barbara Ibrahim, and Tawfic Farah, eds., *The Evaluation and Application of Survey Research in the Arab World*, Boulder, CO: Westview Press, 1987, pp. 66–7.

27. Khalil Shikaki, "The Transition to Democracy in Palestine," *Journal of Palestine Studies*, vol. 25, Winter 1996; Isabelle Daneels, *Palestine's Interim Agreement with Democracy*, Jerusalem: Jerusalem Media and Communication Centre, 1998; Maher Massis, "Jordan: A Study of Attitudes toward Democratic Changes," *Arab Studies Quarterly*, vol. 20, Summer 1998.

28. Anderson, "Politics in the Middle East," p. 7.

29. Ibrahim A. Karawan, *Islamist Impasse*, London: International Institute for Strategic Studies, 1997; Dale Eickelman and James Piscatori, *Muslim Politics*, Princeton, NJ: Princeton University Press, 1996.

30. Mark Tessler and Jolene Jesse, "Gender and Support for Islamist Movements: Evidence from Egypt, Kuwait, and Palestine," *Muslim World*, vol. 86, April 1996, pp. 194–222; and Tessler, "The Origins of Popular Support for Islamist Movements."

31. François Burgat and William Dowell, *The Islamic Movement in North Africa*, Austin, TX: University of Texas at Austin, 1993; Azzedine Layachi and Abdel-kader Haireche, "National Development and Political Protest: Islamists in the Maghreb Countries," *Arab Studies Quarterly*, vol. 14, Spring/Summer 1992.

32. Elie Kedourie, *Democracy and Arab Political Culture*, London: Frank Cass, 1994, pp. 1, 5; also Samuel Huntington, "Will More Countries Become Democratic?" *Political Science Quarterly*, vol. 99, Summer 1984, p. 208.

33. Y. Choueiri, "The Political Discourse of Contemporary Islamist Movements," in Abdel Salem Sidahmed and Anoushiravam Ehteshami, eds., *Islamic Fundamentalism*, Boulder, CO: Westview Press, 1996, pp. 21–2; also Bernard Lewis, *The Shaping of the Modern Middle East*, New York: Oxford University Press, 1994, pp. 54–6.

34. Fred Halliday, *Islam and the Myth of Confrontation: Religion and Politics in the Middle East*, London: I. B. Tauris, 1995, p. 116; John Esposito and James Piscatori, "Democratization and Islam," *Middle East Journal*, vol. 45, 1991.

35. Shukri Abed, "Islam and Democracy," in Garnham and Tessler, eds., *Democracy, War and Peace in the Middle East*, pp. 127–8.

36. Mohamed Elhachmi Hamdi, "Islam and Democracy: The Limits of the Western Model," *Journal of Democracy*, vol. 7, April 1996; Fatima Mernissi, *Islam and Democracy: Fear of the Modern World*, Reading, MA: Addison-Wesley, 1992.

37. Donna Lee Bowen, "Pragmatic Morality, Islam, and Family Planning in Morocco," in Donna Lee Bowen and Evelyn Early, eds., *Everyday Life in the Muslim Middle East*, Bloomington, IN: Indiana University Press, 1993.

38. Jamal Al-Suwaidi, "Arab and Western Conceptions of Democracy," in Garnham and Tessler, eds., *Democracy, War and Peace in the Middle East*, pp. 87–8.

39. Bernadette C. Hayes, "The Impact of Religious Identification on Political Attitudes: An International Comparison," *Sociology of Religion*, vol. 56, 1995; Ted. G. Jelen, *The Political Mobilization of Religious Beliefs*, New York: Praeger, 1991; Ted G. Jelen, "Religion and Public Opinion in the 1990s: An Empirical Overview," in Barbara Norrander and Clyde Wilcox, eds., *Understanding Public Opinion*, Washington DC: Congressional Quarterly Press, 1996.

40. James L. Guth and John C. Green, "Salience: The Core Concept?" in David C. Leege

and Lyman A. Kellstedt, eds., *Rediscovering the Religious Factor in American Politics*, Armonk, NY: M. E. Sharpe, 1993.

41. Martha Abele MacIver, "Religious Politicization among Western European Mass Publics," in William H. Swatos, Jr., ed., *Religious Politics in Global and Comparative Perspective*, New York: Greenwood Press, 1989.

42. Ted G. Jelen, "Religion and Foreign Policy Attitudes: Exploring the Effects of Denomination and Doctrine," *American Politics Quarterly*, vol. 22, 1994.

43. Ted G. Jelen, "Swords, Plowshares, and Philistines: A Comparative Analysis of Religion and Attitudes toward Security Policy," paper presented at the American Political Science Association, San Francisco, 29 August – 1 September 1996.

44. David C. Leege and Lyman A. Kellstedt, "Religious Worldviews and Political Philosophies: Capturing Theory in the Grand Manner through Empirical Data," in Leege and Kellstedt, eds., *Rediscovering the Religious Factor in American Politics*; Peter L. Benson and Dorothy Williams, *Religion on Capitol Hill: Myths and Realities*, San Francisco: Harper & Row, 1982.

45. Georges Sabagh, Jodi Nachtwey, and Mark Tessler, "Islam, Gender, and the Demographic Challenge in North Africa," paper presented at the annual meeting of the Middle East Studies Association, Chicago, 1998; Mark Tessler, "The Contribution of Public Opinion Research to an Understanding of the Information Revolution and Its Impact in North Africa," in Jamal S. Al-Suwaidi, ed., *The Impact of the Information and Communication Revolution on Society and State in the Arab World*, London: I. B. Tauris, 1998; Mark Tessler, "Morocco's Next Political Generation," in Roel Meijer, ed., *Alienation or Integration of Arab Youth: Between Family, State, and Street*, Richmond, UK: Curzon Press, 2000.

46. Alberto Marradi, "Factor Analysis as an Aid in the Formulation and Refinement of Empirically Useful Concepts," in Edgar F. Borgatta and David J. Jackson, eds., *Factor Analysis and Measurement in Sociological Research*, London: Sage, 1981.

47. Mark Tessler, "Islam and Democracy in the Middle East: The Impact of Religious Orientations on Attitudes toward Democracy in Four Arab Countries," *Comparative Politics*, vol. 34, April 2002, pp. 337–54; Mark Tessler and Jodi Nachtwey, "Islam and Attitudes toward International Conflict: Evidence from Survey Research in the Arab World," *Journal of Conflict Resolution*, vol. 42, October 1998, pp. 619–36.

48. Yun-han Chu, Larry Diamond and Doh Chull Shin, "Halting Progress in Korea and Taiwan," *Journal of Democracy*, vol. 12, January 2001, pp. 122–36; Rose, Mishler and Haerpfer, *Democracy and Its Alternatives*; Gibson, "The Resilience of Mass Support for Democratic Institutions and Processes in the Nascent Russian and Ukrainian Democracies."

49. Laurie Brand, *Women, the State and Political Liberalization*, New York: Columbia University Press, 1998.

Part III

National and regional experiences

7

The democratic process in Syria, Lebanon, and Jordan

Kamel S. Abu Jaber

Some have suggested that, because of societal and historical circumstances in the Arab world, the term "democratization" does not necessarily imply what it means in the Western world.[1] The idea of electing leaders at specified intervals with a certain agreed-upon procedure; the occasional exchange of leadership roles between government and opposition; and indeed the very idea of loyal opposition have not yet taken root anywhere in the Arab world.[2] Freedoms generally associated with human rights, including a free press, remain in the painful process of asserting themselves. Throughout the Arab region, the democratization process is ongoing, with some regimes more liberal than others.[3] This is in spite of the fact that legislative institutions in accordance with constitutional provisions do exist, although the degree of their docility to the executive differs from country to country. Full compliance with the written constitutions, however, remains for the large part a promise against the future. Constitutions are merely a step in the right direction, not living documents venerated by rulers and ruled alike. In many instances the democratization process has hardly begun, with the very term "democracy" not yet fully understood by either leaders or society.

What is meant by democracy?[4] A distinction should be made between formalized democracy and liberalism. If democracy merely means the process of electing officials through the vote to legitimize or, as in many cases in the Arab world, give the illusion of legitimacy, then some may conclude that a certain type of democracy does exist in the Arab world.

However, if democracy is coupled with the practice of liberalism based on constitutional government, the rule of law, and the protection of human rights, the system can then be called democratic. For, in certain circumstances, a system may be liberal yet not democratic or an illiberal democracy.[5] What matters is not the formality of suffrage alone, but the spirit and official practice in accordance with the limits set by the constitution. In the three countries discussed in this chapter – Jordan, Lebanon, and Syria – the success of the advance toward such a system varies. Personality and charisma prove to be the most important factors in the political life of the state.

In the Western industrialized countries, the institutional structures, the procedures, and the spirit of a democratic system based on a venerated living constitution have become a fact of life. Although personalities are important, it is the constitutional set-up that is the final arbiter in the process of decision-making in public life. The situation is different in the Arab world, where the personalization of power reigns supreme. Often a country is identified with the ruler, rather than the other way around: Qaddafi's Libya, Saddam Hussein's Iraq, al-Assad's Syria, or Mubarak's Egypt. Institutionalization may take a long time.[6] At the moment, liberalization – the creation of a liberal atmosphere in which the regime begins to respect the minds and bodies of individuals, and in which concepts of civil society and human rights find fertile soil to take root – is of great concern to the intellectuals and the peoples of the region. We have to remember that the three countries under discussion were catapulted into the twentieth and the twenty-first centuries from societies not vastly different from those of the Middle Ages, and they are now attempting to achieve in one or two generations the political, economic, and cultural revolutions that took centuries to achieve in Europe and the West as a whole.

What does the term "democratization" mean in the Arab world? Two points need to be made immediately. The first is that, whatever liberality exists,[7] it is essentially a gift by the state rather than a sacred right emanating from the people and possibly expressed in a constitutional document.[8] As such it is not a constant institution or process whose existence can be relied upon by all persons at all times; its parameters can be expanded or restricted at the will of the state and the ruler(s) at the top. The second point is that the parameters of liberality depend, in turn, on two factors. The first is the degree to which the state and its security apparatus determine the power of the local opposition, and the danger they pose. The second factor refers to the intensity of regional and local crises taking place at the moment. The Arab–Israeli conflict, for instance, has always been a convenient excuse for many Arab regimes to curtail civil and political liberties. It is claimed that the state of war necessitates the marshaling of all resources to confront that challenge. It is also emphasized that this would not be the right time to allow debate, political liberalization, and the possibility of political dissension. Similarly, radicalism – often expressed in nationalist authoritarian ideologies – or the politicization of Islam have tended to find sustenance in existing, seemingly intractable, conflicts.

Of course there is a variety of groups clamoring not only for minor offers of political liberalization but for a serious commitment to the institutionalization of the democratic process. The crisis atmosphere in the region, however, has been a major factor in turning the state's attention inward, with the result that stability has overtaken democracy as a supreme value. This, in turn, has meant the strengthening, indeed enlargement, of the security apparatus and the expansion of its functions.

Almost all Arab states now have a legislative council in their institutional set-up; yet this remains a mere mechanical instrument to pass and legitimize laws proposed by the executive branch. What is more relevant at this stage is the creation of a liberal atmosphere, a major re-education of political leaders and decision-makers, and the education of both authorities and citizens about the meaning of democracy and its potential value for society and government. Competing opinions must be given a place in the political process, and the government's legitimate concern for stability must not cause it to resort to violence against its own people. Similarly, there is a need to instill the values of civic society and respect for the "other." It should also be remembered that terror on the street is often more frightening and effective than that of the state.

Global pressures in a rapidly changing political environment and the accumulation, indeed confluence, of internal pressures and external challenges simultaneously have been major factors behind the maintenance of authoritarianism throughout the region. Some countries remain locked into medieval autocracy. The degree of liberalization and relaxation that may exist depends on the personalities, the circumstances, and the feeling of legitimacy that a regime may have or thinks it has. Traditional regimes as well as so-called "progressive" or "revolutionary" ones advance different claims for their legitimacy. Hereditary regimes often advance dynastic and religious foundations for legitimacy. "Progressive" and "revolutionary" regimes, sometimes dominated by a single party, claim legitimacy in the name of the masses and their "revolution." Throughout most of the past 50 years, all Arab regimes have continued to expand their legitimacy through economic development. Social justice, social democracy, indeed all economic dimensions have been the state's primary focus, in the hope of steering attention away from politics and the authoritarian nature of the regime.[9] This blurred atmosphere leaves the average person quite uncertain about the permitted limits for movement and thought. Thus, for those who care to do so and are willing to take the risks, a process of constant testing takes place.[10]

The transition from an authoritarian political heritage is not easy either for the individual or for the state itself. Confronted with the challenges of the times, the state seeks stability above all else, which of necessity often places it on a collision course with the demands to expand the frontiers of political liberalization.

The traditional state has always been distant, authoritarian, and more or less an object of fear. The Ottoman Empire, in which the three countries under discussion shared a common legacy, rarely interfered in the lives of its subjects, either economically or socially; its justice, or sometimes injustice, was speedy, and its sticks were heavy and without procedure. By and large the attitude of the state toward its subjects – *Ra'iyyah* (flock) – was that they were mere objects to be manipulated, not citizens with sacred rights. Subjects were expected to obey, not to question, and certainly not to hope to participate in the decision-making process. This political legacy inherited by the modern Arab state system also explains the difficulty of attempting to replace it or graft on a new liberal political culture. The attempt is an ongoing one pursued by the elite and the intelligentsia; resistance, however, remains great, not merely from the regimes but often from the masses, whose sentiments continue to be more attuned to the traditional order.

The hope of most Arabs today is to avoid getting into trouble with the government. Over the past 50 years they have learned that they have no chance of winning a contest against the state. Although mass communications and mass media have reduced time and space limitations, the mental distance between the masses and their state is as great as ever. The best Arabs can hope for is to participate in the physical benefits that the state offers. They remain basically skeptical of its enticements to feel a strong sense of belonging and identity. The lesson of the last few decades of the twentieth century is that in the interests of one's well-being and prosperity it might be better to stay as far away from the state as one's ancestors.

The mass media, which should have deepened and expanded people's political awareness, have become a handy tool for governments to expand their own power. In this era of globalization, the mass media have further diverted attention to consumerism and the economic dimension of life. For the most part, Arab societies have become polarized between a well-off minority and the impoverished masses, who read about or view on their television screens the by-products of the global consumer culture without being able to enjoy any of its benefits.

All Arab regimes claim to be democratic. The intelligentsia continue to exert pressure for the institutionalization of a participatory system, but the majority of the people have only a vague idea what this means. Considering the continuous crises that have been a recurring feature of the politics of the area and the prevalent authoritarian character of the regimes, mass expectations regarding the possibility of establishing a liberal democratic system are not high. Of course a few intellectuals maintain the dream, yet intellectuals and masses alike realize that it is a remote dream. Throughout the Middle East, the government is far stronger than the governed, and all that the latter hope for from their government is some degree of political opening and fewer violent or repressive measures against them. Democracy in the Western sense, based on institutions, remains a stranger to the region.

There is a realization that the adoption of a constitution is not enough, that a constitution is no more than a purely mechanical vehicle, and that time is needed – time to acculturate the rulers and the ruled alike. Over recent decades the Arab peoples have learned that the state, if it wishes, can always find ways to ignore the constitution and the will of the people. They have also learned that even the voting exercise, and not only in one-party states, is no more than a formality and does not necessarily reflect genuine democratic values. The use in many Arab countries of plebiscites to reconfirm the already selected head of state with astronomical majorities, sometimes reaching over 99 percent, has exacerbated the cynicism of both the masses and the intelligentsia.

The rapid and sometimes violent regime changes in the area have caused many to hope for no more than stability, an improvement in living conditions, and a milder, less repressive state apparatus; that is, a return to the traditional idea of al-Mustabid al-Adil, the Just Tyrant. A just tyrant is one who will not be too cruel in administering the affairs of the state, and who will have the interests of the people at heart.

Syria

The shock and trauma that accompanied Arab societies' entrance into the modern age in the wake of the collapse of the Ottoman Empire at the end of World War I remain a salient feature of Arab political life. The Arab world as a whole, and the peoples of Greater Syria in particular, remain in the grip of an identity crisis of vast dimensions. With the umbrella of the Ottoman state removed, the peoples of Syria suddenly had to face the challenges of modernity and the need to build a secular nation-state.[11]

In the Arab world, the state of transition seems to be lasting much longer than elsewhere in the developing world. Nothing seems certain any more, and the new identities attempting to replace the once familiar

Ottoman identity continue to face great resistance. Even Syria's honorific title of Um al-Urubah (Mother of Arabism) has not given the people of Syria an adequate and satisfactory sense of identity. The lure of Arab unity as a nationalist goal remains very attractive, more so than Syrian, Jordanian, Lebanese, or Palestinian patriotism. Over the course of the twentieth century, disillusionment deepened into frustration as the nascent national feelings were further wounded by the successive defeats in Palestine, the loss of Iskanderun (Alexandretta), and the failure of successive regimes to deal even semi-adequately with either domestic or external challenges.

Curiously enough it was easier for Lebanon, despite its fractionalized state and sectarian divisions, to achieve a sense of Lebanese identity than was the case with Syria. This phenomenon is perhaps accounted for by the emphasis of successive Syrian regimes on Arab unity and the insistence that Syria must play a leading role in Arab and regional politics, thus placing it at odds with its neighbors, who are not interested in Arab unity and wish to maintain their independence.

Syria's historical development throughout the twentieth century was intertwined with the seemingly intractable crises of the area, especially the Palestine question. Although Syria was less affected by this conflict than Jordan, and in some ways even less than Lebanon, Syrian domestic and international politics continue to be influenced by the Arab–Israeli conflict. Whereas Lebanon attempted to legitimize its regime through its fragile sectarian-based democratization process, and Jordan, being heir to the Great Arab Revolt, experienced continued efforts to establish a liberal civic society, Syria's legitimization is still based on confronting Zionism and achieving military parity with Israel. All else has had to be of lower priority by comparison. Since the 1940s, the perceived Zionist threat, not only to Syria but also to the entire Arab world, took precedence. Human and natural resources were marshaled to face this challenge. In a state of war, it was reasoned, certain sacrifices had to be made, including the possibility of establishing a civic society. At the same time, however, the struggle necessitated a serious socio-economic development effort in which the government had to take a leading role. State socialism became the natural vehicle to direct all resources and means of production into serving the goals of the state. It was hoped, no doubt, that an improvement in living conditions would divert attention away from the oppressive practices of an authoritarian regime.

I should point out that, in all Arab societies, government is the largest pool of resources and talent. However, this phenomenon is more noticeable in some Arab governments than in others. In the management of change, the Syrian regime has always placed the democratization process below stability and economic development. The pressure of rising expectations and population explosion account for only part of this prioritization; external threats account for the rest.

The need for stability is certainly still uppermost in the mind of Syrian leaders. They are faced with many problems, and have hardly any experience or precedents to rely on. The Syrian regime, like that of Jordan and many other Arab regimes established in the twentieth century, had to be built block by block from the ground up. During the centuries of Ottoman rule, the Arabs had little practice in governing themselves. Moreover, the historical political legacy was an authoritarian one. There were no liberal institutions, no contrary opinion was tolerated, and only the whim of the ruler at the top really mattered. In his hands the ruler combined the executive, legislative, and sometimes the judicial powers. There was no procedure for decision-making, which was simply the prerogative of the ruler alone.

Thus, whatever breath of liberalism may have existed in Syria in the wake of the Ottoman Empire, it soon expired in the searing heat of the attempt to confront the internal and external challenges that arose at the same time. After the initial experiment with trying to fashion a liberal constitutional system following independence from French colonialism, the country was beset by a succession of military coups d'état. It took but a few years for the first coup d'état, of Husni al-Zaim, to happen, followed by that of Sami Hinnawi and, in quick succession, that of Adib Shishakli. Although the 1950 Syrian constitution, which replaced the 1930 constitution, was a liberal document, it was soon ignored by the successive unstable regimes of the 1950s and 1960s. In fact, Shishakli staged his second coup d'état, in November 1951, to pre-empt conservative politicians attempting to curtail his power. He was overthrown in 1954, ushering in the ascendancy of the Ba'th Party and its control of the state. This was interrupted only briefly by the era of the union of Syria and Egypt in the United Arab Republic under Nasser and the right of center coup government that took over at the end of September 1961. That government was ousted a few months later, in March 1962, by left-wing elements paving the way for the 1963 Ba'th military coup d'état. Syria's instability ended with the advent of the "Correctionist" movement of Hafez al-Assad in 1970.

Since independence, Syria has been governed by more than six different constitutions.[12] The constitution outlines the theoretical framework of political life, which is at variance with actual practice. The National Front, led by the Ba'th Party (which in turn was led by its Secretary-General, President Hafez al-Assad, until his death in 2000), delineated the parameters of political life in Syria and, in theory, the Ba'th Party's ideology, woven into the constitution, dominates political life. In reality, however, it is the army, dominated by the Alawite minority, that uses both ideology and party as a legitimizing cover. Since independence, Syrian politics have basically revolved around the military, which explains the coups d'état and abrupt changes of regime.[13]

During the rule of President Hafez al-Assad (1970–2000), Syria experienced a period of stability unprecedented in its modern history. This was the longest period that a regime had remained in power. Although at times the regime resorted to repression, as was the case with the Muslim Brotherhood, or the treatment of Sunnis in Hama in 1982, there were attempts in the last two decades of al-Assad's rule to relax the grip of the state on public life. However, this was more evident in the economic than in the political field, which faces considerable uncertainties even under al-Assad's successor, his son Bashar.[14]

The elections to the legislature, Majlis al-Sha'b (the People's Council), have remained essentially a formality to approve Ba'th candidates. What the Syrian constitution gives with one hand, it takes with the other. It achieves this through the dominance of the one-party system as well as the provision that, although freedoms may be practised, such practice must be within the parameters of the law and national interest as defined by the Ba'th Party. Popular participation remains within the confines outlined by the state. Genuine change in leadership can only be accomplished through the instrument of a coup d'état. With Bashar al-Assad succeeding his father, the republic of Syria has been turned into a hereditary republic.

Lebanon

In an interview in 1989, the newly elected president of Lebanon, Emile Lahhoud, emphasized his desire to maintain national unity based on the Taif Agreement of 1989, which in turn is based on proportional sectarian representation for all Lebanese.[15] Although different in manner, style, form, and content from sectarianism in Syria, that in Lebanon remains the salient feature of Lebanese political life. Yet, whereas in Syria sectarianism is denied, in Lebanon, especially after the fierce civil war of the 1970s and 1980s, it is openly promoted and defended as the only path to social peace. The prominent Lebanese politician Michael Edde states that sectarianism is no more than an adherence to the right to be different while admitting the right of the other to hold a contrary belief, which, in his words, is the essence of democracy.[16] Other politicians and intellectuals, both internally and externally, take a different view, emphasizing that sectarianism essentially maintains separation, not integration, and strengthens the selective memory of each sect. This explains why

Lebanon has not one common history but several histories, corresponding to the number of sects in Lebanon.

Lebanon stands unique in its social as well as its political orientation – a forward-looking liberalism that even 15 years of civil war could not stifle. Accounting for this partly was the geographical isolation of the country during the Ottoman period, which allowed for a certain measure of autonomy. This semi-autonomous status, characterized by pro-Western sentiment on the part of the Maronites, who, until the civil war started in 1975, accounted for almost 50 percent of the population, was strengthened by special ties with Rome. At the end of the sixteenth century, Pope Gregory XIII founded a special seminary for the Maronite clergy. In 1649 this pro-Western orientation was further strengthened when the Ottoman sultan permitted King Louis XII of France to "adopt" the Maronites. To this day the Maronites refer to France as al-Um al-Hanoon, the "gentle Mother."[17]

It was thus natural for Lebanon to adopt a liberal constitution in 1926, which has survived in a variety of revisions.[18] In conjunction with the constitution, relations between the different sects were organized along the lines of the unwritten National Pact of 1943, whereby the Maronites promised to forgo their traditional dependence on France and the Muslims promised to forgo their desire for a union with Syria.

Sectarianism spelled out the division of power within the state: positions in government were distributed in accordance to sects. The president was a Maronite, the prime minister a Sunni, the speaker of parliament a Shia', and the ratio of Christian to Muslim deputies in parliament was to be 6:5. Other executive and administrative positions within the state were divided in a similar fashion.[19] At the same time, the 1943 constitution stipulated that all Lebanese were equal, regardless of the sect they belonged to.

Following the civil war, the parliament met in Taif on 24 October 1989. It reached the Agreement that kept the presidency as the prerogative of the Maronites, the prime minister a Sunni, the speaker of parliament a Shia', while this time dividing the seats in parliament equally between the Muslim and Christian sects. As a result, Salim al-Hoss, who would later become prime minister, emphasized that, although Lebanon offers some political freedoms, there is little democracy.[20] He also criticized the system as undemocratic, stating that although Lebanon has 18 officially recognized sects, one monopolizes the presidency, only three can assume the three other prominent posts, and only eight can assume a ministerial post. The remaining sects have no chance of assuming any of the high state offices.[21] Although the composition of the population has changed, with the Christian sects now a minority, this unusual and anachronistic system is still maintained. It is important at this juncture to emphasize that sectarianism, which is a carryover and a legacy from the traditional Ottoman *millet* (communal system), is not confined to the political dimension of life but informs the social dimension as well. The different sects are independent in personal matters.[22]

It is important to note that the Lebanese brand of liberalism, which is enshrined in the sectarian system, is a unique experiment. Its continued survival and resilience are living proof that democracy has as many faces as it has interpretations. Democracy, after all, is designed to structure the distribution of power and authority in a rational, representative, and just manner. The objective factors behind the distribution and division of power must ultimately reflect the countervailing interests and forces within society.

Although each sect internally maintains its spiritual separateness, at the same time there exists a Lebanese sense of loyalty and belonging. Especially since the civil war few Lebanese harbor any serious attachment or sense of belonging to places other than Lebanon. This factor alone distinguishes Lebanon from Syria, where a sense of identity is still in the process of formation, or Jordan, where the Palestinian factor is hampering the development of a sense of Jordanian identity. In all three states, however, the process is ongoing, and the dialectic is constantly at work. In all countries under consideration it is safe to say that, although the apparatus of the state is well advanced, a sense of nationhood has not yet matured.

In spite of the terrible civil war, the Lebanese sense of nationhood remains more prominent than that of Syria or Jordan. The state has developed into a nation with strong feelings of belonging. This has undoubtedly been strengthened by the country's free press, a functioning parliament, and a more advanced sense of civil society. It is not only the constitution that accounts for this atmosphere of political freedom, but also the modern participatory system, in which the head of state and other politicians realize that their power, indeed their sphere of influence and operation, is governed and limited by the power of other groups and parties. Very limited room is available to the president to act freely or to manipulate, as occurs in both Jordan and Syria. In Lebanon, groups, parties, and sects compete, and, within each of these, individuals also compete for primacy and ascendancy.

Jordan

Since its establishment as a modern nation-state in 1921, Jordan's political life, and indeed its socio-economic development, have been dominated by the personalities of King Abdullah I, founding father of the kingdom, his grandson King Hussein, and, since February 1999, his great grandson King Abdullah II. The Hashemite lineage and the legacy of the Great Arab Revolt confer on the Jordanian regime a secular as well as a religious aura of legitimacy. This legitimacy has been further buttressed by the sustained effort by the Jordanian government to maintain a liberal atmosphere and the attempt to institutionalize the country's democratic structures.

In spite of the crisis atmosphere that continues to engulf the region, the Jordanian experiment to bring about good governance through the institutionalization of a rational, moderate political system has been steady. The process was at times more formal, reflecting no doubt the heat and the intensity of the crisis at that particular historical moment. Yet resort to violent and repressive measures, except in very brief emergency situations, was rare.[23]

The present 1952 liberal constitution of Jordan, which amended the more conservative document of 1946, outlines the structure and the distribution of power in Jordan. Alongside it, a patriarchal style of governance dominated by the king has emerged, which was no doubt the result of the semi-primitive socio-economic and political conditions of the country in the early days of the establishment of the state. Although Jordan has experienced tremendous strides in its socio-economic development from its original simple social structure, the traditional symbolism of the primacy of the patriarch has not diminished.

Unlike both Syria and Lebanon, Jordan's population is basically a homogeneous Arab Sunni society, with a small minority of about 6–7 percent Christian Arabs and yet smaller minorities of Circassians and Chechens. The election law provides for the proportional representation of these three minorities, as well as for the Bedouins. Currently, there is a considerable debate in Jordan concerning the wisdom of such a quota system, or indeed its necessity. Debate is also raging about whether women should be guaranteed a quota in view of the election of only one woman to the twelfth parliament, elected in 1989, and of the failure to elect any women to the thirteenth and current parliament.

Jordan's political life, like that of Syria and Lebanon, also continues to be affected by the trials and tribulations of the Arab–Israeli conflict. For Jordan especially, the Palestine question is both a domestic and a foreign policy issue. This is explained partly by the fact that the population is divided almost equally between what were once called East and West Bankers, and partly by geographical proximity and the historical association between Jordan and Palestine. Until a comprehensive, final, and just settlement of the Arab–Israeli conflict is reached, including not only a settlement with the Palestinians but also settlements with Syria and

Lebanon, the politics of Jordan, indeed of the entire Arab world, will continue to be erratic. Should the countries of the region become free of the fetters and the entanglements of the Arab–Israeli conflict, the chances for the establishment and success of liberal systems will be greatly enhanced. Until then, the factors of geography, demography, and history will continue to cast their heavy shadow on the politics of both Jordan and the region, giving sustenance to peace rejectionists, radicals, and political Islamists.[24]

Jordan's democratization process may have been more formal at some times than at others, but the non-violent liberal style of governance and atmosphere has rarely been abandoned. Jordan is unique in that the Islamists have always been able not only to exist but also to function openly, holding rallies, publishing newspapers, and putting up candidates for parliament. Between 1958 and 1993, when political parties were officially banned and martial law existed, repression, as practiced in other third world regimes, was kept to an absolute minimum. None lost their lives because of politics, and in fact the supposedly banned political parties continued to operate. In the by-elections to parliament in 1984 and then in the elections of 1989, opposition parties openly entered the race with their own candidates.

Jordan's pragmatic, centrist, non-violent regime has other attributes that allowed it not only to survive but also to prosper and possibly become a model for other Arab regimes to study and emulate. It is thus one of the few regimes in the third world that allows opposition movements to survive, and that purposefully maintains a dialogue with them. Jordan has also managed to co-opt some of its most prominent opposition leaders to become some of the most loyal defenders of the regime.

Over the years, once-rebellious "free officers," Ba'thists, communists, Islamists, and various types of nationalist pan-Arabists have been rehabilitated to assume some of the highest political and security positions in the state apparatus. These include the sensitive positions of ministers of Foreign Affairs and of the Interior, and chief of the state security and police and public security departments. Once reabsorbed into the system, they have become elements of the regime's resilience and strength.

The factors of lenient and enlightened governance have of course been sustained by the longevity, style, pragmatism, and legitimacy of the Hashemite leadership. Abdullah I ruled from 1921 to 1951, Hussein from 1953 to 1999, with the short rule of King Talal in between, and King Abdullah II from February 1999. The common denominator of the four monarchs has been a patient, mild, pragmatic, and non-violent patriarchal system. Each in his own way has addressed the people as "My Jordanian Family." The monarchy and the institution of the throne have become the rallying point of Jordanian politics and a nascent sense of

Jordanian nationhood and belonging is emerging. No doubt this sense of belonging and national unity will be enhanced once the Palestinian–Israeli conflict is resolved and an independent Palestinian state becomes part of the state system of the region.

The merits of the Jordanian approach

Of course if one were to adhere strictly to the restricted definitions of democracy offered by some intellectuals, Jordan's democratization process might be called a merely "defensive democratization" process. Such narrow definitions, however, emanate from a strictly Western orientation, and do not take into account either the time factor or the circumstances.[25]

Robinson's understanding of the democratization process is essentially a bottom–up process in which social changes instigate institutional reform. This was true of the experience in the West where social classes, indeed the great upheavals of the age of enlightenment, either preceded the existence of the modern nation-state or were independent of it. Neither the capitalist revolution nor the processes of socio-political and economic development were initiated by the state. This is not the case in Jordan, or indeed in most developing countries, where the government initiated the processes of socio-political and economic development. In fact, without the very prominent role that the state continues to take in the process of development it would be difficult to see how these societies would move forward. It is also important to note that Jordan and for that matter Syria and Lebanon, as well as most Arab societies, do not have Western societies' class structure and refined division of labor. The social structure in Arab societies in transition is extremely fluid, making party differentiation along socio-economic interests and lines very difficult. This explains at least in part why most Jordanian parties, and Arab political parties in general, are very broad-based and inclusive. This also explains why the parties continue to fail "to influence the political behavior of the citizens."[26]

The question of democratization in Jordan should go beyond whether it adheres to criteria developed in the West over a long period of time, and consider whether there is respect for human rights and a genuine attempt to increase the process of participation. Jordanian society, semi-primitive when the state was established in 1921, found itself suddenly in the twentieth century with hardly any experience in governance. From day one of its existence, Jordan was almost always in the eye of the storm of the Palestine question and, later, the Arab–Israeli conflict. Considering the confluence of internal pressure for development and external challenges, it had to steer a slow but sustained course toward democracy.

Notes

1. See Fuad Zakaria, "The Rise of Illiberal Democracy," *Foreign Affairs*, vol. 76, November–December, 1997, pp. 22–43. See also Quintan Wiktorowicz, "The Limits of Democracy in the Middle East: The Case of Jordan," *Middle East Journal*, vol. 53, no. 4, Autumn 1999, pp. 606–20; Beverly Milton-Edwards, "Façade Democracy and Jordan," *British Journal of Middle Eastern Studies*, vol. 20, no. 2, 1993, pp. 191–203; and Iliya Harik, "Pluralism in the Arab world," *Journal of Democracy*, vol. 5, no. 3, July 1994, pp. 43–56.
2. The only possible exception is Lebanon, during the period between the mid-1950s until the outbreak of the civil war in 1975, and the presently emerging opposition and its acceptance in Jordan. In the first weeks of January 2000 a heated debate between opposition elements and the prime minister took place. Opposition deputies accused the prime minister and his family of engaging in corruption and demanded his resignation, which he resisted; they also demanded that the judiciary should investigate the matter. Such a debate is unprecedented in any Arab country, where opposition is usually repressed by violence. The event was hailed by many Arab intellectuals as a great step forward toward a genuine democratization process in Jordan.
3. See *Jordan Times*, 13 January 2000, p. 1; Abdelfattah Rashdan, "Recent Developments in Democratization in the Middle East: The Case of Jordan," *METU Studies in Development*, vol. 3, 1997, pp. 413–28.
4. Quintan Wiktorowicz states: "I use the term democracy to denote a political system where popular political participation, civil liberties, and civil rights are protected by law and the enforcement of that law," in "The Limits of Democracy in the Middle East: The Case of Jordan," p. 606.
5. For a distinction between what is meant by democracy and by liberalism, see Zakaria, "The Rise of Illiberal Democracy," pp. 22–43; and Marc Piattner, "From Liberalism to Liberal Democracy," *Journal of Democracy*, vol. 10, no. 3, July 1999, pp. 121–34. Most Arab countries go through the process of electing deputies to a legislative assembly, which is given different names in each country. However, many of these assemblies are no more than a rubber stamp to legitimize the actions of the executive branch. Debates are a mere formality. In essence many are arenas for the executive to present issues to the public through the legislature and give them some publicity. Exceptions where genuine debate occurs are Jordan and Lebanon.
6. The term "institutionalization" is used here to denote a process whereby decisions in public life are taken not by an individual but through a formalized rational procedure in a freely elected legislative body.
7. The term "liberality" refers to a certain measure of liberalism in the conduct of public life.
8. The situation may be similar to that in some European monarchical regimes of the nineteenth century that later evolved into liberal democracies.
9. On this point see Wiktorowicz, "The Limits of Democracy in the Middle East," p. 608, and also Glenn Robinson, who calls Jordan's liberalization "defensive democratization" in "Defensive Democratization in Jordan," *International Journal of Middle East Studies*, vol. 30, 1998, pp. 387–410.
10. In most Arab countries the presence of a constitution does not necessarily guarantee human rights in general or the freedom of expression in particular. At times a particular regime may allow a certain space for debate and opposing opinions; yet that depends on the mood of the day and can change at any time.
11. See David Roberts, "The Background and the Role of the Ba'th in Syria," presented at the conference on "Politics and the Economy in Syria," London, SOAS, 20 May 1987; "The Republic of Syria," in Don Peretz, *The Middle East Today*, 4th edn, New York: Praeger, 1983, pp. 396–427.

12. Article 8 of the Syrian constitution identifies the Ba'th as the leading party in society and the state through the mechanism of a National Front which includes other parties. See also Roberts, "The Background and the Role of the Ba'th in Syria," p. 100.

13. For a discussion of the Alewites see *Al-Mawsu'ah al-Syasiyyah* [The Political Encyclopedia], vol. 4, Beirut: Al-Mu'assaseh al-Arabiyyah li al-Dirasat wa al-Nashr, 1995, p. 181. See also S. al-Din Ibrahim, *Al-Milal wa al-Nihal wa al-Araq: Humoom al-Aqqliyyafi al-watan al-Arabi* [*Millets*, Creeds, and Ethnicity: Worries of the Minorities in the Arab World], Cairo: Ibn Khaldun Center for Developmental Studies, 1994, p. 82.

14. For further details see Kamel Abu Jaber, *The Arab Ba'th Socialist Party: History, Ideology and Organization*, Syracuse: Syracuse University Press, 1986. Also Roberts, "The Background and the Role of the Ba'th in Syria," pp. 101–4; Mustafah Al-Filali, "Al-Democratiyyah wa Tajribat al-Hizb al-Wahid fi al-watan al-Arabi-I'tibarat Nazariyyah [Democracy and the System of One Party State in the Arab World: Theoretical Considerations]," in *Azamat al-Democratiyyah fi al-Watan al-Arabi* [The Crisis of Democracy in the Arab World], Symposium Proceedings, Beirut: Markiz Dirasat al-Wihdah al-Arabiyyah, 1987.

15. See "President Lahhoud is a Maronite," *Al-Hawadith*, 22 October 1999, p. 10. In the same issue and in a separate interview with a member of parliament, Marwan Hamadeh emphasizes the need to maintain Lebanon's "balance" by adhering to the Taif Agreement (pp. 22–3).

16. See M. Edde, "Al-Democratiyyah was al-Salam Bina' Qawmi [Democracy and Peace: A Daily Affair]," in Antoine Mossarah, *Al-Bina' al-Democrati: Al-Ishkaliyyah wa al-Takhtit li Luban Ba'd al-Harb* [The Democratic Edifice: The Problem and the Planning for Lebanon after the War], Beirut: al-Mu'assaseh al-ahliyyah li al-Siem al-Ahli, 1994, p. 17.

17. For a quick historical overview, see "The Republic of Lebanon," in Don Peretz, *The Middle East Today*, pp. 358–95.

18. Ibid., p. 365.

19. Ibrahim, *Al-Milal wa al-Nihal wa al-Araq: Humoom al-Aqqliyyafi al-watan al-Arabi*, pp. 572, 590. See also Article 95 of the constitution.

20. In a lecture at the Shoman Foundation in Amman entitled "Al-Demogratiyyah fi Lubanan [Democracy in Lebanon]," *Al-Mustaqbal al-Arabi*, vol. 7, no. 64, June 1984.

21. "Al-Huriyyat wa al-Democratiyyah fi Lubnan [Freedoms and Democracy in Lebanon]," *Al-Mustaqbal al-Arabi*, vol. 7, no. 64, June 1984, p. 137.

22. See B. Hashem, "Al-Tawaif wa al-Tawa'ifiyyah fi Lubnan: Hal Min Makhraj [Sects and Sectarianism in Lebanon: Is There an Exit?]," in Massarah, "*Al-Bina' al-Democrati*," pp. 119–22; see also Article 9 of the constitution.

23. See Kamel Abu Jaber, *Tajribat al-Hukm fi al-Urdun* [Jordan's Experience in Governance], Amman, Jordan: Jordan Institute of Diplomacy Occasional Papers, 1999.

24. A number of fine studies have been published on the socio-economic development of Jordan. Two are of particular relevance: Arthur Day, *East Bank/West Bank*, New York: Council on Foreign Relations, 1986; and Valerie York, *Domestic Politics and Regional Security: Jordan, Syria and Lebanon*, Brookfield, VT: Gower Publishing Company, 1988.

25. See Wiktorowicz "The Limits of Democracy in the Middle East," and Robinson, "Defensive Democratization in Jordan." See also Rashdan, "Recent Developments in Democratization," for a milder critique of Jordan's democratization process. The time factor refers to the time it takes for the idea of true democracy really to take root, and the circumstances refer to the need for a certain level of education and standard of living, and for a process of acculturation, for the idea of democracy to take root in a traditional society undergoing a transition from one mode of life to another.

26. See the interesting study by Maher Masis, "Jordan: A Study of Attitudes toward Democratic Change," *Arab Studies Quarterly*, vol. 30, no. 3, 1998, pp. 37–63.

8

"Democratic peace" and the Jewish political tradition

Gerald M. Steinberg

In considering the relationship between democracy and religion in the Middle East in the context of "democratic peace" theories, Israel is clearly a unique case. The political institutions of the modern state of Israel – a "Jewish state" (or a state for the Jews) in a region characterized by states in which Islam is the official religion and dominant culture – were modeled on the conceptions developed in Europe during the late nineteenth century. As a result, democratic institutions and principles are an integral part of the Israeli political culture, in a manner that is fundamentally different from that of the rest of the region.

The effort to merge the long and complex Jewish tradition with Western liberal democracy created considerable tension in Israeli society. The Jewish population (which constitutes 80 percent of the total and is the main focus of this chapter) is sharply divided between secular and religious communities. The religious or traditional sector, constituting between 20 percent and 60 percent of the population (depending on definitions and issues), is itself split across a number of dimensions (national religious, ultra-orthodox, Sephardic, etc.) but is characterized in general by a major emphasis on Jewish history and tradition. Historically, the acceptance of divine authority is at the core of Jewish practices and beliefs. According to most rabbinical edicts, in clashes between religious requirements and the demands of secular political leaders or institutions, the former must prevail. In recent years, the increasing role of the secular court system in Israeli society has led to major protests and mass demonstrations involving religious opponents and secular supporters.

Following the 1991 Madrid Middle East Peace Conference and the 1993 Declaration of Principles (the "Oslo" agreement), the discourse in Israel has focused increasingly on the intersection and interaction between democracy, the Jewish tradition, and peace negotiations. The changing relationship between these three central aspects of Israeli society, and the tension between them, is reflected in many areas and dimensions. Israeli political and religious leaders, as well as educators and journalists, often address themselves to the relationship between these factors.[1]

The uniqueness of the Israeli case is also the result of the religious tradition that emphasizes the centrality of the Land of Israel. Jewish sovereignty and settlement in this Land, based on the biblical Covenant, beginning with Abraham, and associated religious commandments, are fundamental aspects of the tradition. As a result, changes in the status of the territory and, in particular, the exchange of "land for peace" are very important religious issues to many Israelis.

In this context, the roles of democracy and secular political institutions are sources of intense controversy, both within the religious community and between this sector and secular Israeli society. The 1993 Oslo agreement and subsequent pacts unleashed an intense and often violent debate. While opponents closed highways and sought to prevent implementation of the agreements, proponents accused them of using violent and undemocratic means to obstruct the policies of the government chosen by the majority in a democratic and free election. In response, critics of the process, both religious and secular, argued that, despite the formal trappings of democracy, the broader concepts of transparency, accountability, free and open debate, and minority rights are not always respected or even recognized by a narrow political elite.

Criticism was exacerbated by a political system that focused power in the hands of a few individuals, elected indirectly. Until 1996, the prime minister was the head of the party that succeeded in building a governing coalition in the Knesset (the Israeli parliament). Because the government has a parliamentary majority in the Knesset, this legislative body does not play an effective role in terms of checks and balances. For some religious Israelis, the narrowly secular government lacked a mandate for the far-reaching changes embodied in the Oslo agreements. (The secrecy of the negotiations and the sudden reversal of long- and strongly held policies that had prohibited any contact with the Palestine Liberation Organization contributed to the intensity of the disaffection among opponents.) Others rejected the authority of the government to make decisions that violated religious precepts regarding the sanctity of the Land.

The assassination of Prime Minister Rabin in November 1995 occurred in the context of these conflicts. This tragedy, in turn, triggered a national re-examination of the different strands and interpretations of the Jewish tradition, the relationship between the Jewish and democratic aspects of Israeli society, and the impact of the peace process. As a result of these events, the roles of pluralism and democracy are increasingly the subjects of discussions and debates within religious society.[2] Interpretations of Jewish tradition and law (*halacha*) that stress the legitimacy of pluralism and secular democratic government are gaining support. In addition, a number of rabbis and religious intellectuals have stressed the need to balance the importance of sovereignty in the Land of Israel with the precepts emphasizing peace and the preservation of human life (*pikuach nefesh*). Indeed, the external events related to the Middle East peace efforts triggered an intense internal debate on the interpretation of the Jewish tradition. The results of this debate, as well as the substance of the negotiation process and the developments toward democracy and pluralism in neighboring Islamic states, will also determine the future policies that are adopted by Israel.

Nationalism and democracy in Israeli society

As an ethno-national community unified by an ancient religious tradition, and tracing its legitimacy to events that took place over 2,000 years ago, Israel is an exceptional political entity.[3] The foundations of the Zionist movement and the modern state of Israel are based on a combination of both ancient Jewish and modern Western political traditions. In Jewish history, the concept of a nation-state long predates modern nationalism, which developed in the wake of the French Revolution.[4] Indeed, the principle of national sovereignty in a territorial state with defined borders is inherent in centuries of Jewish history and tradition. According to Jewish commentators, the objective of the biblical narrative from Genesis through the Exodus and the wandering in the desert is to establish the rights of the Jewish people to sovereignty in the Land of Israel.[5] These concepts remained central to Jewish philosophy and practice during 2,000 years of exile following the destruction of Jerusalem and the Roman conquest.

With the modern revival of Jewish nationalism, nineteenth- and twentieth-century Zionism was also strongly influenced by modern democracy and nationalism. Many of Israel's secular "founding fathers," who were responsible for forming its political institutions, came from Eastern Europe, and they incorporated many of the concepts and institutions that were then current. The governmental system is a parliamentary democracy with universal suffrage, and the basic freedoms of speech and of the press are protected under law. Furthermore, the North American and European Jewish Diasporas are strongly committed to democratic norms, and their close links with and strong influence in Israel have reinforced these norms.[6]

However, for over 50 years, during both the pre-state and post-independence periods, most aspects of Israeli society were controlled by a single dominant group, embodied in Mapai (the Israeli Workers' Party). As Yonathan Shapiro has noted, Israeli political processes were characterized by procedural democracy based on majoritarian hegemony, in contrast to pluralistic liberal democracy and the protection of minority rights.[7] The power structure controlled all aspects of public life (the economy, the media, health care, education, and even sports and entertainment), and often furthered its objectives through illegal and less than democratic means.[8] This elite was also militantly secular, substituting socialist Zionism and statism for religious tradition.[9]

The dominance of the Labor Party was broken in 1977 (following the "earthquake" of the 1973 War), but narrow electoral victories in 1992 and 1999 revived the tendency toward formal majoritarian definitions of democracy, in which concepts of minority rights and consensus based on compromise and pluralism are often overwhelmed. On issues of religious tradition in the public sphere, religious Israelis often feel that they have been relegated to the status of a "besieged minority." Similarly, the ultra-orthodox majorities in parts of Jerusalem, Bnai Brak, and other areas are often intolerant with respect to secular and even other religious groups.

The nature of the Israeli population and the lack of experience with democratic institutions have constituted an additional obstacle to the adoption of more pluralistic and tolerant norms. Following the establishment of the state of Israel in 1948, the Israeli population increased tenfold, from 600,000 to over 6 million. During the 1950s and 1960s, many of these immigrants were Jewish refugees from the Middle East (from North Africa to Iraq and Iran); later, the majority of immigrants came from the former Soviet Union. The vast majority had no previous exposure to liberal democracy. Although participation in party politics and elections is very high (often exceeding 90 percent of the eligible voters, excluding those abroad at the time, as Israel has no provisions for absentee voting), the strong emotions regarding the expression of opposing views, and, in some cases, the violence that has characterized election campaigns, may be attributable to the briefness of the democratic tradition.

Immigrants were absorbed into a political culture that used elections and political processes as vehicles for dominance and control over the allocation of public resources. As these groups formed their own parties and developed political power (that is, Shas or Russian parties), they have followed this pattern, seeking to use the process to enhance narrow sectoral interests. As a result, although democratic processes and institutions are firmly entrenched, pluralistic institutions and norms remain relatively weak and vulnerable.

Religion and democracy in Israel

Zionism is rooted deeply in Jewish tradition, and the concept of "Return to the Land of Israel" was nurtured as a central aspect of religious precept and practice during 2,000 years of exile. The conditions required for the Return were heatedly debated throughout this period, with some religious authorities supporting individual *aliya* (literally, "going up") from exile to the Land in a practical sense. Their opponents prohibited this, requiring divine intervention and restoration of the Temple in Jerusalem (which, according to one interpretation, would descend as a complete entity from heaven) prior to the end of exile. However, throughout this period, the concept of the Return remained a central precept of the Jewish religion.[10] As Rabbi Zvi Yehuda Kook wrote, "[t]he quintessential value of the entire Torah, including its commandments that are not dependent on Eretz Israel, lies in the Land of Israel."[11]

With the inception of political Zionism, these approaches were also manifested in the attitudes of religious groups. In 1948, the Declaration of Independence proclaimed Israel as *Medinat HaYehudim* – a Jewish state – founded on the principles of liberty, justice, and peace as conceived by the Prophets of Israel, and guaranteeing the full social and political equality of all its citizens.[12] (Christians, Muslims, Druze, and others are acknowledged as members of minority groups in the predominantly Jewish environment. From the Jewish perspective, the Arab–Israeli conflict is not the result of religious antagonism. Judaism and Jewish tradition view Islam in a positive light, in part because Islam is monotheistic and is based on Jewish precepts and texts,[13] and in part because Jews have been treated relatively well under Islamic rule, despite being relegated to second-class status as *dhimmis*.)

From the beginning of the Zionist movement, Jewish society in Israel has been divided between religious and secular communities, and each group, as well as the numerous subgroups, has held strong ideological and value-oriented views on the future of Israel and the Jewish people. For religious Israelis, the state of Israel was seen as the seed from which the Jewish nation would re-emerge following the decimation of the Jewish people in the twentieth century, culminating in the Holocaust. Indeed, in Jewish tradition, the return to the Land of Israel and an end to the exile were equated with Messianic redemption. In this context, the religious Zionists (Mizrachi) saw the establishment of a sovereign Jewish state as marking the first steps in this redemption.[14] In a manner consistent with this view, the physical return to the Land was seen as requiring and providing the conditions for a religious framework for society. "The religious Zionist sees no justification for a separation between national social life and [Jewish law]."[15]

In the first decades following independence, the tension between the Jewish and secular democratic (majoritarian) emphases was reflected in the difficulties in developing national policies in a number of areas of friction. These included education, personal status (marriage, divorce, burial, etc.), kosher food regulations, and the operation of public services on the Sabbath (transportation, entertainment, etc.).[16] Continuing the Ottoman *millet* system, personal status was regulated according to membership of a particular recognized religious group (Jewish, Catholic, Protestant, Muslim, Druze, etc.), and every citizen was expected to be a member of one of these groups. Separate secular and religious (rabbinical for the majority Jewish population) court systems were established, as was a Chief Rabbinate, all financed by the state. Religious Israeli children attended separate religious schools, whereas secular Israelis attended secular schools. Equal status was an important principle but, in contrast to Western liberal democratic norms, this equality was group based and not individual. Each person was entitled to rights and bound by obligations as a member of a recognized religious group.

During this period, efforts to develop a written constitution failed owing to differences over the official status of the Rabbinate and fundamental principles relating to the nature of a Jewish state and the role of the religious establishment.[17] The "ultra-orthodox" community did not (and does not) recognize the legitimacy of the secular state and, in contrast to the "modern orthodox" approach, linked political salvation, in the form of restored Jewish sovereignty in the Land of Israel, with religious salvation. For some, a secular Jewish state was and is considered an abomination.[18]

In the absence of agreement, the Knesset began to adopt a series of Basic Laws dealing with specific issues and institutions, which formed the constitutional skeleton. In many cases, the drafting and adoption of these Basic Laws were also the result of negotiation and compromise between the religious and secular factions in the Knesset.

In order to avoid internal divisions during the 1948 Arab–Israeli war, which threatened national survival, conflicts in this area were resolved by acceptance of the status quo in areas of disagreement. Thus, for example, the separate school systems that had existed during the Mandate period were continued, and the level of official Sabbath observance with respect to public transportation, which varied from place to place (the buses operated on the Sabbath in Haifa but not in Jerusalem or Tel Aviv), was continued. In a broader sense, the Israeli political system was consociational in nature, incorporating different groups (cleavages) into the government by dividing resources among the groups, while allowing each group a high level of internal autonomy.[19]

Beyond these specific policy differences, the role of democracy and the authority of the secular political system are also points of contention. Commentators note that the Jewish tradition and religion are not, per se, anti-democratic, and the governing concept of a covenant between the people (*edah*) and God is central.[20] Popular acceptance and ratification of rulers, including kings, are an important norm with roots in biblical and Talmudic sources. The tradition and legal framework emphasize popular participation in government,[21] and in later periods many Jewish communities adopted democratic practices.[22]

The Bible and the Talmud (Tractate Sanhedrin) also emphasize the importance of establishing a clear and accepted political authority, and a number of passages suggest that, even during Talmudic times, democratic concepts were important. Jewish sages declared that the legitimacy of different forms of government is based on first securing the consent of the governed.[23] During the Mandate period, Chief Rabbi Avraham Yitzchak Hacohen Kook and other authorities expanded the traditional frameworks to include a democratic state and its president or prime minister.[24]

However, as Schweid notes, "there is a substantial difference between socio-religious democracy, which in the Jewish religion carries a significant portion of its values, and secular democracy, which was adopted recently as the basis for government on the basis of external European origins ... Religious democracy is based on the concept of the supremacy of the Torah, whose authority is super-human (al enoshi)." It is up to the human leaders (rabbis, prophets, etc.) to interpret the words of the Torah and to make the legal rulings on this basis, but they receive their authority, or are recognized by the religious institutions, consistent with popular will. "In this sense, democracy is expressed in the requirement that the religious leadership respond to the legitimate demands of the populace, on the one hand, and from the popular desire to obey the rulings of the religious leaders according to Torah principles, on the other."[25] According to Liebman,[26] in principle the differences are sharper, but in most cases "[t]here is no major or peculiar incompatibility between halakah and democracy in practice because Jewish law is subject to interpretation."[27]

As a result of both religious/ideological and political/cultural factors, the consociational model appears to be weakening, and the clash between the secular and religious norms has become particularly pronounced.[28] The expanded authority and scope taken on by the secular court system in the past decade have contributed to the undermining of the status quo. Under the influence of Judge Aharon Barak (Chief Justice of the High Court of Appeal), the courts have entered into areas and assumed powers that had, in the past, been rejected by the secular courts as outside their areas of jurisdiction. The secular courts have ruled on cases pertaining to religious conversion practices, property division in divorce, public allocations to religious institutions, and other areas that had previously been considered "off limits." In response, religious (primarily, but not exclusively, ultra-orthodox) groups organized protest movements, and in 1999 over 100,000 people participated in a major rally in Jerusalem. The ultra-orthodox groups have also sought to use their political power in the Knesset and the government to trim the powers of the secular courts. Thus, the nature of Israeli democracy is still highly dynamic and evolving.

Religion, democracy, and the peace process

In the first two decades of Israeli statehood, foreign and security policy (issues of war and peace) did not play a significant role in the religious–secular debate. The armistice lines resulting from the 1948 War created the territorial boundaries of the state of Israel, and the question of settlement outside these lines was moot.[29] The prospects for formal peace were also remote, given the widespread Arab rejection of the legitimacy of the state of Israel and repeated vows to destroy the Jewish state.[30] In this period, frequent cross-border terror attacks, Israeli military responses, and periodic wars were the dominant elements of the political environment.

This situation changed radically following the 1967 War, in which the Israeli forces took control of East Jerusalem and the West Bank areas that were occupied and then annexed by Jordan in 1948–9. These areas, known to Israelis as Judea and Samaria (based on their biblical names), include many biblical sites, such as Hebron, Bethlehem, Beth El, Shechem (Nablus in Arabic), which had been closed to Jews since 1948.

The return to the ancient Jewish quarter of Jerusalem and the Temple Mount was of great historic and religious importance. This small area contains the remains of Solomon's Temple, the Second Temple, as well as synagogues and other sacred sites. Throughout the 2,000 years of exile, Jews continued to pray daily for the restoration of Jerusalem, and Jewish weddings include a ritual in which a glass is broken to symbolize mourning for Jerusalem. The loss of this area during the 1948 War and the subsequent destruction and desecration of much of the Jewish quarter were and continue to be a source of contention and emotion.[31]

For many members of the religious community in Israel, the outcome of the 1967 War provided a divinely ordained opportunity to re-establish

Jewish control over the Sacred City of Jerusalem and all of the Land of Israel, and to observe the religious commandments that pertained to this Land. Settlement in these areas became the primary objective for religious nationalists but not, at the time, for the ultra-orthodox (Haredi) communities – as will be discussed in detail below.

The results of the 1967 War also changed Israeli democracy in a fundamental manner, and altered the approach of the religious sectors of society with respect to issues of security, territory, and borders. Immediately after the 1967 War ended, movements were organized with the goal of building Jewish settlements in the captured areas, including Sinai, the Golan, and the West Bank. These settler movements included many religious Jews, but this was not an exclusively religious cause and also encompassed secular Israelis. However, the religious parties and leaders were prominent, and their role increased over time.

Their political power was enhanced by the stalemate between the two secular political blocs (Labor/Left and Likud/Right). The religious parties, and the National Religious Party (NRP) in particular, used this power to lobby the government to provide incentives for the settlements, and they consistently worked to expand and strengthen Jewish sovereignty and control in these areas. (Initially, the secular community was divided, with some joining forces with the religious settlement movement to form the Greater Land of Israel Movement, while others called for withdrawal from the "Occupied Territories" in the context of a peace treaty.)

Shortly after the 1967 War, Rabbi Zvi Yehuda Kook published a list of biblical quotations and passages to demonstrate that withdrawal from "the eternal land of our forefathers" was prohibited under religious law and unacceptable.[32] Members of the Gush Emunim movement declared that "in the Jewish tradition lies the key to the understanding of the uniqueness and mission of the people and the Land of Israel ... Forfeiting Jewish roots puts into question the very value of Israel's survival and their adherence to Eretz Israel."[33]

From this perspective, democratic procedures, particularly with respect to settlement activities, were not central considerations. Settlements were established without the permission of the government, and led to intermittent confrontations with the police and army (for example, Sebastia, 1974; later known as Kadum and Elon Moreh). The settlers were often able to negotiate a compromise, allowing them to maintain a presence on state-owned land nearby, and eventually growing into larger settlements.[34] Although religious objectives were given priority over obedience to the law, the culture of "illegalism," fostered by the secular founders of Zionism and Israel, also contributed to this pattern of behavior.[35]

The tension between democracy and religious hierarchy in the context of Middle East peace negotiations increased during the negotiations between Egypt and Israel following the 1978 Camp David Accords, and the agreement by the Israeli government to dismantle settlements in the Sinai. Although the Yamit settlement and the rest of Sinai are outside the biblical boundary of the Land of Israel, religious Jews and rabbis led the protests and resistance efforts, in large part to demonstrate their commitment to maintaining control over the settlements in Judea and Samaria.

At the time, the Israeli government was headed by Menachem Begin and the Likud Party, and the National Religious Party was a member of the ruling coalition. This government could not be accused of being militantly secular and anti-religious or oblivious to Jewish values and history. Nevertheless, the confrontations with the government (including the army sent to dismantle the settlements) were very intense and often violent. The religious leaders declared that the secular political power structure lacked the authority to violate Jewish law. This group called on soldiers to ignore government orders to dismantle settlements, rather than violate religious edicts.

The confrontations resumed and intensified following the 1993 Oslo agreement, when the territory involved was the heartland of Jewish settlement in Judea and Samaria. The creation of the Palestinian Authority, and the transfer of territory to it, were anathema to the concept of exclusive Jewish sovereignty in the Land of Israel. This situation, combined with the waves of Palestinian suicide bombings and other forms of violence, and the continued rejection of Israeli legitimacy among Palestinians, led to the massive protests that developed in 1994 and 1995. This atmosphere, in turn, provided the background for the assassination of Prime Minister Yitzchak Rabin by a fellow Jew in November 1995.

As the negotiation and implementation of withdrawal agreements proceeded, these issues continued to be highly contentious. However, as will be seen below, the public debate in the Jewish religious community (as distinct from the majority secular and Arab communities in Israel) crystallized into three different approaches.

Three religious responses

The Jewish religion is by no means monolithic, and there are many different schools of interpretation. In a broad sense, the confrontation between religious and democratic authority in Israel generated three responses within the religious authority. Each response emphasizes a different central principle in considering the relative importance of the three primary values: (1) sovereign control over the Land, (2) the sanctity of life and the prevention of war, and (3) the role of democracy and avoidance of civil conflict. (There is also a fourth approach, which opposes maintenance of control over inhabited occupied territories, based on the biblical injunction to treat the stranger with dignity, "for you were strangers in the land of Egypt" (Exodus 22: 21). This approach often overlaps with the third group and will be discussed in a further development of this chapter.)

The primacy of sovereignty over the Land of Israel

The centrality of settlement in the Land of Israel became a major focus of religious nationalist ideology after the 1967 War, and the principle was essential to the rise of the Young Guard in the NRP, beginning in 1963.[36] For this group, settlement in the territories and opposition to any withdrawal are a religious requirement that is not open to compromise and bargaining.[37] The commandment is based on the biblical verse: "And you shall take possession of the land and settle in it, for I have given the land to you to possess it" (Numbers 33: 53).

Building on the commandment to settle the Land, this group relies on the religious messianic ideology of Rabbi Zvi Yehuda Kook, in which the state of Israel is viewed as the beginning of the flowering of Jewish redemption. The Israeli military successes are interpreted in terms of miraculous divine intervention, precisely in order to implement the commandment of settlement in the Land of Israel.[38] Major leaders of this movement include former Chief Rabbis of Israel such as Rabbi Avraham Shapira, Rabbi Haim Druckman, who headed the religious youth group Bnei Akiva, and Yitzchak Levy, head of the NRP and cabinet minister from 1996 until 1998. In addition, some ultra-orthodox groups, such as the Lubovitch (Chabad) movement, have taken a similar position.[39]

In the 1973 elections, a substantial portion of religious Zionists who traditionally supported the NRP voted for other parties, in large part as a result of policies that were not sufficiently vigorous on security policy and support for settlements in the territories. In 1977, however, following a change in leadership and a more "Land of Israel" centered platform, support for the NRP increased.[40] Since then, the NRP has emphasized the territorial issue.

Adherents of this group support a policy that gives priority to Jewish sovereignty in the land and they oppose territorial withdrawal. In 1981–2, following the signing of the Egyptian–Israeli peace treaty and prior to the evacuation of Yamit in the Sinai region, a number of rabbis issued an edict forbidding the transfer of any part of the Land of Israel to non-Jewish control.[41] In 1985, the Council of Jewish Settlements in Judea, Samaria, and Gaza declared that any surrender of territory in these areas would "represent a prima facie annulment of the State of Israel ... whose purpose is to bring Jews to the sovereign Land of Israel."[42]

In December 1993, following the Oslo agreement, the late Rabbi Shlomo Goren, a former Chief Rabbi, published a ruling forbidding Jews to evacuate any settlement in the biblical Land of Israel, which includes Judea, Samaria, and Gaza, and declared that Israeli soldiers should disobey any such evacuation orders: "according to Halacha [Jewish law], a soldier who receives an order that runs contrary to Torah law should uphold the Halacha, and not the secular order. And since settling the land is a commandment, and uprooting the settlements is breaking the commandment, the soldier should not carry out an order to uproot settlements."[43] He was not alone in his opinions, and many other rabbis issued similar statements and rulings.[44]

In April 1994, discussion of possible evacuation of the Jewish residents of Hebron caused a number of rabbis, including Chief Rabbi Avraham Shapira, Rabbi Moshe-Zvi Neria of the Bnei Akiva movement, and Rabbi Shaul Yisraeli, to direct soldiers to reject any order to evacuate Jews from Hebron or other settlements.[45] Citing the religious importance of Hebron to Jews, an NRP member of the Knesset, Hanan Porat, declared that "[t]his would be a palpably illegal order, which I could not carry out, as it goes against my conscience and everything I believe. I would be willing to pay the price by going to jail."[46]

In July 1995, during the intense national debate that took place following the Oslo Declaration of Principles and the Cairo implementation agreements, seven rabbis (eight more joined the ruling later on) belonging to the Council of Religious Zionist Rabbis and headed by former Ashkenazi Chief Rabbi Avraham Shapira issued another religious (halachic) edict. It declared that "there is a Torah prohibition against uprooting [IDF] Israeli Defense Force bases and transferring the sites to Gentiles, since this contravenes a positive [Torah] commandment and also endangers life and the existence of the state."[47]

Subsequently, another decree stated that the peace process would open "the way for [Arabs] to conquer the entire land" and therefore "it is forbidden, under any circumstance, to hand over parts of Eretz Yisrael to Arabs." Rabbi Nachum Rabinovich, head of the Birkat Moshe Yeshiva in Ma'aleh Adumim, and one of the signatories of the ruling, also cited the precept of protecting life. "Wherever the Israeli army pulls out, settlers' lives will be endangered. There is a fundamental moral issue here and the moral law supersedes any government."[48]

These edicts explicitly emphasized the view that rabbinical authority supersedes the secular authority of the government (whether democratic or in any other form). Its authors based their argument on Maimonides (twelfth century, Spain) who wrote that, "[e]ven if the king ordered [one]

to disobey the Torah, he should not be listened to."[49] From this perception, a secular government has no right to violate Jewish law, which
places primacy on control over the Land of Israel.[50] The rabbinical authorities also cited threats to national security resulting from territorial
withdrawal, claiming precedence of their analysis over the judgment of
the professional military and political leaders. This is an extraordinary
development in the context of Jewish religious authority, although consistent with the overall trend toward *daat Torah* – the doctrine that attributes expertise and authority in all public issues to prominent rabbinical figures.[51]

These edicts had a quick and substantive impact. In August 1995, a
soldier was sentenced to 28 days in military jail for refusing to evict settlers encamped without permission near Hebron. He stated that he refused the order on ideological grounds and that he did not join the army
to fight Jews.[52]

The reactions to these developments were intense and came from all
sections of the Israeli population. Secular Israelis generally condemned
the rabbinical edicts; among the religious sectors of society, the responses
were mixed. As will be seen below, many rabbis criticized the edicts for
undermining the military command structure and for paving the way for
anarchy and disorder.

The assassination of Prime Minister Rabin in November 1995 shocked
some leaders and members of this group, and led them to a fundamental
reassessment of philosophy and policy. This process accelerated during
the Netanyahu period (1996–9) and contributed to strengthening the
support for alternative positions within the religious community, as will
be discussed in the following sections.

In the 1999 election campaign, the NRP's more militant supporters of
the settlers and opponents of concessions in the peace process, such as
Hanan Porat, lost power and were replaced by more dovish members of
the party.[53] (Porat then joined a new party, The National Union, which
placed territorial issues at the forefront. This party did quite poorly in the
elections, and Porat resigned his Knesset seat. However, at a later stage,
the NRP leadership asked Rabbi Haim Druckman, whose positions on
territorial issues are similar to those of Porat, to take the second position
on the Knesset list.) At the same time, two alternative approaches based
on Jewish law and tradition were developed and gained strength.

*The primacy of human life and prevention of war over sovereignty
in the Land of Israel*

From the beginning of the Oslo process, some prominent rabbis and religious leaders ruled that, although settling the Land of Israel is an im-

portant commandment, negotiating peace is of even greater importance, citing the importance placed on *pikuach nefesh*, the preservation of human life, in the Torah. They based this ruling on the Biblical verse: "I have put before you life and death, blessing and curse. Choose life – if you and your offspring would live – by loving the Lord your God" (Deuteronomy 30: 19).

This approach was articulated by the late Rabbi Yosef Dov Soloveichik, who lived in the United States and was regarded by many modern orthodox Jews, including Israelis, as the leading authority of his generation. Opposing the rabbinical rulings that gave exclusive emphasis to sovereignty in the Land of Israel, and noting the centrality of *pikuach nefesh*, his view was that policy decisions on these issues are best left to the professional military and political authorities.[54]

Rabbi Ovadia Yosef, the former Sephardic Chief Rabbi of Israel and founder of the Shas political party, adopted a similar position. (Poll data suggest that Shas supporters have tended to be more hawkish than its leadership, but in most cases the voters are willing to accept the religious and political authority of the rabbinical leadership. Shas was a member of the Netanyahu coalition government, but often attempted to exert a moderating influence on policies related to the peace process.) In Rabbi Yosef's opinion, the positive commandment to settle the land is overridden by the commandment to avoid unnecessary loss of life. Thus, he has declared that, "[i]f the heads of the army with the members of the government, declare that lives will be endangered unless territories in the Land of Israel are relinquished, and there is the danger of an immediate declaration of war by the neighboring Arab [states], ... and if territories are relinquished, the danger of war will be removed, and that there are realistic chances of lasting peace, then it appears, according to all the opinions, that it is permissible to relinquish territories of the Land of Israel ... [according to the principle of] pikuach nefesh."[55] In the same discourse, however, Rabbi Yosef noted that military officers, government officials, and security experts are divided and some have concluded that returning territories could increase the dangers to Israel, and that these views should also be considered.

During this period, Rabbi Yosef was also active in meeting with Arab leaders. In July 1989, Rabbi Yosef met with Egyptian President Hosni Mubarak, and in May 1997 a Palestinian official said Yasser Arafat would welcome Rabbi Yosef's help in renewing the stalled peace talks and getting the process back on track.[56]

The members of the Meimad religious group, founded by Rabbi Yehuda Amital, share this position. The Meimad movement began in protest against the 1982 Lebanon war and its aftermath, and some of its members were associated with Netivot Shalom, a small religious group parallel to the secular Peace Now movement, which provided an alternative to groups such as Gush Emunim and the NRP. Meimad became a political party in 1988 but, after a poor showing in the elections, was transformed into an ideological movement in 1992; it was reconstituted as a party in 1999. Its founders included rabbis, academics, and other professionals who were disaffected with the religious establishment. For this group, policy decisions on issues of war and peace made by a democratic government take precedence over edicts of the religious leadership (see the detailed discussion of this position below).

For members of Meimad, religious law does not require opposition to the "land for peace" formula. In contrast to the messianic interpretation, Rabbi Amital declared that the "miracle of the [1967] Six Day War" was not primarily the conquest of the biblical Land of Israel. "People at the time were concerned about another holocaust, they were receiving letters pleading with them to send their children abroad. So when we won the war, it was a feeling of great relief, a feeling that God saved us from destruction. That was the miracle. It had nothing to do with Judea and Samaria."[57]

Based on this perspective, in 1993–4, Meimad supported the Oslo process, and in the 1996 elections its leaders endorsed the Labor Party and Shimon Peres. Similarly, in 1999 the leadership endorsed Ehud Barak for the office of prime minister, and entered the "One Israel" list (based on the Labor Party). As a result, Meimad placed one member in the Knesset, and joined the governing coalition, and Rabbi Michael Melchoir also became a government minister responsible for religious–secular relations. This process reflected the gradual increase in the relative strength of the approach that places the principle of *pikuach nefesh* (preservation of life) above that of sovereign control over the Land of Israel.

In 2001, following the collapse of the Oslo process, the outbreak of large-scale violence, and the collapse of the Barak government, which led to the election of Ariel Sharon as prime minister, Meimad remained in the government (following the lead of the Labor Party) and Melchior became deputy foreign minister. Although increasingly angry regarding the perceived betrayal of the Palestinian partners in the peace process, Meimad members and leaders continued to be active in seeking ways of restoring the shattered fabric of this relationship.

The primacy of the democratic process and the avoidance of civil conflict

As noted, the Jewish religious tradition also includes interpretations that give primacy to the decisions of the secular government, even when these decisions may be seen to violate other religious principles.

As tension increased in Israeli society, along both the secular–religious and the left–right dimensions, a growing number of rabbis began to emphasize the need for authoritative decision-making based on the primacy of the democratically elected government. The emphasis on the legitimacy of secular political institutions and policies was voiced in 1982 during the confrontation over the evacuation of the Yamit settlement in the Sinai. Religious leaders and rabbis warned that "[t]here is a danger that, in an atmosphere of violence, soldiers may be killed, God forbid. Such a war would stain the people of Israel to the extent that will not be wiped out."[58]

This approach has also been emphasized by Meimad, whose platform opposes coercive religious legislation, emphasizes democratic practices in the Jewish state, and actively supports education regarding democratic values in both the religious and secular school systems.[59]

These themes were underscored and became primary issues in November 1995, following the assassination of Prime Minister Yitzchak Rabin. Many religious leaders, including those previously associated with the more "nationalist" and "hawkish" approaches and parties, expressed concerns regarding the impact of internal divisions, violence, and civil conflict on the future of the Jewish people. Examples from history, and, in particular, the internal divisions and senseless hatred (*sinat chinam*) that commentators have cited as the main cause of the destruction of the Second Temple and the long period of exile, were repeated as warnings of future catastrophe. Rabbis from many different groups stressed the theme of national unity and political stability based on the accepted democratic norms and institutions.

The assassination followed months of intense and often violent demonstrations against the policies of the Rabin government (particularly in the wake of terrorism and suicide bombings).[60] In this period, nationalist rabbis issued edicts declaring the prime minister and the government to be in violation of Jewish law (according to their interpretations) by endangering lives through their policies of territorial withdrawal.

In this environment, the assassination, and the perception that some elements in the religious sectors of Israeli society provided justification for this act, led to a fundamental change among many rabbis and religious leaders. Some, such as Rabbi Yoel Ben Nun, who had been a major leader of the territorialist Gush Emunim approach, renounced their earlier views and emphasized the importance of national unity and democracy. In the curricula of the national religious school system (although, not in the ultra-orthodox system), programs to emphasize democracy as a core Jewish value have been introduced.

Despite the catastrophic end of the Oslo process, beginning in September 2000, these programs have continued in the religious school systems and in other societal frameworks. Participation in various religious–secular dialogues continued to increase and, in terms of the formal political framework, the establishment and maintenance of a wide government following the election of Ariel Sharon in 2001 had broad backing. These developments indicated that, among the religious population, support for this approach emphasizing national unity based on democratic processes is likely to increase in the future.

"Democratic peace"?

Before examining the Israeli case in the light of "democratic peace" theories, the nature and limitations of these models should be considered. Universal theories that attempt to explain war and peace in relations among nations in terms of their respective levels of democracy are problematic, at best.[61] Critics have argued convincingly that shared cultural backgrounds and norms, rather than democratic political institutions and practices, seem to account for the absence of military conflict between Western liberal democracies.[62] In regions where democracy is formalistic and procedural and where intense ethno-national conflicts continue, such as South Asia or the former Yugoslavia, democratic peace theories lose much of their explanatory power.

In the Middle East, some political leaders, particularly in Israel, support the view that democratization in the Arab and Islamic states would promote peace agreements.[63] However, even if these societies were to evolve toward greater acceptance of democratic procedures and processes, there is also evidence that democratization, at least in the short term, could increase the salience of the ideological and religious aspects of the conflict with Israel, rather than leading to greater support for negotiated solutions. Even in relatively progressive states such as Jordan, the peace agreement with Israel is widely considered to be the result of external pressure and expediency ("the King's peace"), lacking wide popular support. Some analysts warn that Arab democracies would likely be more virulent in their opposition to Israel, at least until an agreement was reached and a new generation could be raised in the spirit of intercultural tolerance and understanding.[64]

In the Israeli case, the attempt to evaluate the validity of democratic peace theories is complicated by the heterogeneous nature of Israeli society, particularly along the religious–secular dimension, and the close link between the Jewish religion, Zionism (as the expression of Jewish nationalism), the territorial boundaries, and the question of sovereignty. In the few publications that attempt to examine the application of "democratic peace" theories to Israel, these dimensions have largely been overlooked.[65] However, as has been demonstrated in this chapter, for a significant segment of Israeli society, the mix of attitudes toward the religious significance of the Land of Israel, democracy as the basis for national unity, and other religious issues, such as the commandment to preserve life, are determining factors.

In this sense, it is important to recognize the dynamic nature of the situation. Although democratic institutions and processes in Israel are firmly established, the tensions between the secular political structure and the traditions and legal norms of the Jewish tradition can be expected to remain and perhaps intensify. Although the majority of Jewish Israelis define themselves as secular, rather than religious, identification with Jewish norms and practices has been growing in the past two decades. (Poll data show that close to half of the population maintains traditional Jewish practices such as lighting candles on the Sabbath or kosher dietary rules.[66]) Religious parties, such as Shas, led by Rabbi Ovadia Yosef, have grown in strength in the past decade. (Shas is also an ethnic party, encompassing Sephardi Jews, but members of this group, in general, are far less likely to be secular compared with the Ashkenazi Jewish population.) As the narrow and short-lived support for the post-Zionist ideology demonstrated, Israel will continue to be a Jewish state, in a cultural, social, and political sense, and the debate over the meaning and substantive impact of this framework will also continue.

However, the presence or growth of religious influence in Israeli politics does not mean that inherent religious/ideological opposition to the "land for peace" formula will also increase. As noted, the Shas leadership, the Meimad movement, and many prominent ultra-orthodox rabbis and leaders subscribe to the school that gives priority to the preservation of human life (*pikuach nefesh*) ahead of maintaining total sovereignty in the Land of Israel.

This change is also reflected in support for major changes in Israeli policy with respect to the peace process. Public opinion polls and recent election results show that the majority of Jewish Israelis, including significant portions of the religious population, are now willing to accept a Palestinian state in the context of a permanent status agreement and an end to the threat of violence. In addition, although support for Jewish sovereignty in the Land of Israel, based on religious commandments, is still quite strong, the possibility of dismantling some settlements and of consolidating others in settlement blocs gradually gained support in this community during the period of optimism following the Oslo agreement.[67] This optimism was reflected in the result of the 1999 elections, in which Netanyahu was defeated by Ehud Barak, on a platform emphasizing accelerated negotiations toward full peace agreements with both Syria and the Palestinians. It was clear that such agreements would require major Israeli territorial withdrawals, essentially to the 1948 armistice lines (with the exception of Jerusalem). Nevertheless, a significant portion of religious voters (although by no means a majority) seemed willing to accept this framework.[68] The Shas party, under the "spiritual guidance" of Rabbi Ovadia Yosef, became the third largest in the Knesset, with 17 seats (out of 120), and joined Barak's government. In addition, the representative of Meimad, Rabbi Michael Melchior, became a cabinet member.

However, the failure of the Camp David summit in July 2000, which was designed to complete the Oslo process with the promised "permanent status agreement," and the massive violence that began at the end of September led to fundamental changes in Israeli perceptions of the Palestinians. Within a few months, as casualties mounted and cease-fire efforts failed, the Barak administration lost public support and a number of parties, including Shas, withdrew from the government. Barak lost his parliamentary majority and, in special elections held in February 2001, opposition leader Ariel Sharon was selected as prime minister by an overwhelming and unprecedented majority. This outcome was a clear signal of a major shift in Israeli public opinion, across the political spectrum, in which the negotiation process with the Palestinians was widely seen to have ended in failure. Instead, in the wake of continued violence and high casualties, including numerous suicide bombings, the focus shifted to security. Religious leaders and voters supported Sharon, and their views were largely indistinguishable from the broad national consensus on these issues.

If and when peace and permanent status negotiations between Israel and the Palestinians resume, this period of intense violence is likely to influence public attitudes toward the "land for peace" formula, the question of a Palestinian state, and related issues. Like other sectors in Israeli society, the leaders of the religious parties and their supporters have become embittered and disillusioned with the failed promises of peace. The more hard-line positions, emphasizing the sacredness of the Land of Israel and the centrality of Jewish sovereignty in Jerusalem, regained some support in this period of violence. However, an end to terrorism and a fundamental change in relations with the Palestinians and neighboring Arab states could lead to a recovery in support for compromise. Within the religious sectors, the emphasis on national unity has continued to increase, and in the future, should a government be elected that adopts policies involving major territorial concessions, it is likely to receive support in order to prevent internal division.

In more general terms, although the tension between the religious and democratic secular authority will also continue and perhaps intensify, the situation is dynamic. The religious tradition and leadership provide a wide range of options, and the support for these different approaches, particularly with respect to possible agreements with the Arab states, is variable. The relative impact of these views on Israeli policy with respect to the peace process will depend on a combination of internal and external factors, including the perceived benefits and risks of agreements and the success in implementing them in ways that clearly demonstrate the understanding of and sensitivity to Jewish history and tradition.

Notes

This chapter is dedicated to the memory of Professor Daniel Elazar, whose pioneering work on the Jewish political tradition provided the foundation for academic analysis of this important topic.

1. Arye Carmon, "Political Education in the Midst of a National Identity Crisis: The Compatibility of Judaism and Democracy as a Pedagogical Theme," in Ehud Sprinzak and Larry Diamond, eds., *Israeli Democracy under Stress*, Boulder, CO: Lynne Rienner, 1993, pp. 293–308.
2. See, for example, *The State of Israel as a Jewish and Democratic State (Medinat Israel K'medinah Yehudit V'Demokratit): Proceedings of the 21st World Congress of Jewish Studies* (in Hebrew), Jerusalem: World Union Jewish Studies, 1997.
3. Bernard Susser and Eliezer Don-Yehiya, "Democracy versus Nationalism: Israel as an Exceptional Case" [in Hebrew: *Tarbut Demokratit*], Ramat Gan: Bar Ilan University, vol. 1, 1999, p. 18. For an English version, see Bernard Susser and Eliezer Don-Yehiya, "Israel and the Decline of the Nation-State in the West," *Modern Judaism*, May 1994, pp. 187–202.
4. Susser and Don-Yehiya, "Democracy versus Nationalism," p. 19; Yosef Salmon, "Tradition and Nationalism," in Jehuda Reinharz and Anita Shapira, eds., *Essential Papers on Zionism*, New York: New York University Press, 1996, p. 98.
5. Rashi [Rabbi Shlomo Yitzchaki], eleventh-century Jewish commentator, in his commentary on the book of Genesis.
6. Susser and Don-Yehiya, "Democracy versus Nationalism," citing Jacob Katz, *Emancipation and Assimilation*, Westmead, Farnborough: Gregg International, 1972, p. 131.
7. Yonathan Shapiro, "The Historical Origins of Israeli Democracy," in Sprinzak and Diamond, eds., *Israeli Democracy under Stress*, pp. 65–82.
8. Ehud Sprinzak, *Ha'Ish Hayashar B'enav: Illegalizm BeChevrah HaYisraelit* [Illegalism in Israeli Society], Tel Aviv: Sifriyat Poalim, 1986.
9. Eliezer Don-Yehiya, "Religion, Social Cleavages, and Political Behavior: The Religious Parties and the Elections," in Daniel J. Elazar and Shmuel Sandler, eds., *Who's the Boss: Israel at the Polls, 1988–90*, Detroit, MI: Wayne State University Press, 1992, p. 91.
10. See, for example, Moshe Hallamish and Aviezer Ravitzky, *The Land of Israel in Medieval Jewish Thought* (in Hebrew), Jerusalem: Yad Izhak Ben-Zvi, 1991.
11. Zvi Yehuda Kook, "Ha-Torah Ve'Ha-aretz [The Torah and the Land]," *Yuval Ha-Mizrachi*, Jerusalem, 1952, cited by Salmon, "Tradition and Nationalism," p. 97.
12. *Palestine Post*, 16 May 1948, pp. 1–2, reprinted in Itamar Rabinovich and Jehuda Reinharz, eds., *Israel in the Middle East*, New York: Oxford University Press, 1984, p. 12.
13. This position was taken by Maimonides, the Jewish scholar and legal authority who lived in the twelfth century.

14. This theme was emphasized in the writings of the proto-Zionists who preceded Herzl, such as Alkalai, Kalischer, and Friedland. See Arthur Hertzberg, *The Zionist Idea*, New York: Atheneum, 1959; Salmon, "Tradition and Nationalism," pp. 94–116; Aviezer Ravitzky, *Messianism, Zionism, and Jewish Religious Radicalism*, Chicago: University of Chicago Press, 1996, pp. 1–2.

15. Salmon, "Tradition and Nationalism," p. 99.

16. Charles Liebman and Eliezer Don-Yehiya, *Religion and Politics in Israel*, Bloomington, IN: Indiana University Press, 1984; Norman L. Zucker, *The Coming Crisis in Israel*, Cambridge, MA: MIT Press, 1973; Eliezer Don-Yehiya, *Conflict and Consensus in Jewish Political Life*, Ramat Gan: Bar-Ilan University Press, 1986.

17. Emanuel Rackman, *Israel's Emerging Constitution 1948–1951*, New York: Columbia University Press, 1955. These issues also arose in 1948 with regard to the wording of the Declaration of Independence. "For the secularist, anti-religious left ... any mention of Divine providence was anathema. For religious Jews ... the proclamation of the re-establishment of the Jewish state could not appear without such a reference." The compromise was to use the phrase "Rock of Israel" to allude to, but not specifically mention, God. See Daniel J. Elazar, *The Constitution of Israel*, Jerusalem: Jerusalem Center for Public Affairs, 1996, p. 2.

18. See, for example, Menachem Friedman, "The Ultra-Orthodox and Israeli Society," in Keith Kyle and Joel Peters, eds., *Whither Israel: The Domestic Challenges*, London: Royal Institute of International Affairs, 1994.

19. Liebman and Don-Yehiya, *Religion and Politics in Israel*.

20. Daniel J. Elazar and Stuart A. Cohen, *The Jewish Polity: Jewish Political Organizations from Biblical Times to the Present*, Bloomington, IN: Indiana University Press, 1985.

21. Ibid., p. 6.

22. There is a vast literature on Judaism and democracy, reflecting the centrality of this issue in Israel and the Jewish community. See, for example, *Jewish Political Studies Review*, vol. 12, nos. 3 & 4, 2000 (special issue on Communal Democracy and Liberal Democracy in the Jewish Political Tradition); and vol. 5, nos. 1 & 2, 1993 (special issue on Israel as a Jewish State); Eliezer Schweid, *Democracy and Halakhah*, Lanham, MD: University Press of America, 1994; Shlomo Dov Goitein, "Political Conflict and the Use of Power in the World of the Geniza," in Daniel J. Elazar, ed., *Kinship and Consent: The Jewish Political Tradition and Its Contemporary Uses*, Ramat Gan: Transaction Publishers, 1997, pp. 281–3; Eli Clark, " 'After the Majority Shall You Incline': Democratic Theory and Voting Rights in Jewish Law," *Torah U-Madda Journal*, New York: Yeshiva University Press, 1999, pp. 97–133; Charles Liebman, *Religion, Democracy and Israeli Society*, Reading: Harwood Academic Publishers, 1997.

23. See Daniel J. Elazar, "Judaism and Democracy: The Reality," *Jerusalem Letter*, no. 48, 17 March 1986, Jerusalem: Jerusalem Center for Public Affairs.

24. Amnon Bazak, " 'And You Shall Live by Them' – A Test of Principles: An In Depth Look at the Question of the Sanctity of Life and the Completeness of the Land" (in Hebrew), *Meimad Journal*, Issue 3, April 1995, p. 17.

25. Schweid, *Democracy and Halakhah*, p. 182; see also Eliezer Schweid, "The Jewish State and Democracy," *Jerusalem Letter*, no. 298, 15 July 1994, Jerusalem: Jerusalem Center for Public Affairs.

26. Charles S. Liebman, "Religion and Democracy in Israel," in Sprinzak and Diamond, eds., *Israeli Democracy under Stress*, p. 274.

27. Indeed, from the perspective of Jewish tradition, it is not only democracy but, more broadly, the concept of the modern sovereign state that lacks legitimacy. As Elazar and Cohen note, "the Jewish political tradition does not recognize state sovereignty in the modern sense of absolute independence. No state – a human creation – can be sover-

eign. Classically, only God is sovereign and He entrusts the exercise of His sovereign powers to the people as a whole, mediated through His Torah-as-constitution as provided through His covenant with Israel." Elazar and Cohen, *The Jewish Polity*, p. 5.

28. For a development of this thesis, see Asher Cohen and Bernard Susser, "From Accommodation to Decision: Transformations in Israel's Religio-Political Life," *Journal of Church and State*, vol. 38, Autumn 1996. For a contrasting view, see Eliezer Don-Yehiya, *The Politics of Accommodation: Settling Conflicts of State and Religion in Israel* (in Hebrew), Jerusalem: Floersheimer Institute for Policy Studies, 1997.

29. Liebman and Don-Yehiya, *Religion and Politics in Israel.*

30. Given the long history of anti-Semitism, culminating in the Holocaust, religious Jews were and remain particularly suspicious of the intentions of the outside world. This historical memory contributes to general skepticism regarding the possibilities for peace. As Amos Oz has written, "Perhaps it was a lunatic proposition; to transform, in two or three generations, a mass of persecuted, intimidated Jews, consumed with love-hate toward their countries of origin, into a nation serving as a shining example to the Arab surroundings, a model for the entire world." *Po Ve-sham Be-eretz Yisrael* [Here and There in the Land of Israel], Tel Aviv: Am Oved, 1983, p. 189.

31. In the late 1930s and during the 1940s, religious Zionist leaders "reluctantly" accepted partition, and accepted the policy of restraint in response to Arab terror attacks. See Itamar Wahrhaftig, "The Position of the Rabbis in the Controversy over Partition (1939)" (in Hebrew), *Tehumin*, vol. 9, 1988, pp. 269–301, cited by Stuart A. Cohen, *The Scroll or the Sword? Dilemmas of Religion and Military Service in Israel*, London: Harwood Academic Publishers, 1997, p. 28.

32. Zvi Yehuda Kook, *Lemaan Daat and Lo Taguro*, cited by Yael Yishai, *Land or Peace: Whither Israel?* Stanford, CA: Hoover Institution Press, 1987, p. 130.

33. Shlomo Aviner, "A Double Crisis," *Nekuda*, vol. 14, 15 May 1980, cited by Yishai, *Land or Peace*, p. 131.

34. Yishai, *Land or Peace*, pp. 116–19.

35. Sprinzak, *Ha'Ish Hayashar B'enav: Illegalizm BeChevrah HaYisraelit.*

36. Don-Yehiya, "Religion, Social Cleavages, and Political Behavior," p. 91.

37. See, for example, Yaakov Filber, *Ayelet HaShachar* [Sunrise], Jerusalem: Hamachon LeCheker Mishnat Hara'ayah, 1991.

38. Zvi Yehuda Kook, *Or Lenitavati* [A Light to My Pathway], Jerusalem: Hamachon Al Shem Rav Zvi Yehuda Hacohen Kook, 1989.

39. Menachem Friedman, "The First Non-Zionist Right Wing," *Meimad Journal* (in Hebrew), Issue 7, May–June 1996, p. 14.

40. Don-Yehiya, "Religion, Social Cleavages, and Political Behavior," p. 9.

41. See Cohen, *The Scroll or the Sword?*, p. 27.

42. Davar (Tel Aviv), 4 November 1985, cited by Liebman, "Religion and Democracy in Israel," p. 276.

43. Herb Keinon, "Goren Tells Troops: Disobey Orders," *Jerusalem Post*, 20 December 1993.

44. Cohen, *The Scroll or the Sword?*, p. 31.

45. Sarah Honig, "NRP: IDF Commands Should Be Obeyed 'Unless They Are Illegal,'" *Jerusalem Post*, 1 April 1994; Liat Collins, "Rabbinate Defers Decision on Soldiers' Disobeying Orders to Evacuate Jews," *Jerusalem Post*, 5 April 1994.

46. Honig, "NRP."

47. Herb Keinon, Batsheva Tsur, and Evelyn Gordon, "Rabbis: Soldiers Must Stay in Areas. Rabin Asks A-G to Probe if Decree Is Seditious," *Jerusalem Post*, 13 July 1995.

48. Hillel Halkin, "Israel, Rabbis Battle for Soul of Their Army," *Forward*, 21 July 1995.

49. Keinon et al., "Rabbis." A detailed discussion of this issue is presented by Yaakov Blidstein, "And Even if They Tell You Right Is Left: The Strength of Institutional Authority in Halacha and Its Boundaries," in Avi Sagi and Zeev Safrai, eds., *Between Authority and Autonomy in Jewish Tradition* (in Hebrew), Tel Aviv: Hakibbutz Hameuchad, 1997.

50. Eliezer Don-Yehiya, "Jewish Messianism, Religious Zionism, and Israeli Politics: The Origins and Impact of Gush Emunim," *Middle Eastern Studies*, vol. 23, April 1987, pp. 214–23.

51. Gershon Bacon, "Daat Torah v'chevli Hamashiach: LeSheyalat Ha'ideologiya Shel 'Agudat Yisrael' BiPolin," in Sagi and Safrai, eds., *Between Authority and Autonomy in Jewish Tradition*, reprinted from *Tarbiz*, vol. 52, no. 5743, 1983, pp. 497–508; see also Lawrence Kaplan, "'Daas Torah': A Modern Conception of Rabbinic Authority," in Moshe Sokol, ed., *Rabbinic Authority and Personal Autonomy*, Northvale, NJ: Aronson, 1992.

52. Alon Pinkas, "Soldier Jailed for Refusing to Evict Settlers," *Jerusalem Post*, 17 August 1995.

53. Gerald M. Steinberg, "Foreign Policy and Security Issues in the 1999 Elections," in Daniel Elazar and Ben Mollov, eds., *Israel at the Polls* 1999, London: Frank Cass, 2000.

54. Cited by Adam Doron, *Medinat Yisrael V'Eretz Yisrael* [The State of Israel and the Land of Israel], Tel Aviv: Beit Berel, 1988.

55. Ovadia Yosef, "Hachzarat Shtachim Me'eretz Yisrael Bimkom Pikuach Nefesh [Ceding Territory in the Land of Israel vs. the Sanctity of Life]," in Yitzchak Rafael, ed., *Lectures Presented at the 21st National Conference on Torah She'baal Peh*, Jerusalem: Mosad Harav Kook, 1980, p. 14; see also Ovadia Yosef, "Me'sirat Shtachim Me'eretz Yisrael Bimkom Pikuach Nefesh [Giving Territories of the Land of Israel vs. the Sanctity of Life]," in Yitzchak Rafael, ed., *Lectures Presented at the 31st National Conference on Torah She'baal Peh*, Jerusalem: Mosad Harav Kook, 1990. These analyses generated an exchange of articles, religious edicts, and responses in this and other publications, which are beyond the scope of this paper.

56. Michal Yudelman and Sarah Honig, "Arafat Wants to Meet Yosef," *Jerusalem Post*, 30 May 1997.

57. Herb Keinon, "Extraordinary Events," *Jerusalem Post*, 25 November 1994.

58. Itamar Warhaftig, "The Soul Should Not be Granted," *Nekuda*, no. 41, 19 March 1982, cited by Yishai, *Land or Peace*, p. 241.

59. *Meimad Journal* (in Hebrew), Issue 14, September 1998, back page.

60. Gerald M. Steinberg, "Peace, Security and Terror in the 1996 Elections," in Daniel J. Elazar and Shmuel Sandler, eds., *Israel at the Polls 1996*, London: Frank Cass, 1997.

61. See, for example, Jack S. Levy, "Domestic Politics and War," *Journal of Interdisciplinary History*, vol. 18, no. 4, Spring 1988, pp. 653–73. For a critical review of this literature, see James Lee Ray, "The Future of International War," in David Garnham and Mark Tessler, eds., *Democracy, War and Peace in the Middle East*, Bloomington, IN: Indiana University Press, 1995, pp. 3–33.

62. Errol Anthony Henderson, "The Democratic Peace through the Lens of Culture, 1820–1989," *International Studies Quarterly*, vol. 42, no. 3, September 1998, pp. 461–84.

63. Garnham and Tessler, *Democracy, War and Peace in the Middle East*, Introduction, pp. xvii–xviii.

64. Jo-Ann Hart, "Democracy and Deterrence," in Garnham and Tessler, eds., *Democracy, War and Peace in the Middle East*, p. 37.

65. This omission can be found in Gabriel Sheffer, "Israel and the Liberalization of Arab Regimes," in Garnham and Tessler, eds., *Democracy, War and Peace in the Middle East*,

pp. 268–88; and Gad Barzilai, *Democracy at War: Argument and Consensus in Israel* (in Hebrew), Tel Aviv: Sifriat Poalim, 1992.

66. Shlomit Levy, Hanna Levinson, and Elihu Katz, "Observances and Social Interaction among Israeli Jews," Jerusalem: Louis Guttman Israel Institute of Applied Social Research, 1993.

67. In the wake of the Oslo agreement (the "Declaration of Principles") in 1993, support was widespread and opposition was too limited to affect public policy. However, following waves of terrorism and the continued hostile rhetoric from Palestinians, including Yasser Arafat, protest grew. These factors led to the defeat of the Labor Party and Shimon Peres in the 1996 elections. See Gerald M. Steinberg, "Peace, Security and Terror in the 1996 Elections," *Israel Affairs*, vol. 4, no. 1, Autumn 1997 (special issue on Israel at the Polls 1996).

68. Gerald M. Steinberg, "Foreign Policy in the 1999 Israeli Elections," *Israel Affairs*, vol. 7, nos. 2&3, Winter/Spring 2001 pp. 174–98 (special issue on Israel at the Polls 1999).

9

Democracy and peace in Iran and Iraq

Amin Saikal

As an ideal of government, democracy has become as much a catchword in the Middle East as in most other parts of the world. Whatever their degrees of commitment to it, most Middle Eastern leaderships do not disown the *vocabulary* of democracy as a useful means of claiming political legitimacy and branding their regimes as popular, representing the will of the majority of their respective publics. Many can point to the existence of *some* forms of "popular representation" and "electoral legitimacy" to substantiate their claim to popular sovereignty and ultimately a democratic system of governance. Yet in most Muslim Middle Eastern countries what is practiced is a form of either absolutism or authoritarianism or veiled authoritarianism, in which the ballot box cannot be used effectively to change governments. All serious post-war attempts at democratizing politics and society in most Middle Eastern states, whether Egypt or Iran or Algeria, have ended up, at best, in the institution of concealed authoritarianism.

There is a very important message in this: a Western-style democracy may be unsuited to the political and socio-cultural conditions of these states. The goal of political reform should not therefore be to create a system and implement a mode of social and economic development that would meet Western standards, but rather to develop the constituents of a civil society relevant to the particular conditions and cultural traditions of the given country. In this context, the course of political evolution pursued by the Islamic Republic of Iran in the past few years is most pertinent and warrants a serious focus. What President Muhammad Khatami has been attempting to achieve is what he has called "Islamic civil society" and "Islamic democracy," as distinct from their Western counterparts and yet not entirely inconsistent with them. It may also be pertinent to contrast the Iranian case with another case in the region where, by all accounts, no distinct notion of civil society or democracy is in operation. That case is provided by the neighboring state of Iraq.

This chapter has three main objectives. The first is to explain, although briefly, the dimensions of the concept of democracy and how incompatible a Western understanding of it has so far proved to be with the fundamental conditions in the Muslim Middle East. The second is to outline the diverse courses undertaken in relation to democratization in two particular Middle Eastern constituent states – Iran and Iraq – as two contrasting cases. The third is to conclude with the need for building a civil society that is conducive to democratization.

Dimensions of democracy

Needless to say, democracy is an overloaded concept. Historically, it has meant different things to different people. It has been applied to many different formations and, in interaction with different socio-cultural traditions and practices, it has produced diverse forms of government – some more representative, participatory, and stable than others. Even in Western democracies, there is no consensus on what precisely the concept means and how best to express it as an ideal. There is not even widespread agreement among theorists and practitioners about whether it is a form of government or a method of choosing a government or a term applied to a whole society, as intimated in Alexis de Tocqueville's study of *Democracy in America*, which is essentially about American society.[1]

Whatever the diversity of views, there is a core or minimalist definition beneath all the interpretations and uses of the term. As Anthony Arblaster writes, this core definition "is necessarily general and vague enough to make such variations possible, but it is not so vague as to permit any meaning whatsoever to be placed on the word. At the root of all definitions of democracy, however refined and complex, lies the idea of popular power, of a situation in which power, and perhaps authority too, rests with the people. That power or authority is usually thought of as being political, and often therefore takes the form of an idea of popular sovereignty – the people as the ultimate political power. But it need not be exclusively political."[2] Obviously, the mechanisms for achieving this minimalist position can vary from country to country: they can be either

electoral or non-electoral, although an election based on universal suffrage is often regarded as the best means.

The Iranian and Arab regimes have constantly been pressured both
from outside, especially by the West, and from within to conform at least
to this minimalist position as a foundation for the development of a liberal, pluralist, tolerant, and stable society. If one adopts the principles of
popular power and popular sovereignty as the minimum for instituting
democracy, one can argue that Iran and several Arab states, notably
Egypt, Jordan, and Kuwait, have already made some progress in this
direction. They have succeeded in establishing electoral and representative processes of popular legitimation, whereby citizens are given the
opportunity to participate (either directly as in the case of Iran since the
revolution of 1978/79, or directly and indirectly as in the case of Egypt,
especially since 1981) in the making of legislative and executive powers,
although these processes have been more robust in Iran than in the other
states. The Jordanians have also managed to establish a more representative legislative body, with a noticeable role in making the government
accountable, than may be the case in many other countries in the region,
although the Jordanian monarch still remains in possession of very strong
powers. Even Kuwait has put in place a kind of crypto-Athenian democracy[3] with its election of 1992, in which some 80,000 Kuwaiti males, who
constituted about 13 percent of the total population, were allowed to
elect a pluralist national assembly. Meanwhile, closed regimes such as
those of Syria and Libya also have resorted to such processes, albeit in
sham form, to substantiate a claim to popular power and authority.

However, the fundamental problem with this minimalist form of democracy is that it can be utilized either to lay the foundation for building
a comprehensive or liberal democracy, or to construct or reinforce a wide
range of authoritarian systems. In the Middle East, the latter have been
most prevalent. When prompted to institute some minimalist democratic
reforms, a majority of leaderships have done so on a selective and exclusive basis and within procedural frameworks that have not substantially
affected their personal or family or elite powers. They have conveniently
designed and applied the reforms in such a way as to produce nothing
more than systems that may be termed "democratic in form but authoritarian in content," ensuring that the basic principles of separation of
powers, political pluralism, and individual rights and freedoms are not
secured against the open-ended, arbitrary needs of rulers. Thus, whether
operating within a traditional or traditional–modernist or revolutionary–
modernist mold, they have shown a marked reluctance to venture beyond
the minimalist position in the direction of creating liberal polities.

The few regimes that have sought to venture beyond the minimalist
position, because of either genuine reformist convictions or domestic and

external pressures, have not aimed at creating a widely inclusive and competitive system. They have sought to exclude from the process those groups perceived as popularly threatening. As a consequence, their reforms have frequently resulted in political polarization and violent conflicts – a development that has served as a strong deterrent to the others. One can draw on the experiences of a number of countries to illustrate this point, in particular those of Iran, Egypt, and Algeria. The Iranian case is especially instructive.

Case studies

Iran

In Iran, the revolutionary transition from the Shah's pro-Western autocracy to Khomeini's anti-Western (or, more specifically, anti-American) "theo-democracy" provides a clear example of the danger and violence that a process of even limited pro-Western democratization can involve in the Middle East. There is no doubt that a variety of factors, ranging from the Shah's failure to institute a legitimate political system and an effective process of change and development, to his ill-conceived and badly implemented program of socio-economic modernization and military build-up, to his alliance with the United States and his regional ambitions, contributed to the creation of a revolutionary situation that eventually caused the Shah's fall. With the benefit of hindsight, however, it is clear that what decisively opened the way for his downfall was his mishandling of the process of limited liberalization as a precondition for the democratization of the polity that he sought to implement, especially from 1976.[4]

From his reinstallation on the throne with the help of the CIA in 1953, the Shah, together with his main ally the United States, was all along conscious of the legitimacy problems that he faced. As a result, and at Washington's urging, he had made a number of attempts in the 1960s to popularize his rule. In fact, his "White Revolution" was designed to achieve this purpose. However, like many leaders in the region, he was prepared to implement only political reforms that would not undermine his autocratic powers but rather would allow him to manifest some ostensible commitment to creating a democratic system of government. He focused his reform efforts to benefit mainly those politically minded or active Iranians who were easily co-optable and lacked the potential to pose a serious challenge to his powers. This meant that he not only excluded the radical religious and secularist groups from his reforms, but actually directed the reforms against them.

The Shah appeared to believe in intertwined autocratic secularization and modernization as the best way to popularize his rule. In the process, he lost sight of the fact that, after four centuries of power struggle between the Shi'ite establishment and political authority in Iran, his reforms needed to have the support of the religious establishment, which was still the only force capable of influencing the minds and capturing the emotions of the Iranian public against his reforms in the right circumstances. Despite being warned about the danger of his approach, he persisted into the 1970s with a policy of doing everything possible to suppress and marginalize the religious establishment rather than to entice it to become a genuine participant in his reform endeavors.

Nonetheless, under pressure from President Jimmy Carter's emphasis on human rights as an issue in the conduct of US foreign policy, the Shah finally found it necessary and expedient to introduce more substantial political reforms. Hence, from 1976 he inaugurated a phase of limited but serious liberalization. His ultimate goal was not clear, but it is evident that he had intended to institute a wider degree of public participation in the policy formulation and policy implementation processes, with a measure of freedom for the people to criticize the government, highlight human rights abuses, and demand greater social justice and equity. Although still opposed to dealing with his traditional religious and political opponents in anything other than an autocratic manner, he wanted to open avenues of participation for the new social and economic groups that his process of pro-capitalist modernization had generated.

However, in a country where political suppression had been the central instrument of governance for a long time and the public had not been educated in political pluralism, even this amount of reform was sufficient to enable a variety of groups, both old and new, to air their grievances with great ferocity. Yet although these groups quickly succeeded in instigating a nationwide anti-Shah protest movement by mid-1978, they were not able to develop a shared platform beyond a general desire to overthrow the Shah's regime and the hope of replacing it with something better. Consequently, following the fall of the Shah in January 1979, the revolutionaries headed in different ideological directions. This opened the way for a long and violent power struggle between a cluster of Islamists, whose Shi'ite Islamic message and promises were easily discernible to the overwhelming majority of the Iranian people, and a variety of semi-secularist and secularist groups, whose ideological pronouncements in support of creating a pluralist and liberal system proved bewildering to a large proportion of the Iranian public.

In the process, Ayatollah Khomeini and his committed Islamic followers gained political ascendancy, with wide public support. This occurred only at the cost of brutally suppressing other groups and demonizing the West, especially the United States and its regional supporters, as dictated by the need to establish their brand of Shi'ite Islamic government and transform Iran into an Islamic republic.[5] In its early years, the Khomeini Islamic regime evolved in many ways as the mirror image of the Shah's regime. It adopted an Islamic constitution and created an electoral process of political legitimation and citizen participation in politics. But it failed to establish an inclusive political order that could allow Iran to be defined as more than a theocratic state and be treated as such by all those outside forces that found its behavior threatening to their interests. It became as exclusive and intolerant of opposition as the Shah's regime, if not more so. This, together with the Islamic regime's inability to fulfill its promises of good government and a better life for a majority of Iranians, gave rise to the risk that any future structural political change might be as violent as the one that brought the regime to power. The regime remained vulnerable to spontaneous popular uprisings of the kind that initially opened the way for the destruction of the Shah's rule.[6]

This, however, does not tell the full story. It explains only the Islamic *jihadi*[7] (or "resistant and exertive") dimension of Khomeini's leadership. This dimension involved ideological and policy behavior that enabled the regime, first of all, to integrate politics with religion, to consolidate its own position, and thus to achieve a Shi'ite Islamic transformation in hostile circumstances as rapidly as possible. Its emphasis was naturally more on resistance, defense, and reassertion in pursuit of securing the revolution to bolster the regime, enabling it to deflect those internal and external forces that either actively opposed it or perceived it as dangerously threatening.

Once this objective had been achieved, another related dimension in Khomeini's leadership was waiting to emerge at an opportune time. This was the *ijtihadi* (or "creatively interpretive") dimension,[8] which had been working in tandem with the *jihadi* dimension but had been eclipsed by it because of the conditions in the early years of the Islamic regime. In the tradition of Iran's Shi'ite establishment, Khomeini had been regarded as a Mujtahid (or creative interpreter of Islam) long before the revolution, because of his emphasis on the need for a creative interpretation of Shi'ite Islam and its application in accordance with changing conditions and the course of history.

In other words, Khomeini had never believed in Islam being frozen in time; he had upheld Islam as a religion for all times, peoples, and conditions. This was evident not only in the series of lectures that he had delivered in Iraq in the early 1970s, compiled subsequently as a volume entitled *Islamic Government*, but also in numerous *fatwas* or religious rulings that he issued both before the revolution to oppose the Shah's regime and its US ally, and after the revolution to establish a very complex but nonetheless modern Islamic governmental system. Although Khomeini founded the governmental system on Islam and vested the final religious-based temporal authority in the Vilayati Faqih (or "Supreme Jurisprudent" or "philosopher-king"), he ensured that the system was participatory, enabling the public to be involved in the processes of political legitimation and policy formulation and implementation; hence his notion of popular elections and a popularly elected president.

This had generated a generic division within the ruling clerics, giving rise to two main factions. One was the Jihadis, who upheld a *jihadi* or what some might label "combative" interpretation of Shi'ite Islam and who became popularly known as Islamic "conservatives" or "hardliners." Indeed, it was this group that, under the conditions of post-revolutionary internal strife and the eight-year war between Iran and Iraq (1980–8), initially managed to achieve political ascendancy, gaining control over most of the instruments of state power. The other main faction was the Ijtihadis, who adopted a more liberal interpretation of Shi'ite Islam and who were called Islamic "pragmatists" or "moderates." While alive, Khomeini was regarded as a leading Jihadi and Ijtihadi, with paramount constitutional and revolutionary powers successfully to establish some kind of a balance between the two factions of his followers.

Khomeini's death in June 1989 changed the situation. Whereas the Ijtihadi faction's approach was at least partly reflected in the policy behavior of President Hashemi Rafsanjani (1989–97), the Jihadi faction was patronized by Khomeini's successor to the position of Vilayati Faqih, Ayatollah Ali Khamanei. Given the ending of the Iran–Iraq war in a stalemate – a war that had enabled the Jihadis to divert people's attention from the revolution's original promises of democratic freedoms and a higher standard of living – as well as Iran's deepening economic and social problems, its persistent international isolation, and the rapid growth of post-revolutionary youth's dominance in the electorate, the scene was set for a sharpening of the Jihadi–Ijtihadi division in Iranian politics. Nonetheless, Rafsanjani managed to keep a lid on the situation by cooperating closely with Khamanei and refraining from stepping too far outside the ideological parameters set by the Jihadis.

However, this situation could not endure for too long. It was clear that the parameters of the ideological framework had to be widened to accommodate a more accelerated process of *ijtihadi* reform in support of the revolution's original goals. By the early 1990s, one prominent clerical thinker and activist who had already placed the issue of the expansion of ideological parameters on the agenda was Abdulkarim Soroush.[9] His argument about the compatibility between Islam and democracy and the elasticity of Islam as a religion to be applied in time–space under changing conditions had already given a dimension to the debate between the Jihadis and Ijtihadis that clearly provided wider legitimacy to the Ijtihadis' position. What boosted this shift further was the fact that, despite the Jihadis' dominance in the state power structure, the electoral process that had been put in place was robust and inclusive enough to produce the main catalyst.

It was against this backdrop that Muhammad Khatami rose from the ranks of the Ijtihadis to be elected President of Iran in a landslide victory in July 1997. This is not to claim that he does not defend Iran and Islam whenever necessary, but clearly his platform from the beginning was one of *ijtihadi*. He was firmly convinced that the time had come for Iran to move rapidly from a political culture of *jihad* to one of *ijtihad* if it was to stay in tune with changing conditions in Iran and in the international environment. To realize this objective, Khatami called for the intertwined goals of achieving "Islamic civil society" as a precondition for and in tandem with "Islamic democracy," and of rationalizing Iran's foreign relations, based on the principles of "dialogue" between civilizations and cross-cultural understandings within the international system of nation-states.[10] In essence, he was calling for the advent of a new Shi'ite Islamic vision in accordance with the changing times and conditions – a vision that Khatami claims Khomeini would have shared if he were alive.[11]

Although Khatami treats Iran's Islamic constitution as sacrosanct and operates within it, he has stressed not only that Islam enshrines its own concepts of civil society and democracy, but also that the Iranian Islamic constitution is committed to the promotion of such concepts as a means to serve the common good. He has emphasized that these concepts, although different in their roots from their Western counterparts, are not necessarily in "conflict and contradiction in all their manifestations and consequences" with those arising from Western traditions of rationalism and liberalism. He claims that "[t]his is exactly why we should never be oblivious to the judicious acquisition of the positive accomplishments of Western society."[12]

He states that in an Islamic civil society, "although it is centered around the axis of Islamic thinking and culture, personal or group dictatorship or even the tyranny of the majority and elimination of the minority has no place; ... man ... is venerated and revered and his rights respected; ... and citizens enjoy the right to determine their own destiny, supervise the governance and hold the government accountable. The government in such a society is the servant of the people and not their master, and in every eventuality, is accountable to the people whom God has entitled to determine their own destiny." He stresses that an Islamic civil society is not one "where only Muslims are entitled to rights and are considered citizens. Rather, all individuals are entitled to rights, within the framework of law and order." To Khatami, "respect for human rights and compliance with their relevant norms and standards is ... the natural consequence of ... [Islamic] teachings and precepts." Furthermore, he makes it clear that an Islamic civil society "seeks neither to dominate others nor to submit to domination," but at the same time, "as instructed by the Holy Qur'an, [it] considers itself entitled to acquire all requisite means for material and technical progress and authority."[13]

Khatami places a high premium on the notion of freedom in the construction and operation of a stable and vibrant Islamic civil society, although he stresses that, in practice, freedom – whether at the individual or societal level – cannot be limitless. "We want a system based on abstinence and high morality that only comes through relentless endeavor and the courage to embark upon moral and spiritual growth. This is true freedom, but people need to be taught to see it this way."[14] He considers freedom of thought and expression and a diversity of views to be central to the substantiation of an Islamic civil society. He quotes Imam Khomeini, who argued that "[i]n Islamic government there should always be room for revision. Our revolutionary system demands that various, even opposing, viewpoints be allowed to surface."[15] Khatami notes: "We must achieve a new vision and understanding. Relying on current religious leadership is necessary but not sufficient."[16]

He condemns censorship and the banning of opposition as a solution to Iran's problems. He shuns those who seek to impose "their rigid thinking on Islam and call it God's religion [because] they lack the intellectual power to confront their opposite side's thinking on its own terms" and thus "resort to fanaticism."[17] He argues for the plurality of views and the freedom to express them as a condition for the development of an Islamic civil society. He states, "we cannot expect any positive transformations anywhere unless the yearning for freedom is fulfilled. That is the freedom to think and the security to express new thinking."[18] "[T]ransformation and progress require thought, and thought only flourishes in an atmosphere of freedom. But our history has not allowed human character to grow and to be appreciated, and thus the basic human yearning for thinking and freedom has been unattended at best and negated at worst."[19]

Khatami's concept of Islamic civil society is thus more conditioned on moral than on material standards. Although it involves a measured degree of separation of politics and capital, political and social pluralism, freedom of thought and expression, and government intervention in public life to help the needy and to ensure justice and the implementation of Islamic-based laws, ultimately it relies on moral force to win the day. Like many other religious–political thinkers, Khatami is keen to emphasize that it is moral, virtuous, and humane existence that delivers a better standard of living in economic and social terms, rather than vice versa.

This belief also strongly shapes Khatami's international outlook, which stresses the importance of peaceful coexistence and mutual respect and of a dialogue of civilizations among peoples and states in world politics. Ever since coming to power, he has persistently underlined the need to promote the common aspect of humanity that can bond peoples together in peace rather than those earthly distinctions that lead them to conflict. He has sought to apply this approach to the conduct of Iran's relations with not only its arch enemy (the United States) but also its traditional regional rivals, such as Saudi Arabia.

Of course, as could have been expected, Khatami has not had a smooth run with his reform agenda in either the domestic or the foreign policy arena. On the domestic front, he has been seriously challenged by those Jihadis who have been unable to make the leap into his *ijtihadi* culture as rapidly as required. These Jihadis have used their domination of the judiciary, the security and armed forces, and numerous decision-making councils and committees, as well as close association with the Vilayati Faqih, to frustrate some of Khatami's Islamic civil society reforms as extra-*Ijtihadi*, extra-constitutional, and pro-Western. They have also rejected some of Khatami's overtures for wider and better foreign relations, including a possible rapprochement with the United States, as undermining the strength of Islam and pleasing the West and Western-dominated forces of globalization. They have argued that Khatami's reforms in general are bound to unravel the fabric of the revolutionary Islamic Iran that Khomeini left behind, and to provide the necessary opportunities for the West, especially the United States, to restore its influence in Iran. As the reform process has moved forward, the Jihadis have increasingly targeted one of the issues at the heart of the process – that is, freedom of thought and expression.

Khatami's response has been to make judicious use of his public mandate in dealing with his Jihadi opponents within the bounds of the law and the principle of maintaining peace and order. He has acted within the framework of the constitution not only to pursue a peaceful and orderly *ijtihadi* course of change, but also to educate his opponents to behave in a similar manner. He has repeatedly condemned extra-legal means as a substitute for non-violent debate and behavior. Although his reforms have not been altogether free of generating some violent confrontations, as manifested in the July 1999 and subsequent student demonstrations, which brought disproportionate use of force by the Jihadis, on the whole his methods of peaceful dialogue and conciliation have proved to be fairly credible, but at one important price. That is, he has managed his reforms only within a strategy of "two steps forward one step back," which has inevitably slowed the pace of reform, to the dismay of some of his supporters.

Even at this pace, Khatami still maintains overwhelming public support and has succeeded in persuading a number of leading Jihadi clerics to move to his *ijtihadi* mold. Such clerics include Ayatollah Khalkhali (known as the "hanging judge" in the early days of the revolution), Abdullah Nouri, and the leaders of the student militants who in November 1979 took some 50 American diplomats hostage in Tehran for 15 months: they are all now firmly lined up behind Khatami's reforms.[20] Whatever Khatami's difficulties so far, he scored a stunning electoral victory in May 2001 for a second term, which followed a similar victory by his supporters in the February 2000 Majlis (National Assembly) elections. This would indeed make it more difficult than ever for his opponents to reverse his course of reform.

Khatami has undoubtedly put Iran on something of an indigenous course of civil and democratic change that would contain a number of elements that would at the very least fulfill the criteria for what is regarded as a minimalist model of democracy in the West. However, the success of Khatami's reforms will ultimately depend on the maintenance of the process of reform within the Islamic framework, because there is a danger that it could, especially beyond Khatami's presidency, evolve into something outside that framework. Khatami's ability to bridge the gap between the Jihadis and Ijtihadis, in such a way as not to seriously compromise the process itself, and to improve Iran's economic conditions, which have increasingly become very difficult for many of those very people who voted him into office, will also be very crucial. The US attitude toward Iran will be another factor. So far, the policy behavior of the administration of President George W. Bush has not been very helpful to the Iranian reformists. President Bush's branding of Iran in late January 2002 as a member of the "axis of evil" (together with Iraq and North Korea) has simply played into the hands of Khatami's opponents, who have taken Bush's remarks as evidence of Washington's unbending hostility toward Iran. These are the issues that are most likely to determine the pace and outcome of Khatami's reforms. Indeed, Khatami's experiment is followed closely not just by the Iranian population, but also by the Muslim countries in the region. Whatever the ultimate direction of this experiment, it will have deep repercussions for both Iran and its neighbors.

Iraq

Iraq, in contrast, is presently at the opposite end of the ideological and political spectrum from Iran. There is no evidence of democratization or liberalization of any kind in the country. It is ruled by what is essentially the pro-secularist dictatorial regime of President Saddam Hussein. Neither the nature nor the governing methods of the regime have substantially changed over the 30 years since Saddam Hussein came to power through a military coup. The personality of Saddam Hussein continues to loom large in the conduct of every aspect of Iraq's domestic life and foreign relations. This situation is not expected to change for as long as Saddam Hussein is in power. However, the situation must be understood in the context of the evolution of the Iraqi state, the circumstances of President Saddam Hussein's rise to power, and the president's unusual personality.

Ever since its formal independence in 1932, Iraq has rarely experienced any form of political liberalization or democratization. It has progressed from one form of dictatorship to another, with personalization rather than institutionalization of politics determining the mode of change and development, as well as the political continuity and survivability of the state. As such, any regime change or socio-economic structural change in the country has come about as the result of either large-scale political violence or suppression. This was the manner in which Iraq was born and it is more or less in this manner that Iraq has evolved and been governed as a state.

A number of factors have interacted to contribute to this situation. The first is the demographic profile and national identity of Iraq. Ethnic and sectarian divisions have frequently posed a serious threat to the country's territorial integrity and its claim to nation-statehood. Iraq's significant Kurdish Sunni minority, who inhabit mainly the north of the country, have persistently revolted for autonomy or independence either on their own or in affiliation with their cross-border kindred in Iran and Turkey. The country's Arab population is divided between Shi'ites and Sunnis, with the former constituting 55–60 percent of the total population, but the latter dominating the ruling elite. The Sunnis' sectarian affiliation with the wider Arab world has been crucial in giving them the advantage over the Shi'ites, who have been viewed as the natural allies of the Arabs' regional rival, Shi'ite Iran.

The second factor is related to the problems associated with the historical entity of Iraq. Following the decline of the Abbasid dynasty, which embodied much of the Arabs' Islamic civilizational achievements from the eighth to the eleventh centuries, Iraq by and large ceased to exist as an identifiable political unit. Under the Ottomans it was reduced to an imperial province, and it was only under British mandate rule after World War II that it was finally reshaped into a political unit in its own right. Some historians claim that this was done artificially, without much consideration given to Iraq's long-term viability. As was the case with their rule in most of the Middle East, the British did little to encourage the development of democratic norms, values, and practices in Iraq. Pro-British absolute monarchical rule became the order of the day until the

Arab nationalist coup of 1958 swept away the monarchy, and with it the vestiges of British influence, and declared Iraq an Arab republic. This opened the way for a radical transformation of the Iraqi political land-scape and thus another, but as violent as ever, phase in the evolution of Iraqi politics. The coup brought various militant sections of Iraqi society into conflict, ushering in an era of bloody coups and counter-coups which lasted for at least a decade.

The third factor was that after 1958, with the heightening of the Cold War, Iraq was surrounded by fairly powerful rival neighbors, whose cross-border ethnic, cultural, and sectarian affiliations provided them with strong anti-Iraqi leverage. A US-backed Iran was positioned to ex-ploit its linkages with the Iraqi Shi'ites and Kurds against Baghdad, and a pro-Western Turkey emerged to treat Iraq as a growing bastion of Arab radicalism and to aid Iraqi Kurdish groups in order to neutralize their possible support for the Kurds of Turkey in their bid for independence. In the meantime, the growing ideological rift and rivalry between Bagh-dad and Damascus left Iraq vulnerable to its most important Arab neighbor, Syria.

The fourth factor related to the nature of and the manner in which the small Arab socialist Ba'ath Party (with no more than 3,000 members) seized power in July 1968, and to the personality of Saddam Hussein. Saddam was rapidly able to combine the use of violence as a means to governance with a brutal manipulation of Iraq's volatile internal situation and complex external relations (as well as oil wealth) to establish a unique personal dictatorship. If it had not been for favorable and oppor-tune conditions generated by Iraq's changing national and international circumstances, the Ba'ath Party could not have seized power, and Sad-dam Hussein – relatively poorly educated and inexperienced, but politi-cally shrewd, brutal, and deceptive – could not have taken the helm.

Although for the first ten years Saddam held the position of vice-president, until he took over from President Hassan al-Bakr, he was from the beginning regarded as the strongman of the regime. He grew out of the violent, repressive political culture that had come to dominate Bagh-dad as the nerve center of the Iraqi polity, and remained committed to that culture in ensuring his own rule and the transformation of Iraq into a Stalinist, modern state. The Ba'athist Arab socialist ideology, as es-poused by its founders Michel 'Aflaq and Salah al-Din Bitar, soon proved to be of little relevance to Saddam Hussein other than to enable him to claim an ideological framework within which he could justify and achieve his personal ambitions. He transformed the Ba'ath Party into a personal refuge within which and around which he could build an elaborate secu-rity–bureaucratic–administrative system, dominated by Sunni Iraqis and more specifically by his Taqridi clan and more narrowly by trusted mem-bers of his family.

As Iraq's oil income quadrupled in the early 1970s and the border and political conflict with Iran subsided following the signing of the 1975 Algiers agreement between the two sides, Saddam was able to expand this system dramatically and to equip its security–military wing with the best arms available. Although initially he befriended the Soviet Union, ultimately he would not allow any friendship to provide comfort to the domestic opposition or stand in the way of the strengthening of his absolute power and his growing ambition to become the paramount regional actor. He showed no hesitation in executing pro-Soviet Iraqi communists at the height of Iraq's public friendship with Moscow at the turn of the 1970s. Nor did he hold back from attacking Iran and fighting one of the longest, bloodiest, and costliest wars of the modern era, or from drawing on regional Arab fear of Khomeini's Islamic regime and Washington's hostility toward it to present himself as the main regional Arab bulwark against Iran in order to win American and Arab support in the war. Furthermore, when he found it necessary and opportune for a variety of reasons, he was more than content to invade the neighboring Arab state of Kuwait in August 1990. In so doing, he appeared to have given little or no consideration to the possible damage that his actions might cause to the Iraqi people and Arab unity, or to the possibility that the invasion could provide more excuses for the United States to bolster its military presence in the Gulf. The latter was the very development that he supposedly wanted to avoid.

Up to the time of the Kuwait invasion, Saddam had succeeded in building a fairly powerful state – both economically and militarily – with a noticeable degree of geopolitical clout in regional politics and an assured place in the international system, but the invasion simply blew all this. Following the reversal of that invasion by a UN-backed but American-led international coalition, by the end of February 1991, Iraq was forced to pay a very heavy price for Saddam's military defeat.

The Western members of the international coalition, more specifically the United States, and the United Nations declared Iraq's Kurdish territory north of the 36th parallel a "safe haven" to protect Iraq's rebellious Kurdish minority against Saddam Hussein's repression, with a "no fly" zone for Iraqi planes over the area. They similarly imposed an air exclusion zone over southern Iraq, covering an area up to the 34th parallel – a limit that in mid-1996 was extended further to the 32nd parallel. This was partly to protect the Iraqi Shi'ites, who are concentrated in the south and had joined the post-war revolt against Saddam Hussein, and partly to reduce any chances of more Iraqi threats against Kuwait and other member states of the pro-Western Gulf Cooperation Council.[21] Further, they empowered the United Nations to undertake an extended mission to destroy, without impunity, all Iraq's weapons of mass destruction and to circumvent its capacity to produce any in the future. In so doing, in the context of Iraq's demographic divisions, they also made northern Iraq vulnerable to Turkish and Iranian intrusions in pursuit of leverage against their respective Kurdish opposition groups.[22]

All this, together with the widespread infrastructural damage that the war inflicted upon Iraq and the devastation that the comprehensive regime of UN economic sanctions brought to the country, has substantially weakened Iraq's domestic structures, virtually destroyed its middle class, and rendered it a divided state. Ever since, Iraq has functioned only partly under the sovereignty of the Baghdad government, and largely under the shadow of the United States and some of its allies. This situation has remained largely unchanged to date, although three new developments are worth stressing. The first is that the United Nations found it necessary in 1996 to sign an "oil for food" agreement with the Iraqi government to allow it to sell a limited amount of oil to meet the humanitarian needs of the Iraqis and pay war reparations to Kuwait. The second is the difficult relationship that has developed between the United Nations and Iraq, with Baghdad finally succeeding in discrediting and halting the work of the UN weapons inspection team (UNSCOM) by mid-1998 because of its claimed use for espionage purposes by the United States and some of its allies. This prompted the United States and the United Kingdom to launch retaliatory attacks on Iraq in November 1998, marking the start of a war of attrition that has continued to date and has apparently been designed to contain the Iraqi regime until such time that conditions become receptive to an alternative. The third development is a growing rift in the UN Security Council between the United States and the United Kingdom on one side, and France, Russia, and China on the other, over the usefulness of maintaining the sanctions, which have done no serious damage to Saddam Hussein's rule but have caused much suffering to the Iraqi people. As a result, the regime of sanctions has lately crumbled, with not only France but also many other countries, including some of the Arab countries, deliberately ignoring the sanctions.

These developments, and the survival of Saddam Hussein's regime, may have constituted a victory for Baghdad, but at a great cost. Iraq has been subjected to severe limitations on the exercise of its political and territorial sovereignty, undermining its position as a sovereign state. Even if there is a change in Iraqi circumstances, such as the forcible removal of Saddam Hussein by the United States, the country may not recover from its present ordeal for quite some time. As a result, it is likely to remain a fairly weak state for the foreseeable future.

As the situation stands, Iraq has no more than a few democratic pretensions, such as tightly state-controlled and state-run presidential and legislative elections every few years and a totally compliant National Assembly. Any opposition is completely suppressed, and the middle class as the main agent of change is virtually destroyed. Freedom of thought and expression is the sole property of the leadership. What President Saddam Hussein has succeeded in instituting is more than a mono-organizational society, which characterized Stalin's rule in the Soviet Union. It is what one might call a "mono-personalized" society, in which one man is all-powerful and supreme; no one else has any security and everyone is a potential target of state suppression. Even the assistance provided under the "oil for food" deal or any other international humanitarian scheme has been actively used to bolster his political and social control. Iraq stands more or less as a pariah in the international system, lacking the very basic elements of civil society and principles of democracy.

The tragedy facing the international community is that, ever since the Gulf War, Saddam Hussein has been able to justify this in the name of UN sanctions and American aggression. The Iraqi opposition in exile remains deeply divided and incapable of providing a viable alternative, so the biggest loser for the foreseeable future will be the Iraqi people. Thus, Iraq's autocratic circumstances are diametrically opposite Iran's robust processes of building an Islamic civil society and Islamic democracy. Whatever the outcome of the Iranian experiment, the problem with Iraq is that it is doing nothing at all. Whereas Iranians may be looking into a window of opportunity, the Iraqis can only wait painfully for such a window to open. As long as President Saddam Hussein is in power and Iraq is placed under international sanctions, which have made little or no dent in the regime, the Iraqi people will continue to suffer.

Conclusion

A Western process of democratization may not be the ideal for either Iran or Iraq, or for that matter for other Muslim countries in the Middle East or elsewhere in the world, given the cultural, social, and historical factors that set them distinctively apart from the West. The Iranian experiment at least shows that a Muslim country does not have to follow a Western model in order to achieve a civil, virtuous, and decent existence for its citizens. It can draw on its own intellectual and cultural traditions, and has the means and possibilities to construct a process of change whereby it can provide its citizens with those opportunities that may not take them down the path of democratization as required by Western democracies, but will enable them to achieve political liberalization within the framework of promoting a civil society based on Islam. In these manifestations, an Islamic civil society is not necessarily incompatible with some of the basic principles of Western democracies and universal human rights.[23] As a religion and a civilization, Islam does not oppose such a development but strongly endorses it.

Notes

1. For details, see Alexis de Tocqueville, *Democracy in America*, edited and abridged by Richard D. Heffner, New York: Mentor, 1956.
2. Anthony Arblaster, *Democracy*, Milton Keynes: Open University Press, 1987, p. 8.
3. For a discussion of different models of democracy, see David Held, "Democracy: From City-States to a Cosmopolitan Order," *Political Studies*, vol. 40 (special issue), 1992, pp. 10–39.
4. Amin Saikal, *The Rise and Fall of the Shah*, Princeton, NJ: Princeton University Press, 1980, Ch. 8.
5. For details, see Said Amir Arjomand, *The Turban for the Crown: The Islamic Revolution in Iran*, New York: Oxford University Press, 1988, esp. ch. 8; Amin Saikal, "Khomeini's Iran," *Current Affairs Bulletin*, vol. 60, no. 5, October 1983, pp. 18–30.
6. For a critical assessment of the Islamic regime, see Martin Wright, *Iran: The Khomeini Revolution*, London: Longman, 1989, esp. pp. 31–42; Hazhir Teimourian, "Iran's 15 Years of Islam," *The World Today*, vol. 50, no. 4, April 1994, pp. 67–70; Darius M. Rejali, *Torture & Modernity: Self, Society, and State in Modern Iran*, Boulder, CO: Westview Press, 1994, esp. chs. 7–8.
7. For a detailed discussion of the concept of *jihad* in Islam, see John L. Esposito, *Unholy War: Terror in the Name of Islam*, New York: Oxford University Press, 2002, ch. 2.
8. For a discussion and different meanings of the concept, see Joseph Schacht, *The Origins of Muhammadan Jurisprudence*, Oxford: Clarendon Press, 1979; Wael B. Hallaq, "Was the Gate of *Ijtihad* Closed," *International Journal of Middle East Studies*, vol. 16, 1984, pp. 3–41; Bernard G. Weiss, "Interpretation in Islamic Law: The Theory of *Ijtihad*," *American Journal of Comparative Law*, vol. 26, Spring 1978, pp. 199–212.
9. For a discussion of Soroush's ideas, see Valla Vakili, *Debating Religion and Politics in Iran: The Political Thought of Abdulkarim Soroush*, Occasional Paper Series no. 2, New York: Council on Foreign Relations, 1996.
10. Mohammad Khatami, *Dialogue and the New Millennium*, Address delivered to the 30th General Conference of the United Nations Educational, Scientific and Cultural Organisation (UNESCO), Paris, 29 October 1999, p. 2.
11. Mohammad Khatami, *Islam, Dialogue and Civil Society*, Canberra: Australian National University, Centre for Arab and Islamic Studies, 2000, p. 111.
12. "Statement by H.E. Seyyed Mohammad Khatami, President of the Islamic Republic of Iran and Chairman of the Eighth Session of the Islamic Summit Conference, Tehran, 9 December 1997," *Iranian Journal of International Affairs*, vol. 9, No. 4, Winter 1997/98, p. 601.
13. Ibid., p. 603.
14. Khatami, *Islam, Dialogue and Civil Society*, pp. 53–54.
15. Ruhollah Khomeini, *Sahifey-e Noor* [The Book of Light], Tehran: *Markaz-e Madarek Anghlab-e Islami*, vol. 21, 1990, p. 47.
16. Khatami, *Islam, Dialogue and Civil Society*, p. 57.
17. Ibid., p. 104.
18. Ibid., p. 85.
19. Ibid., p. 90.
20. John. F. Burns, "Former Hanging Judge of Iran," *New York Times*, 23 October 1999.
21. For details, see Ofra Bengio, "The Challenge to the Territorial Integrity of Iraq," *Survival*, Summer 1995, pp. 74–94.
22. George Joffe, "Iraq's Strategic Role," *Middle East*, May 1993, pp. 221–4.
23. For an example of the debate, see the special issue of the *Middle East Journal*, vol. 47, no. 2, Spring 1993.

10

State power and democratization in North Africa: Developments in Morocco, Algeria, Tunisia, and Libya

Tom Pierre Najem

Increasing democratization has been a trend in the developing world, particularly since the dissolution of the Soviet Union in the early 1990s. With the apparent failure of the heavily statist, one-party-driven, command economy model of socialist development long advocated by the Soviets and adopted by their allies and many other nations in the third world, the Western pluralist, democratic, and capitalist model of development has in effect become the only system of governance that is perceived by most developing countries as being both viable in practice and attractive in terms of its societal implications. Part and parcel of this perception, of course, is that the victory of Western capitalism in the Cold War has meant that the Western powers are in a position not merely to influence development as exemplars but also to impose their preferences. The increasing globalization of the world economy and the predominance of not only Western countries but also powerful intergovernmental and non-governmental organizations such as the World Bank, the International Monetary Fund (IMF), Amnesty International, and many others has meant that in many cases, and for better or for worse, development capital, trade, and other prerequisites for effective development have become contingent upon the adoption of Western ideals and standards.

To some extent, the past decade has been characterized not only by increasing democratization, but also by considerable triumphalism on the part of some of its advocates. Some scholars, most notably Francis Fukuyama, have suggested that the Western form of liberal democracy can now be recognized as the only truly historically viable and legitimate form of government. Hence, the fall of the Soviet Union and the now presumably unstoppable march of democratization represent the "end of history."[1] Other commentators have been more cautious in their assessment, while nevertheless at the same time maintaining a heavily pro-democratic bias. Samuel Huntington, for example, has identified further and perhaps more dangerous, albeit more geographically limited, rivals to democracy from China and from Islamist movements found throughout the Islamic world.[2] Only time will tell whether Fukuyama's or Huntington's conceptions of the future development of democracy are more valid, but it is worth observing at this point that both perspectives make contested value-oriented assumptions about the historical strength and desirability of the type of democratic government that happens to be prevalent at this point in time.

In any case, irrespective of the causes and historical implications, increasing democratization has undeniably been a dominant trend. According to a recent study, in 1975 at least 68 percent of the world's countries were controlled by authoritarian regimes, but by the end of 1995 only about a quarter of regimes were strongly authoritarian, with the rest having held some sort of competitive elections and having adopted at least formal guarantees of political and civil rights.[3] However, a couple of regions have resisted the trend, most notably the Middle East and North Africa (MENA). This chapter considers the underlying factors that have led to the continuing prevalence of authoritarianism in North Africa, with a focus on Morocco, Algeria, Tunisia, and Libya. After the introduction of the conceptual framework of this analysis, the four case studies are discussed in detail, followed by concluding thoughts on the future of democratization processes in these four countries. In all cases, the overwhelming power of the state, vis-à-vis state–society relations, is the main hindrance to substantive democratization in the near future. Furthermore, in the event that a state crisis did occur in any of these countries, it is unclear, and indeed seems unlikely, that a democratic regime would emerge to replace the existing authoritarian state order.

Conceptual framework

This section looks briefly at some of the key explanatory factors that other theorists have identified as important with respect to the democratization process in various settings. Before proceeding, however, it will be useful to define what I mean by the term "democratization" in this study, because it can be, and has been, defined in different ways by people with different ideological or political goals and biases. For the purpose of this chapter, the definition suggested by David Potter et al. in their 1997 book *Democratization* will serve as the reference point. The authors define democratization as a movement in a society "from less accountable to more accountable government, from less competitive (or non-existent) elections to freer and fairer competitive elections, from severely re-stricted to better protected civil and political rights, and from weak (or non-existent) autonomous associations in civil society to more autono-mous and more numerous associations."[4]

Having defined democratization in terms of progress in four areas, – accountability, elections, civil and political rights, and autonomous associations – I will now look at six factors that many theorists have identified as being important with respect to development in these areas. These are: state and political institutions; economic development; social divisions; civil society; political culture and ideas; and transnational and international engagements.[5]

State and political institutions

As indicated in the introduction, state and political institutions may be the single most important factor in the context of this study. The extent of the state's power in relation to other actors in society is an important indicator of the likelihood of substantive democratization in a society. If the historical, political, and/or economic circumstances of a given country are such that there are powerful actors in society, be they military ele-ments, powerful economic classes, or well-organized social and political associations, that are capable of challenging state power, then the pros-pects for the development of an open political process are much greater than they would be in a society where the state is pervasive and is able to co-opt or effectively suppress potential rivals or play them off against each other.

Economic development

Different schools of theory all assign a great deal of importance to eco-nomic development as a factor that potentially helps to explain the pro-cess of democratization in some societies. However, the exact rela-tionship between development and democratization is not particularly clear-cut. For modernization theorists, when a society develops to a certain extent, demand for participation in the political process tends to increase. However, this is not always the case, and such demands may come about as a result of other factors such as political culture or the establishment of extensive state welfare networks. For structural theorists, the relationship between economic development and democratization is even less clear.

Development can lead to democratization, but can also lead to other kinds of political systems. The decisive factor seems to be the class structure and class interests of a society, sometimes coupled with transnational economic or political processes.

Social divisions

Some theorists have suggested that certain social classes that emerge as a result of capitalist development, particularly the bourgeoisie, have natural pro-democratic leanings in the face of authoritarian regimes. However, there is plenty of historical evidence to suggest that, although this may have been the case in nineteenth-century West European societies, it is not necessarily the case in all societies. It is consequently important, when looking at social divisions, to pay attention to the factors that shape class interests and class alliances within particular social and historical settings. Other types of social divisions, including ethnic and religious divisions, can affect the prospects for democratic development. Crucially, if a society is too divided and its people have no sense of common identity, the prospects for democratization can be quite limited.

Civil society

Civil society can be defined in terms of the number and autonomy of associations functioning outside, or at least partly outside, of the state context in a society. Many theorists see a well-developed civil society as a factor that can potentially balance the power of the state and can consequently contribute to the development and consolidation of a democratic system.[6] It is important to note that civil society closely reflects class and social divisions in society, and that substantial groups within civil society in a state can be anti-democratic. Therefore the development of a large and active civil society will not necessarily promote democratization. Furthermore, the autonomy of civil associations is a crucial element. If many associations exist but they are closely linked to, or regulated by, the state, then they are not likely to be effective democratizing agents.

Political culture and ideas

There is considerable controversy within theoretical circles about the role of political culture and ideas in the development of democracy. Modernization theorists tend to argue that the development of democratic political culture is a key factor, whereas structural theorists contend that the structures of democracy usually pre-date the development of democratic political culture. There is some consensus that institutionally rooted values, such as organized mass religion, can be very important, for either promoting or inhibiting democratic development. Yet many scholars have noted that even religious doctrines are periodically subject to substantive reinterpretation as a result of social developments.

Transnational and international engagements

A fundamental concept, which virtually all theorists accept, is that no society develops in a complete vacuum. Developments in, and pressures emanating from, the international system can have great impact on the course of development adopted by a society. With the post–Cold War advent of globalization, this is perhaps more true today than it ever was in the past. Whether or not the globalization process necessarily encourages democratization is a matter of considerable debate and, interestingly, the case studies in this chapter can be used to illustrate how the globalization process both contributes to democratization and inhibits it.

Having identified and commented briefly on these six key factors, I will now look at how they can be applied to the four North African countries under study in this chapter. Unfortunately, a systematic exploration of how each concept applies to each country is beyond the scope of this study. Consequently, the discussion will simply emphasize the factors that are particularly important in the context of the ongoing political development process in each individual country. It should be reiterated at this point that each of the countries is effectively dominated by a very powerful state and that, consequently, the prospects for substantive democratization are limited. However, it is important to note that different factors have contributed to the strength of the state in each case.

Case studies

Morocco

Since achieving independence in 1956, Morocco has been dominated by a regime controlled by successive monarchs: Muhammad V from 1956 to 1961, Hassan II from 1961 to 1999, and Muhammad VI from 1999 to the present. Although the political system was ostensibly a multi-party pluralist system with an active civil society from the very beginning, in practice the various parties and forces operating within the system have always been under the effective control of the monarchy, a situation that continues to this day and shows no sign of changing substantially in the foreseeable future.[7]

With respect to the six factors outlined in the previous section, the course of development has been fairly complex, but has tended strongly to favor the continuation of the monarchy as the overwhelming political force in the country. The way that the Moroccan state and its institutions are structured has historically been probably the major factor supporting the ascendancy of the monarchical regime, because it overlaps considerably with developments relating to virtually all of the other five factors associated with democratization.

Up until the late 1990s, only political parties controlled by, or at least closely allied with, the monarchy were allowed to form governments, thereby giving the monarch de facto control of the political system. Furthermore, although there were opposition parties, which pressed for greater independence of decision-making, even these parties did not question the fundamental legitimacy of the monarchical system. The state is structured in such a way that the regime has been able to use Morocco's social divisions to its advantage by allowing competing factions to form political parties and then playing them off against each other. To a great extent, the monarchy has used the political system to institutionalize its alliance with the conservative social elements, predominantly the rural elements. In the meantime, elements that have questioned the basis of the monarch's authority, particularly Islamists, have been completely excluded from the political process. Partly as a result of increasing pressures on the Moroccan system, especially economic problems, by March 1998 Hassan II decided to allow the formation of an opposition government under the ostensible direction of Abdelrahmane Youssoufi. However, the advent of this system of "alternance" was a very limited experiment in opening the political system. The most powerful ministerial portfolios, including the interior ministry, the strongest of all, remained in the hands of the king's supporters, and the inclusion of opposition elements not only improved the king's standing on the international stage but also allowed him to deflect some of the blame in the event that economic and social problems continued or became worse. Ultimately, the monarch continues to retain veto power over the entire political system.[8]

The state has to a great extent retained control over the economy and the regime has used this to secure its dominance of the system. Unlike many of the other countries in the region, Morocco has no real oil wealth and is not a rentier state. Consequently, the regime has not enjoyed the same kind of abundant wealth or absolute dominance of the economy that one tends to see in states of this type. Nevertheless, the regime has been a very active player in the economic sphere, and has managed to co-opt or subdue powerful economic elements through incentives, by distributing patronage and economic privileges, or through pressure, for example by threatening to seize control in areas where its interests are threatened. The leading rural and urban economic classes have tended to be quite conservative and have preferred to ally themselves with the regime rather than challenge its influence, perhaps largely because Morocco's economy is not very strong and the state, rather than restricting their opportunities, has historically acted to protect their interests.[9]

Although Morocco's civil society has been fairly large and active throughout the independence period, groups at this level (similarly to political parties in the state context) have generally existed on the sufferance of the regime. The monarchy has to a great extent been able to penetrate and co-opt civil associations, in effect robbing them of any real autonomy. Furthermore, the regime has been able to dictate the boundaries of acceptable discourse about the political system. Limited criticism has historically been allowed in a number of areas, but the most crucial issues, particularly any questioning or criticism concerning the dominance of the monarch, have remained strictly off-limits. By and large, most of Morocco's citizens have been willing to abide by such restrictions and have practiced self-censorship to a considerable degree. This is not only a result of the regime's extensive coercive mechanisms but also ties into Morocco's political culture.[10]

The Moroccan political culture has historically placed a strong emphasis on the monarch's traditional role as a divinely appointed ruler and defender of the Islamic faith. Reverence for the monarch and response to his personal charisma have played an important role in reinforcing the dominance of the regime, particularly during the long reign of Hassan II. The monarch's strong linkage with Islamic traditions and beliefs has been a critical factor in shaping and reinforcing the regime's response to challenges from the Islamic community. In turn, the Islamist opposition in Morocco is less organized and has a smaller power base than that in many of the other countries in the region.[11]

Finally, the state and the regime have also benefited to a great extent from Morocco's transnational and international engagements, although, particularly recently, trends have emerged that may ultimately undermine the regime's power. The regime has been able to use the regional rivalry with Algeria to mobilize support. Initially this was based on concern about the spread of Algeria's socialist model into Morocco, then the Western Sahara conflict became a central focus, and, finally, the regime has been able to benefit from the collapse of the Algerian system by presenting this to its own people as an example of what might happen to Morocco if the monarchical system ever broke down. A further international factor, one that both supports and undercuts the regime, is the impact of the increasing globalization process. Unlike some of the other countries in the region, Morocco has been engaged in the international system since independence. For many years the regime benefited from its alignment with the United States and the Western powers during the Cold War, and this alignment has continued to this day, since the regime is seen as a moderating force in relation to the spread of radical Islam throughout the region. However, in the post–Cold War environment, the regime has been under some pressure to open both its economic and its political systems (particularly with respect to freedom of expression and other human rights) so that the country can be fully integrated into the global economy. Partly this has been active cultural pressure for liberalization on the part of the World Bank, the IMF, and other Western aid donors. Partly it has been a more passive form of cultural pressure arising from the exposure of the population to Western ideals, standards, and modes of behavior. Counterbalancing these influences to some extent is the general desire by Western actors to keep the political system fairly stable – a level of stability that might break down if the government were pressured into radical reforms. After all, there would be no point investing in Morocco if it were on the verge of a revolution or a collapse like the Algerian system.[12]

Since the accession of Muhammad VI to the Moroccan throne in 1999, there have been some developments that have encouraged Western observers. The new king has laid a great deal of stress on his desire to reform the system (ridding it of some of its more unpleasant features), to reduce social inequity, and to provide stronger guarantees of fundamental human rights for all citizens. The regime has been visibly active, particularly with respect to the human rights issue, freeing most of Morocco's political prisoners, compensating families of past victims of regime oppression, extending freedom of expression, and establishing links with international human rights organizations.

However, although the new king has expressed a desire to open the political system, no steps have yet been taken that would limit the overwhelming power of the monarchical regime in any real way, and one must question the extent to which there is any real commitment within the regime to such an objective.[13] Furthermore, even though there are signs of an increasing desire for democratic reforms among the Moroccan public, no social structures are currently in place for translating such aspirations into effective political action. Moreover, ongoing structural processes, such as the overriding transnational desire for political stability, are not conducive to sweeping reform in the short term. Perhaps the best that one can hope for is a very gradual development toward a democratic form of government. If a state crisis should occur, particularly in the event of an economic collapse, it is by no means clear that it would necessarily be driven by pro-democratic forces or would have the result of establishing a democratic regime. The most likely beneficiaries of a crisis would be Morocco's Islamist groups, which have been gaining a following, particularly among the urban poor.

Algeria

It is important to place the structural processes that characterize the Algerian system in the context of that country's historical development, because, more so than with respect to the other case studies, they have been shaped in response to monumental events and/or crises. The post-independence history of Algeria is probably best viewed in three phases: the development and dominance of a one-party state from 1962 up to the 1980s; the economic and state crisis of the 1980s; and the period of military rule following the experiment with free elections in the early 1990s and the subsequent civil conflict.[14]

From 1962 to the 1980s, Algeria could basically be classified as a functional rentier state. However, it should be recognized that the regime drew legitimacy not just from its oil wealth but also from its perceived historic mission as the liberator of the nation and as a non-aligned model of development for the third world. As a result of these factors, the regime of Houari Boumedienne (1965–78) and the National Liberation Front (Front de Liberation National, or FLN) was able to secure virtually complete monopoly over economic and political power in a very heavily statist system.

By the 1980s, however, as Bahgat Korany and Saad Amrani have noted, "[t]he implicit social contract between state and people – based on offering social welfare in return for deprivation of some basic political rights – collapsed after the continuous decline in oil earnings and the state's consequent lack of resources to keep buying off its people. The state's inefficiency became apparent and its legitimacy eroded."[15] The regime's ultimate response to this crisis was to attempt a fairly rapid process of economic and political liberalization. The economic dimension was shaped by the need to diversify the economic base and to open up the economy to outside investment, while the political imperative was to relieve the pressure generated by mass opposition to the one-party state. Political reforms were introduced with the intention of transforming the system into a multi-party system (in which, incidentally, the FLN expected to continue being the most powerful party).[16]

Opening the political process so quickly after an extended period of monolithic government, however, proved unmanageable and resulted in the emergence of a proliferation of poorly organized pro-democratic parties with ethnic or secular interests, as well as a better organized and more radical Islamist opposition. Algeria's first multi-party elections took place in 1990 and 1991 with results that surprised and horrified both the regime and many outside observers – that is, a fairly comfortable victory for the Islamic Salvation Front (Front Islamique du Salut, or FIS), an organization that showed questionable commitment to the continuation of a multi-party political system. The regime suspended the election process, in effect nullifying the Islamist victory; the Islamist response was to attempt to overthrow the regime by violence.[17] A full-scale civil conflict ensued (and continues, with periodically varying levels of intensity, to this day),[18] with tens of thousands of civilian casualties and a nearly complete collapse of social order in the country.[19] Because of a substantial weakening of the FLN, the military took control of the state and set about restoring order, with considerable support from the international community.

The structure of the state, the continuing role of transnational and international actors, and the nature and extent of Algeria's emergent civil society are key elements in assessing Algeria's prospects for democratization.

It is important to recognize not only the state's continuing domination by an authoritarian military elite but also that the institutions are structured in such a way as to concentrate political power very heavily in the executive branch. In short, one obstacle to the democratization of the system is the dominant role of the presidency in the Algerian political process. It should be noted that Algeria did continue its flirtation with at least an ostensible democratic process by holding a presidential election in 1995 and legislative elections in 1997. However, the victory of the military's favored candidate, retired general Lamin Zeroual, in the presidential elections probably represented a consolidation of military rule rather than a genuine opening of the system. Another presidential election was held in 1999, which initially seemed to be more openly contested but it ended in acrimony as six of the seven candidates withdrew, claiming that the election was being rigged in favor of the eventual winner, Abdelaziz Bouteflika. These developments notwithstanding, it is probably safe to assume that the military will continue to dominate the political process for as long as the conflict with the violent Islamist elements continues.[20]

From the point at which the regime nullified the 1990 and 1991 elections to the present time, the international community, particularly the Western powers, has supported the military-dominated regime in its conflict against the Islamists. There has been, and continues to be, widespread international and regional concern about the implications for Algeria and its neighbors should an Islamist regime ever succeed in taking power. As long as this situation holds, there will be little, if any, real transnational or international pressure on Algeria to move from an authoritarian to a more open society and political system.

As for Algeria's civil society, it is still gradually emerging. Although there are some democratic elements, particularly among the middle class and the Berbers, the development of a broad-based democratic political culture, civil society, and institutional base has not occurred and the prospects for substantive democratization of the system are consequently very limited. The point that needs to be stressed above all in this context is that the associations that currently exist are deeply divided on the future nature of Algerian society. There are strongly pro-Islamic groups on the one hand, and strongly secular groups on the other, with very little apparent willingness for compromise on either side. It is possible that the regime may attempt to foster the secular, pro-democracy groups as a counterbalance to the Islamist groups, but it is probably too early to tell whether or not the country will ultimately benefit from such a strategy.[21]

Tunisia

There are a number of similarities between the Algerian case and developments in Tunisia. The post-independence period saw the creation, and the extended rule, of a very strong one-party state. Over time, the economic situation became worse, the demands for an opening of the political system became greater, and the state eventually decided to engage in a reform program. However, whereas the reforms in Algeria led to a collapse of the system and civil conflict, the state in Tunisia refused to allow Islamist elements to participate in the system, curtailed its political reforms in the face increasing Islamist radicalism, and has reasserted its authority over the system through increasing political repression. In discussing the prospects for democratization, I shall once again emphasize the dominant role of the state, the course of economic development, the impact of transnational factors, and the relative underdevelopment of democratic civil society in the Tunisian context.[22]

Tunisia became independent in 1956, and until 1987 it was ruled by Habib Bourgiba and his Parti Socialiste Destourien (PSD), creating a very strong one-party state. The initial post-independence agenda was the establishment of an Arab nationalist state bent on modernizing and secularizing society. However, unlike other regional states with similar agendas (i.e. Algeria and Libya), the Tunisian state was able to obtain only modest levels of revenue from oil and other external rents, and consequently was not in a particularly strong economic position. The Bourgibist state did nationalize the country's industries and exercise strong control over the economy, but had less patronage to distribute in order to placate potential opposition forces. After abandoning the socialist experiment by 1970, the regime experienced a period of steady economic growth, and its pro-Western foreign policy and progressive social agenda (exemplified by the Personal Status Code, in effect a list of formally guaranteed human rights) combined to ensure that the state enjoyed reasonably cordial relations with the Western powers. This set of circumstances freed the regime to continue its monopolization of the political process and its suppression of opposition elements.[23]

During the 1980s, however, the economic situation deteriorated significantly owing to falling oil prices and a growing debt problem. This, combined with frustration at the closed nature of the political system and increasing social inequities, led to a significant increase in mass opposition to the regime, particularly Islamist opposition (which was also inspired by the success of the Iranian revolution).[24] By 1987, even Bourgiba's supporters in the PSD had become disenchanted with his increasingly erratic leadership and his failure to deal with the growing political and economic crises. The result was a "constitutional coup" that brought Zine el Abidine Ben Ali to power. Ben Ali committed the regime to a series of economic and political reforms that led some to believe that Tunisia would embark on a course of truly democratic development.[25]

While pursuing an economic liberalization program with some success, Ben Ali also sought to quell popular dissent by opening up the political process, although the extent to which he was prepared to enact truly democratic reforms is questionable. Certainly he did establish a clearer constitutional distinction between the state and the PSD and allowed the formation of a number of legal opposition parties. He changed the name of the PSD to the Rassemblement Constitutionnel Democratique (RCD) and tried to broaden its popular base. In September 1988, he established the National Pact, which was designed to reconcile opposition elements through dialogue and to commit all of the political parties to a program that would revive the country's political, social, and economic life.[26]

Finally, Ben Ali attempted to engage in a dialogue with the most numerous and most influential opposition element, the Mouvement de la tendance islamique (MTI). However, for reasons that are not clear, he refused to legalize the party and allow it to participate in the 1989 parliamentary elections. Some commentators trace Ben Ali's decision on this crucial matter to his concern that the MTI was undemocratic and was participating in the system only in order to subvert it; other commentators trace the decision to his concern that the MTI would actually displace the RCD in a truly competitive election. Whatever the reasoning behind the decision, it had a disastrous effect on the political liberalization process. Essentially, having been excluded from the political process while other opposition elements were being included led the main Islamist faction[27] to become increasingly radical; the regime responded by becoming increasingly repressive, to the extent that much of the progress that had been made in moving away from authoritarian government was eventually reversed.[28]

The overriding theme of Tunisian politics from 1989 to the present has been the tension between an increasingly repressive regime and the extra-legal Islamist opposition. Contemporary developments in Algeria have only added to the Tunisian state's determination to suppress the Islamist elements, and it should be noted that the repressive measures have been tolerated if not openly supported by the international community as a whole as a result of similar concerns. Given this transnational dimension and the overwhelming power of the state, it is difficult to see how any democratization will be possible in Tunisia in the near future.

Furthermore, the elements within civil society (i.e., non-Islamist elements such as the bourgeoisie) that in other circumstances might champion democratic development remain poorly developed and do not enjoy the same levels of mass support as the non-democratic Islamist elements. As with the Algerian case, it seems that loosening the authoritarian state order in Tunisia was not a sufficient condition for the establishment of a democratic, or even democratizing, regime.

On the basis of the experience of these two states one might question whether a rapid transition from an authoritarian to a democratic state order is possible unless other structural conditions are also present, including, for example, a developed civil society, a democratic political culture (or at least a political culture that is not strongly anti-democratic), and/or powerful pro-democratic social groups.[29]

Libya

The power of the state and the nature of economic development have historically been the most important factors in the slow democratization process in Libya since Colonel Muammar Qaddafi seized power in 1969, creating and maintaining a strongly authoritarian political system. The power of the state has been such that democratic political culture and the development of a democratic civil society have in effect been nonexistent. Furthermore, the course of economic development has limited the political effects of social divisions to a great extent. The main factor that weakened the regime's grip was the impact of transnational forces in the 1980s and 1990s. However, two issues are important in this context. The first is that the opposition to Qaddafi was not pro-democratic, and the second is that the regime so far seems to have completely reasserted its control over the system.

Libya is a fairly typical example of a rentier state. Many theorists have noted that highly asymmetric economic and political development is a feature of this particular state form.[30] Essentially, as economic development proceeds, the authoritarian regime is able to reinforce its dominance of the political system by using the externally generated income from oil revenues to buy off or co-opt potential opposition elements, while at the same time using its financial strength to bolster its internal coercive mechanisms. Libya has certainly historically conformed to this model. Qaddafi's regime has exercised complete control over the economy and has used the advantages derived thereby to dominate society as a whole. Because the government had, and continues to have, complete control over the education system, the mass media, the laws and practices concerning the formation and behavior of non-state associations, and so on, there has been virtually no development of democratic values, political culture, or civil society. Of course, the regime has also been able to retain control of the military, and has exercised complete control over the police force, along with an impressive network of internal coercive mechanisms.

However, particularly from the second half of the 1980s and through the 1990s, the regime's power was challenged by a number of transnational pressures: US military pressure, including occasional direct military action against Libya such as in April 1986; international sanctions; the economic implications of fluctuating oil prices; and the rise of Islamist movements throughout the MENA region. US military pressure was related to Qaddafi's ideological conflict with the West, particularly the perceived association of his regime with terrorist activities, most significantly the Lockerbie bombing in 1988. Qaddafi's refusal to hand over the suspects in the bombing to Western authorities led to the imposition of UN sanctions. These curtailed Libya's economic activity, resulting in high prices on consumer goods and food and the withdrawal of certain financial benefits and perks (such as international travel) that the regime had previously supplied to important groups such as the military. Declining oil prices throughout the period contributed significantly to the economic crisis and led to further erosion of the regime's ability to maintain its control over society. Finally, the emergence of Islamist groups, particularly in Egypt and Algeria, inspired the formation of similar groups in Libya. As a result of these transnational pressures, the Qaddafi regime faced some level of opposition from three sources within Libyan society during the 1990s: elements within the military, certain tribal groups, and Islamist groups.[31]

In 1993, there were reports of an attempted military coup in Bani Wali, 100 miles southeast of Tripoli. The plot failed, 1,500 people were arrested, and hundreds were killed. The attempted coup was apparently motivated partly by dissatisfaction in the military with delayed payment of salaries, the cutting of officers' perks and overseas training, and the cutting of weapons purchases.[32]

The opposition from tribal groups was partly related to the attempted military coup. Members of the Warfalla tribe, for example, were accused of leading the coup and a number of tribal leaders were either executed or imprisoned as a consequence. The grievances of the tribal groups were probably also partly related to the regime's reduced capacity to distribute patronage during this period.[33]

Finally, the opposition from Islamist groups was, as noted previously, inspired to a great extent by the development of Islamist movements within other regional states. During the 1990s, at least four militant Libyan groups were formed and, through activities in Libya and beyond, they pursued policies aimed at destabilizing the regime. There were numerous reported incidents of assassinations and attacks on military posts and government figures. The regime responded by bringing its massive coercive capacity to bear on the Islamist groups with the aim of neutralizing their influence and destroying their capacity actively to oppose the regime. Although it is difficult to obtain reliable data, it seems that the regime's attempts to deal with the resistance have been fairly successful.[34]

Toward the end of the 1990s the Qaddafi regime took steps to reduce its international isolation. Perhaps the most notable development was Qaddafi's decision to hand over the Lockerbie suspects for trial in Europe. Along with his acknowledgement of responsibility in some other incidents and his agreement to provide monetary compensation, this resulted in the lifting of UN sanctions on Libya. This has reduced the economic pressure on the regime and has coincided with a rise in oil prices, which only makes the situation more favorable from the regime's perspective. Consequently, the regime is now in a stronger position than it has been for some time. However, even in the event that the regime should suffer as the result of an unexpected crisis (for example, the death of the Colonel from causes natural or otherwise), it seems unlikely that a democratizing regime would emerge to replace it. None of the socially powerful elements currently operating outside of the state context has serious democratic leanings, and the economy and, indeed, most of the other social structures as they are currently constituted are not conducive to short-term democratic development.[35]

Conclusion

Given the widely perceived importance of the democratization trend, it is not surprising that a great number of scholars have attempted to account for the lack of substantive democratization in the MENA region. There are basically two schools of thought, both of which require some consideration.

The first school of thought, which tends to be associated with the modernization theory of democracy, holds that the continuing authoritarianism of the region is based on its "exclusivity," that is, its unique social arrangements and political culture. The premise of modernization theory, which was originally developed by Seymour Martin Lipset in his 1960 essay "Economic Development and Democracy," and which has been adopted and expanded by many subsequent theorists, is that there is a strong correlation between modernization, in terms of quantitative factors such as gross national product, per capita income, urbanization, and literacy, and the development of democratic institutions and modes of behavior in a society.[36] Modernization theorists looking at MENA have noted that many of the countries in the region have achieved levels of modernization with respect to many, if not most, of these factors that would lead one to expect a concurrent process of democratization. However, democratization has obviously not taken place. In order to account for this, theorists of the modernization school have tended to refer to the prevalence of Islam in these societies, the supposed reason for an inherently anti-democratic cultural system.[37]

The second school of thought, which tends to be associated with the structuralist theory of democracy, rejects the notion of exclusivity and holds that the continuing authoritarianism should be accounted for in terms of ongoing structural processes that must be viewed in the context of both the historical development of the countries in the region and their position in the international system. These theorists have conceded in many cases that Islam can be, and has been, used to support an authoritarian social order. However, they have argued that, given different structural processes, Islam might be interpreted differently and might contribute to, rather than detract from, the development of a democratic political culture. Consequently, although they often incorporate observations about political culture and Islam into their studies, they do not account for the lack of democratization in the region primarily by reference to this factor. Instead, they prefer to view continuing authoritarianism in terms of overlapping structural factors, such as class alignments in society; the extent and nature of economic development; the level of engagement in the international system; and, probably most significantly (being both a cause and a result of the other factors), the overwhelming dominance of the state at the expense of all other actors and forces in society.[38]

This study focused on developments (or lack thereof) with respect to the ongoing process of democratization in the four North African countries of Morocco, Algeria, Tunisia, and Libya. The data presented support the structuralist account of societal evolution rather than the modernization theorists' notion of MENA exclusivity. The exclusivity argument emphasizes the significance of just one causal factor – an Arab/Muslim political culture that is held to be uniquely anti-democratic. This is far too simplistic an explanation. Although the four countries do have certain political cultural elements in common, and although they have all failed to make substantive progress toward real democratization, they are not otherwise particularly similar. On the contrary, they represent an interesting cross-section of the different types of states found in the Arab world on at least three levels: the contrast between rentier and non-rentier states; the contrast between traditional monarchical states and one-party states; and, finally, the contrast between states that are increasingly engaged in the globalization process and the international system generally, and states that are in effect international pariahs, excluded from the system for one reason or another. In addition, and perhaps most significantly in this context, although Islam and its associated political discourse are present to some extent in all four countries, the level and the nature of their impact are by no means uniform.

The structuralist theorists' contention that the failure of these states to democratize should be accounted for by looking at a number of overlapping factors, above all the overwhelming strength of the state, is a much more compelling argument. Although all four countries are, indeed, characterized by very strong states, this is not really explicable in terms of any one readily identified factor. On the contrary, it seems that different processes – structural processes – must be carefully examined to explain the preponderance of the state in each case. The point that must be emphasized is that in each of the four countries the state has become the overwhelmingly dominant player in the political system for different, complex, reasons, and not because of Islam alone.

There is a consensus among theorists of all schools that substantive democratization is extremely unlikely in this kind of state setting. The underlying argument is that ruling elites do not concede power in a society unless they are forced to do so, either by overwhelmingly powerful external elements (as in the cases of Japan and Germany after World War II) or by powerful elements in their own societies (strong middle classes, military elements, working-class elements, well-organized peasant movements, and so on). Where a state is not under strong external pressure and is able to monopolize power in a society to the extent that no internal group, or alliance of internal groups, is strong enough to compete with it, any movement toward an opening of the political process is highly unlikely.

Notes

1. Francis Fukuyama, "The End of History?" *The National Interest*, vol. 16, 1989, pp. 3–18.
2. Samuel Huntington, "The Clash of Civilizations," *Foreign Affairs*, vol. 72, Summer 1993, pp. 22–49.

3. David Potter, David Goldblatt, Margaret Kiloh, and Paul Lewis, eds., *Democratization*, Cambridge: Polity Press, 1997, pp. 1 and 9.
4. Ibid., p. 6.
5. Ibid., pp. 24–31.
6. With particular reference to the Middle East, see A. R. Norton, ed., *Civil Society in the Middle East*, Leiden: Brill, 1995–6; W. Kazziha, *Civil Society and the Middle East*, Tokyo: Institute of Developing Economies, 1997. For more general sources, see CIVICUS, *Civil Society at the Millennium*, Connecticut: Kumarian Press, 1999; and J. Cohen and A. Arato, *Civil Society and Political Theory*, London: MIT Press, 1995.
7. For a succinct look at the Moroccan political system, see Remy Leveau, "Morocco at the Crossroads," *Mediterranean Politics*, vol. 3, no. 3, Winter 1997, pp. 114–22.
8. Ibid.
9. For a detailed look at this, see Azzedine Layachi, *State, Society and Democracy in Morocco: The Limits of Associative Life*, Georgetown, Washington DC: CCAS, 1999.
10. Ibid.
11. Leveau, "Morocco at the Crossroads."
12. See Clement Henry, *The Mediterranean Debt Crescent*, Gainesville, FL: University Press of Florida, 1996.
13. In fact, developments over the past year or so have indicated that the process of improving human rights and expanding freedoms of expression might have come to an abrupt halt. Furthermore, in all likelihood, the terrorist attacks on 11 September 2001 and the American "War on Terrorism" will likely result in a Moroccan government crackdown on the opposition (Islamist or otherwise).
14. For a look at each of these periods, see John Entelis, ed., *State and Society in Algeria*, Boulder, CO: Westview, 1992; Henry, *The Mediterranean Debt Crescent*; Luis Martinez, *The Algerian Civil War, 1990–1998*, London: Ashgate, 1999.
15. Bahgat Korany and Saad Amrani, "Explosive Civil Society and Democratization from Below: Algeria," in Bahgat Korany, Rex Brynen, and Paul Noble, *Political Liberalization and Democratization in the Arab World: Comparative Experiences*, Boulder, CO: Lynne Rienner, 1998, p. 11.
16. Ibid.
17. For a history of the Islamist movement in Algeria, see Michael Willis, *The Islamist Challenge in Algeria: A Political History*, Reading: Ithaca Press, 1996.
18. See Martinez, *The Algerian Civil War*.
19. At the moment, the government clearly has the upper hand in its conflict with Islamists. The conflict has largely ended, although the situation continues to be somewhat fluid. Islamists are able on occasion to perpetrate some sort of violent response to the regime. Without question, the international community is likely to increase its support of the military government, especially post–September 11.
20. For a look at these elections, see William Quandt, "Algeria's Election Fiasco," *Civil Society*, vol. 8, no. 90, June 1999, pp. 13–14; and Yahia Zoubir, "Presidential Elections and Signs of Democratization in Algeria," *Civil Society*, vol. 8, no. 90, June 1999, pp. 15–21.
21. Korany and Amrani, "Explosive Civil Society and Democratization from Below: Algeria."
22. A good series of essays dealing with all of these themes can be found in William Zartman, ed., *Tunisia: The Political Economy of Reform*, London: Lynne Rienner, 1991.
23. For an excellent study examining the dynamics of economic and political change in Tunisia, see Emma Murphy, *Economic and Political Change in Tunisia*, London: Macmillan, 1999.
24. Mark Gasiorowski, "The Islamist Challenge: The Failure of Reform in Tunisia," *Journal of Democracy*, vol. 3, no. 4, October 1992, pp. 85–97.

25. Emma Murphy, "Ten Years On – Ben Ali's Tunisia," *Mediterranean Politics*, vol. 3, no. 3, Winter 1997, pp. 114–22.
26. Ibid, p. 118.
27. The MTI had, by this point, changed its name to Hizb al-Nahda (Renaissance Party) as part of an attempt to distance itself from anti-democratic Islamist radicals.
28. Abdelbaki Hermassi, "The Rise and Fall of the Islamist Movement in Tunisia," in Laura Guazzone, ed., *The Islamist Dilemma: The Political Role of Islamist Movements in the Contemporary Arab World*, Reading: Ithaca Press, 1995.
29. See also the chapters by Majid Tehranian and Amin Saikal in this volume.
30. For a sophisticated yet highly readable account of this observation, see D. Vandewallee, *Libya since Independence*, London: I. B. Tauris, 1998.
31. Mary-Jane Deeb, "Qadhafi's Changed Policy: Causes and Consequences," *Middle East Policy*, vol. 7, no. 2, February 2000, pp. 146–53.
32. Ibid, p. 147.
33. Ibid.
34. Ibid, pp. 146–7.
35. Ray Takeyh, "Qadhafi's Libya and the Prospects of Islamic Succession," *Middle East Policy*, vol. 7, no. 2, February 2000, pp. 154–62.
36. S. M. Lipset, *Political Man*, London: Heinemann, 1960.
37. Rex Brynen, Bahgat Korany, and Paul Noble, eds., *Political Liberalization and Democratization in the Arab World*, vol. 1, *Theoretical Perspectives*, London: Lynne Rienner Publishers, 1991, pp. 6–10.
38. Simon Bromley, "Middle East Exceptionalism – Myth or Reality?" in Potter et al., *Democratization*.

Contributors

Kamel S. Abu Jaber has recently served as president of the Higher Media Council, Jordan. Previously, he served as president of the Jordan Institute of Diplomacy (1997–2001), as a senator in the Jordanian upper house of parliament (1993–7), and as Minister of Foreign Affairs for Jordan (1991–3). He has furthermore held the posts of professor of political science (1971, 1979–80, 1985), dean of the Faculty of Economics and Commerce (1972–9), and director of the Strategic Studies Centre at the University of Jordan; and he was an associate professor of political science at Smith College, USA (1967–9) and a visiting professor at Emory University, the Carter Center, Atlanta, USA (1989). Dr. Abu Jaber holds a doctorate in political science (1965) from the University of Syracuse and has carried out post-doctoral research in oriental studies (1962–3) at Princeton University, USA. He is the author of numerous articles, chapters, and books, including *The Arab Ba'ath Socialist Party* (Syracuse University Press, 1966), *Bedouin of Jordan: A People in Transition* (co-author with F. Gharaideh, S. Khawasmeh, and A. Hill, Royal Scientific Society Press, 1978), and *The Jordanians and the People of Jordan* (Royal Scientific Society Press, 1980).

Tom Pierre Najem is chair of the Political Science Department at the University of Windsor, Canada. Dr. Najem teaches in the areas of international relations and comparative politics (developing world), with a regional specialization in the Middle East and North Africa. He has a wide range of research interests, including: international political economy (especially trade between the European Union and southern Mediterranean countries); economic development; and political development (democratization, human rights, and good governance). He has given numerous lectures on Middle East politics at venues throughout North America, Europe, the Middle East, and North Africa. He has published widely, including two books on Lebanon and one on the Middle East oil monarchies. Previously, he has held academic posts at universities in England (University of Durham) and Morocco.

Amin Saikal is professor of political science and director of the Centre for Arab and Islamic Studies (the Middle East and Central Asia) at the Australian National University. He has been a visiting fellow at Princeton University, USA, Cambridge University, UK, and the Institute of Development Studies (University of Sussex, UK), as well as a Rockefeller Foundation Fellow in International Relations. His publications include: *The Rise and Fall of the Shah* (Princeton University Press, 1980), *Regime Change in Afghanistan* (co-authored, Westview Press, 1991), and *Russia in Search of its Future* (co-edited, Cambridge University Press, 1995).

Albrecht Schnabel is an Academic Programme Officer in the Peace and Governance Programme of the United Nations University, Tokyo, Japan. He received his doctorate in political studies from Queen's University, Canada (1995), and has previously taught at Queen's University (1994), the American University in Bulgaria (1995–6) and the Central European University (1996–8). His work on ethnic conflict, conflict prevention and management, peacekeeping, peacebuilding, refugees, and

humanitarian intervention has appeared in *International Peacekeeping, Journal of Social Affairs, Peace Review, Peace Forum, WeltTrends, Esprit, Etudes Internationales, International Journal, Refuge*, and numerous edited volumes. His recent edited books include *Kosovo and the Challenge of Humanitarian Intervention: Selective Indignation, Collective Action, and International Citizenship* (with Ramesh Thakur, United Nations University Press, 2000), *United Nations Peacekeeping Operations: Ad Hoc Missions, Permanent Engagement* (with Ramesh Thakur, United Nations University Press, 2001), *Southeast European Security: Threats, Responses, Challenges* (Nova Science Publishers, 2001), and *Recovering from Civil Conflict: Reconciliation, Peace and Development* (with Edward Newman, Frank Cass, 2002).

Etel Solingen is professor of political science and international relations at the University of California, Irvine, USA. Her most recent book is *Regional Orders at Century's Dawn: Global and Domestic Influences on Grand Strategy* (Princeton University Press, 1998). Her articles on internationalization, democratization, and international and regional security regimes have appeared in *International Security, International Organization, International Studies Quarterly, Comparative Politics, Journal of Peace Research, Review of International Studies, Journal of Theoretical Politics, Global Governance*, and *Journal of Democracy*, among others.

Gerald M. Steinberg is a professor of political studies and director of the graduate program on conflict management and negotiation at Bar Ilan University in Israel. He received his doctorate in international relations from Cornell University, USA, in 1981, and his research focuses on the role of process in international negotiations, the impact of track-two negotiations, and arms control in the Middle East. He has contributed chapters on the peace process and Israeli elections to the *Israel at the Polls* series (Frank Cass) since 1988, he is the editor of *Jewish Approaches to Conflict Resolution* (Jerusalem Center for Public Affairs, 2000), and his articles have been published in the *Journal of Church and State, NonProliferation Review, Survival, Israel Affairs*, and *Security Dialogue*.

Majid Tehranian is professor of international communication at the University of Hawaii and director of the Toda Institute for Global Peace and Policy Research. A graduate of Dartmouth College and Harvard University, USA, his publications include 20 books and more than 100 articles in over a dozen languages. He edits *Peace & Policy* as well as the Toda Institute Book Series. His latest edited volumes are *Dialogue of Civilizations: A New Peace Agenda for a New Millennium* (I. B. Tauris, 2002) and *Bridging a Gulf: Peacebuilding in West Asia* (I. B. Tauris, 2003).

Mark Tessler is Samuel J. Eldersveld Professor of Political Science at the University of Michigan, USA. He is the author or co-author of 11 books and approximately 100 scholarly articles. His most recent books include: *Area Studies and Social Science: Strategies for Understanding Middle East Politics* (Indiana University Press, 1999); *Democracy and Its Limits: Lessons from Latin America, the Middle East and Asia* (Notre Dame University Press, 1999); and *Democracy, War and Peace in the Middle East* (Indiana University Press, 1995). His current research, which has been supported by the Ford Foundation, the US Institute of Peace, the US State Department, and the US National Science Foundation, deals with the attitudes of ordinary men and women toward issues of international relations, governance, religion, and gender.

Index

Catalogue Request

Name: _____

Address: _____

Tel: _____

Fax: _____

E-mail: _____

To receive a catalogue of UNU Press publications kindly photocopy this form and send or fax it back to us with your details. You can also e-mail us this information. Please put "Mailing List" in the subject line.

United Nations University Press

53-70, Jingumae 5-chome
Shibuya-ku, Tokyo 150-8925, Japan
Tel: +81-3-3499-2811 Fax: +81-3-3406-7345
E-mail: sales@hq.unu.edu http://www.unu.edu